What the critics have said about
Lillian Beckwith's charming bestsellers
of Hebridean life:

THE SEA FOR BREAKFAST

'Hilarious . . . I haven't laughed so much since WHISKY
GALORE' *Maurice Wiggin, Sunday Times*

THE LOUD HALO

'A sparkling book which could well become a Scottish
humorous classic' *Weekly Scotsman*

A ROPE - IN CASE

'As delightfully and unsentimentally drawn as ever'
Sunday Times

LIGHTLY POACHED

'A beautiful book this, smelling of earth and sea,
carrying the atmosphere of the crofts, and forcing you
to laugh aloud' *Oxford Mail*

BEAUTIFUL JUST!

'Its humour is happy, easy and natural' *Daily Mirror*

Also in Arrow by Lillian Beckwith

Beautiful Just!
The Loud Halo
Lightly Poached
A Rope – In Case!
About My Father's Business
Green Hand
The Sea for Breakfast
The Spuddy

Lillian Beckwith

THE HILLS IS
LONELY

Decorations by
DOUGLAS HALL

ARROW BOOKS

Arrow Books Limited
3 Fitzroy Square, London W 1 P 6 J D

An imprint of the Hutchinson Publishing Group

London Melbourne Sydney Auckland Johannesburg
and agencies throughout the world

First published by Hutchinson 1959
Arrow edition 1967
Reprinted 1968, 1969 (twice), 1970, 1971 (twice), 1972, 1973,
1974, 1975, 1977, 1979 and 1980

© Text and illustrations Hutchinson & Co. (Publishers) Ltd 1959

Made and printed in Great Britain
by The Anchor Press Ltd
Tiptree, Essex

ISBN 0 09 906620 3

Contents

1

Arrival

If you have never experienced a stormy winter's night in the Hebrides, you can have no idea of the sort of weather which I encountered when I arrived, travel-worn and weary, at the deserted little jetty where I was to await the boat which would carry me across to 'Incredible Island'. It was a terrible night. A night to make one yearn for the fierce, bright heat of an ample fire; for carpet slippers and a crossword puzzle. Yet here I stood, alone in the alien, tempestuous blackness, sodden, cold and dejected, my teeth chattering uncontrollably. On three sides of me the sea roared and plunged frenziedly, and a strong wind, which shrieked and wailed with theatrical violence, tore and buffeted at my clothes and fought desperately to throw me off balance. The swift, relentless rain stung my eyes, my face and my legs; it trickled from my ruined hat to seep in cheeky rivulets down my neck; it found the ventilation holes in my waterproof and crept exploratively under my armpits.

Somewhere out on the turbulent water a light flashed briefly. Peering through screwed-up eyes, I watched with fascinated horror as it appeared and vanished again and again. With stiff fingers I switched on my torch; the battery was new and the bright beam pierced the blurring rain for a few yards. Quickly I switched it off. To a faint-hearted landlubber like myself the sound of the sea was sufficiently menacing; the sight of it was absolutely malevolent. Nostalgia overwhelmed me. Why, oh why, had I been so foolhardy—so headstrong? And this was supposed to be for the good of my health! Why was I not sitting with Mary in the cosy living-room of our town flat, dunking ginger-nuts into cups of steaming hot tea and following from my own armchair the exploits of my favourite detective? The second question was simple enough to answer. The first presented more difficulty.

An illness some months previously had led my doctor to order me away to the country for a long complete rest. A timely windfall in the shape of a small annuity had made it possible for me to give up a not very lucrative teaching post in a smoky North of England town, and look around for a suitable place where, within the limits of my purse, I might, in the doctor's words, 'rest without being too lazy, and laze without being too restive'.

My advertisement in a well-known periodical had brought an avalanche of tempting offers. England, it appeared, was liberally dotted with miniature Paradises for anyone seeking recuperative solitude, and I had almost decided to remove myself temporarily to a Kentish farmhouse when the postman brought a letter which changed my plans completely. The envelope bore a Hebridean postmark; the handwriting, though straggly, was fairly legible, but the words themselves painted a picture as vivid and inviting as a railway poster. It ran thus:

Bruach.

Dear Madam,

Its just now I saw your advert when I got the book for the knitting pattern I wanted from my cousin Catriona. I am sorry I did not write sooner if you are fixed up if you are not in any way fixed up I have a good good house stone and tiles and my brother Ruari who will wash down with lime twice every year. Ruari is married and lives just by. She is not damp. I live by myself and you could have the room that is not a kitchen

10

and bedroom reasonable. I was in the kitchen of the lairds house till lately when he was changed God rest his soul the poor old gentleman that he was. You would be very welcomed. I have a cow also for milk and eggs and the minister at the manse will be referee if you wish such.

Yours affectionately,
Morag McDugan.

PS. She is not thatched.

Mary, reading the letter over my shoulder, dissolved into laughter. We were still chuckling when we went to bed that night, I to dream of a minister in full clerical garb, tearing frantically around a football pitch, blowing a referee's whistle, while two teams of lime-washed men played football with a cow's egg—a thing resembling a Dutch cheese—and an old man changed furtively in the kitchen.

Deciding privately to postpone acceptance of the Kentish offer, I wrote next morning to Morag McDugan, excusing myself to Mary by saying that a further reply might provide more amusement. I had to admit to myself, however, that the ingenuousness of the letter had so delighted me that the idea of a possible visit had already taken my fancy. The reply from Morag (already we were using her Christian name) did not disappoint us. Her advice regarding travelling arrangements was clear; obviously she had been instructed by a seasoned traveller, but her answers to my questions about quietness and distance from the sea, etc., were Morag's own.

Surely its that quiet here even the sheeps themselves on the hills is lonely and as to the sea its that near I use it myself every day for the refusals.

Mary's eyelids flickered.
'What does she have to say about the water supply?'

'There's a good well right by me and no beasts at it,' I read.

Mary shuddered expressively.

'I'm glad you're not going there anyway, Becky,' she said.

'I believe I am though,' I said suddenly, but I was thinking out loud, not really having made up my mind.

She stared at me, incredulous. 'But you can't, Becky!' she expostulated. 'Surely you can see that?'

'Why not?' I asked defensively. 'I'm interested in meeting people and finding out how they live and I've never yet crossed the border into Scotland.'

'Don't be a fool,' argued Mary. 'I admit the woman sounds fun, and so does the place; but it's ridiculous to let yourself be carried away like that. It wouldn't be in the least funny to live under the conditions suggested by those letters.'

'I'm sure it would be even funnier,' I replied, with a flippancy I was far from actually feeling. 'After all, there can't be many dual-purpose cows in the world and it's time someone did something to cheer up those poor lonely sheeps.'

Mary giggled. 'Don't be a fool!' she reiterated.

Her words goaded me to a decision.

'That's just what I'm going to be,' I replied.

Mary was not the only person to remonstrate with me on my decision to forgo the indisputable attractions of a Kentish farmhouse for the doubtful charms of a Hebridean croft. My doctor was equally incredulous when I told him of my plans.

'I don't think you're very wise,' he said seriously. 'Friends of mine who've been up in the Hebrides tell me the inhabitants are only half civilised.'

'Well,' I replied gaily, 'I'm going to find out for myself,' and added: 'Really, I'm quite determined.'

He stared at me for a few moments, then shrugged his shoulders and rose. 'In that case,' he warned me, 'I think you should let me inoculate you against typhoid.'

12

Inoculated I was, and now, standing embittered and lonely on the pier, I was heartily amazed that I could ever willingly have embarked on such a venture, and heartily glad neither the doctor nor Mary could witness my plight.

The light I had been watching drew unsteadily nearer and with sickening dread I realised that it belonged to the masthead of a tiny boat, and that its appearance and disappearance was due to the boat lifting and plunging on the huge seas. Slowly she lunged nearer, the dark outline of her bow leaping recklessly until it seemed impossible that she could come closer without being smashed to pieces on the stone jetty. But suddenly she was alongside and a figure clad in streaming oilskins and thigh-boots jumped ashore, a rope in his hands.

'Are you off the train?' he shouted as he hitched the rope around a tiny bollard.

The question was directed at me. 'Yes,' I yelled back. 'Is this the ferry?'

'Aye.' He spat with all the dignity of a man presenting a visiting card and obviously considered it sufficient introduction. 'Iss there anybody else for the ferry?' Again the question was for me and I peered vaguely into the surrounding darkness.

'I've no idea!' I yelled.

The man grunted. 'Wass there many on the train?'

Dimly I began to appreciate the degree of familiarity I must expect in my new surroundings.

'There were quite a few people on the train,' I replied, 'but they've all disappeared.' Impulsively I glanced behind and immediately regretted having done so, for the movement had deflected some of the rivulets along chilling new courses.

'Have you been here long?'

I felt that the questions were becoming pointless and was tempted to grossly overstate the ten minutes proclaimed by my watch. But I replied truthfully. Again the man spat.

'You'd best be gettin' aboard, then, if you're goin' the night,' he growled.

This was undoubtedly an example of the dourness I had been warned to expect from the Hebrideans, but to me at this moment it seemed particularly uncalled for. Apprehensively I groped forward. There was a surging gulf of water between the boat and the jetty and I was terrified of stepping down into it.

'Watch your step now!' commanded another voice, brisk and imperious, from the darkness, as I hesitated, waiting for the deck to leap high enough for me to clamber aboard without having to perform something in the nature of a gymnastic feat.

'I can't see!' I wailed. Almost before the words were out of my mouth I was seized by two strong arms and propelled unceremoniously over the gunwale and down into the well of the boat. The calves of my legs came up against something solid and I collapsed heavily. I managed to gasp out my thanks but need not have wasted my breath, for the men, having seen me and my belongings stowed safely aboard, went about their own business. Miserable with fright, cold and vexation, every muscle strained and taut, I clung grimly to the seat to prevent myself from being thrown overboard with each lurch of the boat. There were no other passengers. 'No one else,' I thought dully, 'would be such a fool as to cross on a night like this.' The thought galvanised me into action.

'I'm coming off!' I shouted. My voice shrilled with panic. 'I'm not going to cross tonight. It's too rough.'

'Ach, sit you down,' the answer came scornfully; 'you canna' go jumpin' on and off boats for fun on a night like this.'

'Fun!' I retorted angrily, and was about to tell them the extent of my pleasure when a suffocating stream of spray filled my mouth and effectively choked the words. The boatman may have intended his sarcasm to be reassuring, but before I could attempt further argument

14

there was a staccato command, the men leaped aboard and the slowly ticking engine pulsed into life. We were off, and I must face whatever might come.

That we had left the jetty and were moving I could guess from the sound of the engine, but from the terrific impact of the waves on the bow I considered it more than likely that we were being driven backwards. The boat seemed sometimes to rear supplicatingly on her stern, and then nose-dive so steeply that I was certain each time that her bow could never lift through the water again. My agonised thoughts compared the performance with that of Blackpool's 'Big Dipper', a thrill which I had endured once and subsequently avoided. This, however, was a succession of 'Big Dippers' and my stomach tied itself into knots at each abysmal plunge. While the boat rolled and pitched dramatically the sea belched over each gunwale in turn. Icy water was already swirling and eddying around my ankles. 'How much longer?' I wondered wretchedly. Soon I was sobbing and, in an excess of cowardice, praying alternately for safety and a quick death. I felt terribly sick but fear kept my muscles too tense to permit me to vomit.

A dark shape loomed up beside me, and quite suddenly I knew that disaster was upon us; that this man had come to tell me to save myself as best I could; that the boat was sinking. I smothered a scream and, wrenching the torch from my pocket, looked wildly around for lifebelts. I could see none. The man continued to stand, still and silent, and I guessed that he too was gripped by a fear as strong as my own. I was shaking from head to foot.

'What is it?' I asked weakly.

'Tenpence.' His voice was crisply matter-of-fact.

'Tenpence?' My own voice burst from my throat in an incredulous squeak and relief flooded through my quaking body like a nip of hot brandy. I could almost have laughed. Foolishly I loosed my hold of the seat and a sudden lurch of the boat threw me heavily against him.

'Steady,' he reproved me.

'Tell that to the boat,' I replied pertly. With a feeling akin to elation I fumbled for my purse and handed the man a shilling. Gravely he sought the twopence change and handed it to me along with the ticket. The latter I promptly lost; but the two pennies I clutched like a talisman. It seemed fantastic. Twopence change on a night like this! Twopence change when I had been prepared to abandon my all! I began to feel quite exuberant.

The man disappeared and again I was left alone, but now I could at times glimpse the island jetty with its single light and what looked like a pair of car headlamps piercing the darkness beyond. Though I still had to cling to my seat as the boat performed acrobatics more suited to an aeroplane; though I was not one whit less cold and wet than I had been a few minutes previously, the purchase of a tenpenny ticket had given me new confidence; for had I not heard enough about the character of the Scot to be certain that the tenpence stood a good chance of reaching its destination safely? Otherwise I felt sure the weight of the money would have been left with my body, not added to heavy oilskins and sea-boots.

Like a steeplechaser that had scented its stable that boat romped alongside the jetty and I was promptly hauled out with as little ceremony as I had been stowed in. The headlights which I had noticed earlier had vanished temporarily, but now they flashed on again, spotlighting my woebegone appearance. The slam of a car door was followed by a rich masculine voice.

'Would it be yourself for McDugan's, madam?' it asked.

'It would,' I replied thankfully, almost ready to fall upon the speaker's neck.

'Come this way if you please,' the voice invited politely. 'I have the taxi you were wanting.'

A large overcoated figure picked up my two cases, shepherded me towards the headlamps and, with a flourish worthy of a Rolls, opened the door of an ancient roadster. It offered indifferent shelter, but I climbed in gratefully, and from somewhere in the rear the driver thoughtfully produced a rug which, though coarse and hairy and reeking horribly of mildew, was welcome if only to muffle the knocking of my knees. As we drove away from the pier the wind rushed and volleyed both inside and outside the car; silvery rain sluiced down the windscreen and visibility was restricted to the semi-circle of road lit by the headlamps. The driver, who chatted amiably the whole time, kindly informed me that the road followed the coastline most of the way, and I had to accept his assurance that it was a 'ghrand fiew in fine weather'.

For some miles the car ploughed noisily on, then it turned off abruptly into a ridiculously narrow lane, bounded on either side by high stone walls, vaulted a couple of hump-backed bridges in quick succession and drew slowly to a stop. I wondered if we had run out of petrol, for there were no lights or houses visible; nothing but road and walls and the rain.

'This is what you were wanting,' announced the driver, pushing open the door and slithering out from his seat. He could not have made a more erroneous statement. This was certainly not what I was wanting, but it looked, unfortunately, as though this was what I was getting.

Pulling his cap well down on the side of his face exposed to the wind and exaggeratedly drawing up his coat collar, he uttered a mild curse and flung open the rear door of the car, where he commenced to wrestle with my luggage. In the glare of the headlights the rain still swooped vengefully down as though each drop bore some personal animosity to each and every particle of the gritty lane. In all my life I had never seen such full-blooded rain!

With a despairing shudder I pulled my waterproof

closer about my shoulders and peered anxiously over the driver's back, hoping fervently that he had stopped as near to the entrance gate as was possible. I was disappointed. On each side of the car the stone walls loomed up impenetrably, and I could see that it was not so much that the walls themselves were high, as that the road was a cutting, leaving an earth bank on either side thus forming a fairly inaccessible barrier of about six foot in height between the lane and the field.

'I can't see any entrance,' I complained fretfully.

The driver paused in his attempt to lever my second case through the door of the car. 'Oh no,' he assured me with nimble complacency; 'there's no entrance at all here, but you'll just climb over the wall, d'y' see? The house is beyond there.'

I could not have been more astounded had he told me I must wait for the drawbridge to be lowered! I began to realise that acrobatics were a necessary accomplishment for visitors to Bruach.

'I can't climb walls!' I protested, 'and that one is a good six feet high. Surely,' I went on, 'there must be some other entrance.'

'Oh surely, madam,' he replied in conciliatory tones, 'but the tide's in just now, and you'd be after swimming for it if you were going to use that tonight.' He permitted himself a sardonic chuckle.

'What a welcome!' I muttered.

'Ach, you'll soon nip over the wall easy enough,' the driver assured me blandly. 'I'll give you a leg up myself.'

Now while I do not wish to give the impression that my figure is in any way grotesque, I must disclaim that it is by any means the sort of figure which nips easily over six-foot walls. Agility is not, and never was, my strong point; my figure, though sturdy, being somewhat rotund for anything but a very moderate degree of athleticism. I viewed the prospect of climbing, even with a willing 'leg up' from the driver, with misgivings.

Despondently I climbed out of the car. The wind

caught me off guard and almost succeeded in unbalancing me, and the rain recommenced its furious assault on my waterproof. From the darkness beyond and uncomfortably close came the pounding and sucking of breakers on the shore. To add to my dismay I perceived that a fast-flowing ditch coursed riotously along the base of the wall. I positively yearned for town pavements.

The driver nonchalantly stepped over the ditch (his legs were long) and pulled himself upwards. He was a tall man and the top of the wall was on a level with his nose. He turned an enquiring gaze on me.

'They'll be expectin' you likely?' he asked. I agreed that it was extremely likely, for I had sent Morag a wire announcing the probable time of my arrival.

Once again the driver turned to the wall, and gave a stentorian yell, the volume and unexpectedness of which outrivalled the storm and very nearly caused me to make a premature and undesirably close acquaintance with the ditch. Immediately a shaft of yellow light gleamed in the distance as a door was opened and a voice of equal power, though indisputably feminine, called out interrogatively. The driver answered and in spite of the violence of the weather a conversation was carried on, though as I could make out no word of it I concluded it to be in Gaelic.

The shaft of light was blotted out as the door was shut and then a lantern came swinging rhythmically towards us. A moment later a figure surmounted the wall and climbed quickly down to stand beside me. This then was Morag, my future landlady.

'Well, well, Miss Peckwitt is it? And how are you?' My hand was lifted in a firm grip and shaken vigorously and I only just managed to evade a full-lipped kiss.

'My, my, but what a night to welcome a body. Surely you must be drookit,' she lamented cheerfully. I thought that 'drookit' probably meant 'dead' and I agreed that I was—almost.

'Almost? Sure you must be quite,' she asserted. I decided that 'drookit' meant 'drowned'.

'Ach, but I have a nice fire waitin' on you,' continued Morag happily, 'and you'll be warrm and dry in no time at all.' The softened consonants were very noticeable and to my Sassenach ears the rolled 'r's' sounded as over-emphasised as those of some opera singers.

Morag held up the lantern so that for a moment we were able to study each other's faces and I was surprised, in view of her agility, to see that hers was dry and wrinkled with age, while the wisps of hair escaping from the scarf she had wound round her head were snowy white. She dropped my hand and turned to the driver.

'Will we just swing her up and over between us?' she asked him.

'Aye,' agreed the driver shortly. I bridled and stepped back a pace but, ignoring me, they bent and together swung my two suitcases up and on to the wall. They were swiftly followed by Morag who lifted them down to the other side; then, lissom as a two-year-old, she leaped lightly down again. I gasped at the effortless ease with which she accomplished the feat but her performance did nothing to allay my own apprehension.

'Is there no other way?' I asked timidly.

'No indeed,' she replied, and pointed down the road; 'the wee gate's down there, but the watter's up and all round it at this hour. It's a pity you couldna' have come when the tide was out.' It occurred to me that tides were going to play a very important part in my new life. I smothered a sigh.

'Ach, but you'll find this way easy enough when you put your feets to it,' Morag went on in an encouraging tone. 'Now come.' Cautiously I stepped across the ditch and put my 'feets' to it. 'Now then,' directed my landlady with heavy pleasantry, 'one fine feet here ... now another fine feet here ... that's lovely just ... now another fine feet here. ...' Undoubtedly Morag believed her new guest to be a quadruped. The driver who was waiting on the other side of the wall to haul me over also clucked encouragement. I felt a firm grasp on my ankle. 'Now just another feet here and you'll be near done,' instructed Morag. She was right! In the next instant one of my 'fine feet' slipped on the treacherous wet stone and I was left clinging desperately with my hands, my legs flaying the air, while the wind lifted my skirts above my head and the rain committed atrocities on those parts of my body which had not before been directly exposed to such vengeance. The driver, seeing my predicament, came to the rescue and gripping both arms firmly hoisted me bodily over the wall. My feet landed on solid earth. Very wet earth admittedly, but I cared not so long as I had to do no more climbing. Instantly Morag was beside me. 'You're all right?' she enquired anxiously; 'you didna' hurt yourself?'

I assured her that I was in no way hurt; though I knew that, even if I had not suffered, my stockings at least were irreparably damaged.

'That's all right, then. I'll tell Ruari to see to your boxes directly.'

'Oh yes—Ruari,' I echoed, and had a fleeting vision of a freshly lime-washed Ruari braving this torrential rain, and began to feel better again. After all, I told myself, I had been roughly handled but then I had planned this as something of an adventure.

Opening my purse, I gave the driver his fare plus a moderate tip. He demurred at the latter but on my insistence thanked me courteously and pocketed it. 'It is indeed,' I thought, 'like coming to a different world, where even the taxi-drivers refuse to be tipped.'

Guided by Morag's lantern I followed her across the sodden grass, over cobblestones and into the tiny hall of the cottage where a candle burned lopsidedly in the draught from some hidden crevice. Taking off my dripping outdoor clothes I hung them on the antlers of a pathetic-looking stag's head. Morag opened the door of a room on our left and ushered me inside. 'The room that wasn't a kitchen' was a neat lamplit place with an immense fire burning brightly in the well-polished grate. Half on the fire, half on the hob, a kettle stood spouting steam and rattling its lid in ill-concealed impatience, promising a speedy brew of tea. A small table was spread with a white cloth and on it my supper was laid invitingly. After the appalling conditions outside the whole place gave a welcome so much greater than I had expected that I exclaimed over it impulsively. I dropped into a chair and ignoring its formidable creakings watched while Morag, with a self-satisfied smile on her face, busied herself about the meal.

My landlady was a small woman with a broad back which, though not exactly bent, gave one the impression that it was accustomed to carrying many burdens. The rest of her figure was hardly discernible beneath the bulk of clothing she wore, but her movements were lively enough despite a gait which I can only describe as 'running with one leg and walking with the other'. Her hair, as I have said, was white, her face wizened and freckled. Her eyes, when they were not being soulfully blue, were as mischievous as a small boy's, while her hands were horny as a man's, the stubby fingers resembling calcified sausages. Her clothes, or what I could see of them, consisted of a thick tweed jacket over a homespun skirt, the front of which was partially concealed by a now sodden apron, for she had apparently added nothing to her attire when she left the house to come to my assistance. I judged, however, from the proportion of bulk in relation to size, that there were in all probability a great many insulating layers between her skin and her outer garments, which were no doubt as efficient under Island weather conditions as the more conventional waterproof.

The tea brewed, Morag departed, having first assured herself that she could at the moment do nothing further for me beyond promising to stir Ruari into bringing my cases indoors. Accordingly, soon after she had gone I heard the front door bang, and even while I sat sipping my third cup of tea there was a rumble of voices followed by a thudding on the stairs which indicated that my bags were being carried up to my bedroom. I repressed a desire to peep. A few minutes later there was a knock on my door and Morag entered.

'I'm just sayin' I didna' bring Ruari and Lachy in to see you tonight, seeing you'll be awful tired,' she began. I protested feebly. 'You see,' she went on apologetically, 'Ruari's that deaf his shoutin' near splits the ears off you, and I'm after tellin' him to keep his mouth shut on the stairs for sure he grunts like a bull.'

'But who is Lachy?' I asked, stifling a yawn.

'Ach, he's the other half of the boat with Ruari,' explained Morag obscurely.

'And what time will you be for takin' your breakfast?' she asked.

I suggested about eight-thirty.

'Half past eight,' she agreed; 'and if the Lord spares me I'll have your fire lit by eight then.' I glanced at her enquiringly.

'Aren't you feeling well then?' I asked.

'I'm feelin' fine,' she answered with some surprise; 'why, d'you think I'm lookin' poorly?'

'Not at all,' I rejoined hurriedly, 'but when you said "if the Lord spares me", I thought perhaps you were not feeling quite well.'

'I'm feeling quite well tonight,' replied Morag piously; 'but who can tell if the Lord may call any one of us before the morn comes; and if He chooses to call me in the night then I canna' light your fire in the mornin', can I?'

'I rather take that for granted,' I said with a smile.

'Ah indeed, it's no wise to take anythin' for granted with the Lord,' she rebuked me, and then added determinedly: 'But I'll have your fire lit for eight certain if

I'm spared,' and as though to underline the words she closed the door firmly behind her.

After the long journey, the fright, the bitter cold and now the warmth and food, I became unconquerably sleepy. Wearily I climbed the narrow linoleum-covered stairs to the bedroom which Morag had already pointed out to me. In the room a lamp had been lighted and burned dimly, but more than that everything appeared to be clean and comfortable I could not have told that night. Unpacking the minimum of necessities, I undressed and tumbled into bed, where I lay for a time listening to the storm outside. Conscious of a queer little thrill, I turned out the lamp. It was the first time in my life that I had actually used an oil-lamp and I was not at all sure whether to blow or keep turning the knob until the flame was completely extinguished. I managed a successful compromise, and as I dropped back on to the pillows and drifted into sleep I was aware of the rain spattering against the window and drumming with dogged persistence on the tiled roof.

2

Initiation

I awoke after what seemed a very short time to the realisation that the rain had ceased and that chill, grey daylight was filtering through the lace curtains of my window. My head still echoed the rhythmic jogging of the train, for I am one of those unfortunates who, if they travel five hundred miles in actuality, travel at least another thousand during sleep.

The bed was cosy enough to make the prospect of leaving it seem unattractive and I lay sleepily surveying my room and listening with drowsy intentness to the sounds of the morning. There was a clanking of cans, which I assumed to be milk-pails; the impatient clucking and questioning of hens, interspersed with loud flutterings of wings; a strange intermittent wailing noise which I was quite unable to identify; doors opening and closing and dishes clattering: sounds which seemed to indicate that the Lord had seen fit to spare my landlady for another day's work, and also that the poultry still awaited their morning feed.

The hands of my watch were pointing to half past eight when there were footsteps on the stairs followed by a knock at my bedroom door.

'I've brought you watter and she's fine and hot,' Morag's voice announced.

'Take her away!' I entreated with an involuntary shudder. 'I shall wash downstairs where it's warmer.'

Morag began speaking again, but her words were drowned by an acrimonious bellow which reverberated up and down the stairs and almost dislodged me from my bed.

'Sorry,' I apologised when there was a moment's lull, 'but I didn't catch what you were saying.'

'That's just Ruari,' explained Morag with patient resignation, 'and I'm just sayin' he's fine and warm already for I have him blazin' up the chimney with a dose of paraffin.'

Her footsteps retreated down the stairs. After a moment of confused horror I succeeded in disentangling this rather surprising piece of information; though had I supposed my landlady to be capable of such villainy the strength of Ruari's bellow would undoubtedly have lent credence to her statement.

As I reached the bottom stair Morag came out of her kitchen bearing a steaming bowl of mash.

'Sure I hope you slept well after your long journey,' she greeted me. I agreed that I had.

'Something smells awfully good,' I observed.

'It's just the meal I'm after scaldin' for the hens,' said Morag; 'though it smells that good many's the time I'm takin' a lump of it for my own breakfast. Indeed it fairly makes my teeths watter.'

Although the later part of her reply was patently untrue—over her shoulder I could see her 'teeths' adorning the dresser and they looked positively arid—I could not doubt the temptation of the smell, and had the bowl been a little cleaner I might perhaps have sampled it for myself.

Among the chorus of noises outside I again noticed the strange wailing call I had heard earlier.

'What sort of an animal makes that queer noise?' I asked.

The ghost of a smile curved Morag's lips. 'Why, that's my cockerel,' she explained.

'Really?' I said, then, seeing her smile broaden at my ignorance, added lamely: 'I thought cockerels always said cock-a-doodle-doo, but that one sounds as though he's been crossed with a circular saw.'

'Ach, he's just young yet,' she excused him; 'another six months and he'll be cock-a-doodle-dooin' as well as you can yourself.'

It became plain that my landlady was prepared for a long conversation but I could not, as she did, ignore the greedy clamour of the hens who, in their eagerness for food, had thronged the tiny hall and were endea-vouring to reach perching positions on the edge of the mash-bowl. Out of consideration for the hens as well as concern for the state of the floor I decided to withdraw and hurried into my room.

Now, without the mellowness of lamplight and the contrast of the storm outside, it struck me as repulsively ugly. The floor covering was shabby; the two easy chairs were grey with age and, on closer examination, I dis-covered that their ability to support the human frame was due solely to the circumstance that a famous brand of margarine was packed in wooden boxes. A yellow-grained sideboard took up nearly the whole of one wall of the room; a dreadful monstrosity of a thing, which looked for all the world as though it had been set upon by someone suffering from a fit of delirium tremens, using as a weapon a paint brush dipped alternately in yellow ochre and black treacle.

The table was glaringly home-made and, though a cloth covered its major crudities, I was soon to learn that none of its four legs matched in shape or length and that the only way to keep it steady while eating was to balance it on my knees. The wallpaper, which last night had seemed self-effacing, now intruded its garish pattern of vermilion buttercups with a frieze of neglected false teeth, though the latter were no doubt meant to be autumn-tinted leaves.

Had I embarked on my venture with the full approval of my friends I might have permitted myself some doubts as to the probability of my remaining long with Morag.

As it was I determined to look only on the more comforting side and, after reassuring myself that the curtains, the cushions and the tablecloth were fresh and clean, turned to admire the old-fashioned grate with its deep fire of glowing peat, the gleaming brass fire-irons and the clock which had already ticked its way through a century of time.

A knock on the door heralded Morag's appearance with my breakfast tray, the sight of which effectively dispersed any misgivings for the time being, and soon I was settling down to do full justice to the excellent meal she had provided. There was porridge—my first experience of porridge made with fresh-ground oatmeal—there was cream, thick, smooth and rich; there was sugar, though my landlady shook her head disapprovingly as I spooned the latter on to my plate.

'Ach, mo ghaoil,' she chided, 'but you were never meant to eat sugar with porridge. Sure it'll spoil the grand taste of it.'

'I should never manage it without,' I retorted and tucked into my well-filled plate with a most uninvalidish appetite.

Next a dish of succulent-smelling bacon and eggs was placed before me. As this had been keeping warm on the hob beside the fire I easily ignored the fact that the dish was signed distinctly with a greasy black thumbprint. After all, had I not realised even while contemplating my Island sojourn that I could not afford to be overfastidious? My suggestion that she should join me in a cup of tea, Morag accepted with alacrity.

'I don't know that I ever refused a cup of tea yet, supposin' it was my twentieth,' she admitted ruefully as she helped herself from the ample brown teapot. Subsequent experience convinced me that twenty cups per day was grossly understating Morag's capacity for tea, and that the enormous tea-caddy which dominated the mantelpiece in her own room was not there solely for ornament.

28

After breakfast, as the weather showed a distinct improvement, I set out on a tour of investigation. My own waterproof and shoes were still sodden from their experience of the night before, so my landlady offered me a spare oilskin and a pair of gumboots. I accepted them dubiously, fearing that the boots would be too heavy for my unpractised feet and that the oilskin would be only an encumbrance. But once the initial awkwardness had passed, I wished very much that my friends, particularly Mary, could see me as I clumped about in the strange outfit.

Out of doors the view was unimpressive, for though the rain had ceased it had merely given way to clouds of mist which rolled in from the sea and hovered sluggishly over the surrounding moors, intensifying the roar of the waves and curiously deflecting the sounds of the land. Morag, hopping eagerly about me with her odd gait, pointed out the approximate bounds of her domain; approximate because she shared a croft with her brother Ruari, Morag owning one-quarter and Ruari the remaining three-quarters, with no recognisable boundary between the two. I asked how they managed about letters, since both houses were number fifteen—the numbers being given to crofts only—and the surname common to both. The explanation was simple; the postman was thoroughly familiar with the goings-on of each household and could thus decide for himself which letters were for which person. He rarely made a mistake, but, all the same, I was delighted to learn that official correspondence was addressed to Morag at 'One-quarter of number fifteen', and to her brother at 'Three-quarters of number fifteen'. The preciseness of officialdom is commendable but it does look slightly ludicrous on an envelope.

We strolled towards the elusive entrance gate, which turned out to be nothing more than a gap in the drystone wall across which was placed an old iron bedstead. Though the wind had dropped away to nothing and

Morag murmured something about the tide being half-way out, the swell still slapped and sucked around the bottom of the three stone steps which led from the garden to the shore. Much as I disliked the idea of scaling walls, I decided that climbing would be less destructive to morale than being confined to the house except at negotiable states of the tide.

'It seems to be a choice of two evils,' I remarked sadly to Morag.

'Ach, by the time you've been here a month, you'll be leapin' over yon dyke like a goat,' she predicted cheerfully. Reflecting upon my performance of the night before, I had a vague suspicion that my landlady was being ironical.

For some minutes I had been watching a boat which was now pulling in to the shore a little to our right. Besides the man at the oars it contained five or six women of varying ages, each of whom nursed at least one large milk-pail. As the boat grounded, the women stepped into the water, grasped the gunwales and hauled the boat up the beach as though it were a light toy. In answer to my look of enquiry, Morag explained that some of the cattle were grazed on a small tidal island and, despite the tides being roughly half an hour later each day, the crofters preferred to wait and go by boat to milk rather than walk the two or three miles round the shore. The arrangement struck me as being haphazard, but I had not then discovered that in the Hebrides the cattle are wonderfully accommodating; that time is practically non-existent and that the clocks are as much out of touch with reality as are their owners.

The women milkers, frankly curious, stood holding their heavy pails. As much for their sakes as my own I decided to return to the house and there asked Morag to direct me to the post office.

'Well, you'll need to walk slowly, or she'll no be back from the milkin',' she instructed me.

'What time does she open then?' I asked, for it was nearly eleven o'clock.

'I believe it's nine o'clock rightly,' she answered, 'but the cows have to be milked and she canna' be in two places at once, can she now?'

I admitted the logic of her statement and, unwilling to incur the displeasure of the postmistress, I walked very slowly in the direction indicated to me, deriving a furtive and infantile pleasure from plodding through the deepest puddles and squelching through the thickest mud.

The crofters' houses, some low and thatched, some two-storied and slated, were scattered along both sides of the road. Through their open doors were wafted the sounds of clinking dishes, thudding feet and Gaelic voices engaged in fierce altercation; sounds which ceased with suspicious suddenness as I approached. Once or twice I turned quickly, hoping to see some hidden watcher betrayed by the twitch of a curtain, until I realised that there were no curtains to twitch. Inquisitive dogs appeared in every doorway; collies and cairns; some venturing so far as to smell at my heels, others content to hail me from the sanctuary of their own doorsteps. Here and there a tethered cow grazed, placidly indifferent to its restricting chain. Sheep nibbled contentedly in the circle allowed them by their short ropes. In front of one house a horse moved gingerly, revealing the fine-meshed chain stretching from its hind leg to a stake some distance away. A turkey gobbled forlornly and stood stork-like on one leg, its other leg being secured by a length of parcel string to a nearby bush. The crofters appeared to have brought the science of tethering down to a fine art, and every kind of animal seemed to accept a length of rope and a stake as a matter of course.

Surrounding each of the houses was a small plot of land bounded by a drystone wall, which in England we should call a garden, but which Morag had grandly referred to as 'the park'. This 'park' was distinct from the rest of the croft, which was itself also bounded by the inevitable drystone walls. In every case the entrance gate was achieved by knocking down a few of the stones and placing across the gap an old iron bedstead. Some of the bedsteads were ancient and rusted; others, obviously newly discarded, still sported their ornamental brass knobs and rings. They were of every conceivable pattern, so that I was able to amuse myself by trying to guess which design I should come upon next. That night, when I wrote to Mary telling her of my journey and my reception and impressions so far, I added: *Just imagine, every house I've seen has an old bedstead for an entrance gate and I've already counted at least twenty-two!*

A small sign, 'Post Office', led me to a corrugated-iron shed. I knocked on the door; there was no response, and despite repeated knockings the place remained still and silent. I looked again at the notice. Yes, it definitely said 'Post Office'. I continued knocking, but still nothing happened. A little way along the road some small boys were playing a scuffling game of football and, thinking that they might know the whereabouts of the postmistress, I went towards them. I was not really surprised to find that their football was a much battered brass bedknob. They ceased their game as I approached, but my question stunned them into an embarrassed silence. I repeated it.

'She'll be at her house likely.' One boy vouchsafed the information shyly.

'Is the post office closed then?' I asked, gesturing towards the iron hut.

'That's not the post office just now.' The boy's voice strengthened as he gained courage. 'That's just the post office when there's tourists about in the summer. In the winter the stamps would all stick up with the damp in there, but she'll give them to you from her house.' He indicated a small cottage at the end of a cart track through one of the crofts, but a glance at my watch told me that the postmistress must remain undisturbed until after lunch. I quickly retraced my steps homewards.

In the cooking of my lunch Morag had excelled herself and once again the tablecloth was snowy white. The helping of meat was liberal enough for three appetites, but unfortunately it was served on an afternoon-tea plate, and even without the addition of vegetables the gravy was threatening to spill over the edge. I suggested a larger plate, hastily reassuring Morag, as I saw her woebegone expression, that it was not the inadequacy of the dinner that was disturbing me. Eagerly she hurried from the room, soon returning with an ordinary-sized plate which she was surreptitiously polishing on a corner of her apron. It was a pretty plate and I exclaimed delightedly at its attractive border of what I then took to be tiny yellow crocuses; their subsequent appearance and disappearance, however, was so perplexing that I reluctantly came to recognise them to be splashes of egg yolk, and was inordinately thankful that the green leaves at least showed signs of permanency. I complimented Morag on her cooking; the less said about her dish-washing the better.

I was awakened from my after-dinner doze by the noise of the front door opening and the rumble of a motor. Through the window I could see a lorry, loaded high with coal, jolting slowly down the road past Ruari's house and towards the sea. I went into the hall where Morag was hurriedly tying a scarf over her head.

'It's yon man with the year's coal,' she grumbled in answer to my question; 'and here it is a Saturday too, the rascal! Another two hours and the tide will be takin' it away on me.'

I offered to help but, though it was plain from her manner that she would welcome assistance, Morag refused my offer after a disparaging glance at my neat suit. I changed into an old skirt and jacket and hurried outside. The tide was out now and the entrance gate was high and dry; beside it on the shingle a huge mound of coal had been dumped. Morag was already engaged in bitter recriminations with the lorry driver, whom I recognised as my taxi-driver of the previous evening. They broke off as I approached and the man greeted me with polite warmth.

'It's goin' to rain,' he told me cheerfully, with a knowing glance at the sky.

'Do you think so?' I asked.

'Certain to,' replied the driver emphatically. 'Now, Miss Peckwitt, I'll tell you a good weather sign: if ever you should see trees up in the sky you may be sure it's goin' to rain before very long.'

I thought that if ever I saw trees up in the sky I should expect to see pigs flying in and out of them; but I nodded and stared intelligently at a cloud-patched ceiling of grey, deeming it better to accept his prediction without comment.

'I canna' give you tea, if I'm to get this in before the watter's up,' snapped Morag to the driver.

The latter jumped hastily into the cab of the lorry. 'I couldn't stay for tea supposin' it was waitin' on me,' he retorted. 'I have two tons for the manse tonight yet.'

'Two tons for the manse?' shrilled Morag. 'They'll never take it from you tonight.'

'Then they'll do without it for longer than they care to,' said the driver with a sardonic chuckle. He let in the clutch and the lorry jolted away along the foreshore.

'So the taxi-driver is the lorry-driver too,' I observed to Morag as we set to work with shovels and pails.

'He's not just the taxi-driver and the lorry-driver,' replied Morag caustically, 'but he's the coal merchant, the carrier, the undertaker and the garage'; she counted off his trades on her fingers, 'and I don't know what else besides.'

I began to feel slightly embarrassed. 'He must be quite wealthy in that case,' I said.

'Wealthy?' she returned, 'Why, if I had as many half-pence as he has pounds I'd be comfortable for the rest of my life.'

I recalled the man's disinclination to accept my shilling tip and was glad that my exertions over the coal could account for the flush which spread over my neck and face.

'And swank!' continued Morag, rubbing salt into the wound. 'Why, he's that much swank on him as would suit a duke.'

Abruptly I changed the subject.

'How much coal is there here?' I asked, eyeing the prodigious heap.

'Two tons,' she lamented, 'and in less than two hours the tide will be away with it.'

It seemed an impossible feat for the two of us to transfer the coal from the shore to the coal-shed in under two hours. Morag must have read my thoughts.

'Ruari's away with his cow to the bull or he'd give us a hand,' she explained as we shovelled.

In all my life I have never performed such hard physical labour as I did during those two hours. The coal had to be carried pailful by pailful up the three stone steps and about ten yards beyond to a shed beside the henhouse. The day was dank and chill; our clothes were speckled with mist, but so fierce was our labour that we needed to work without waterproofs or even jackets. Morag wielded a workmanlike shovel, but I had to be content with a small fire-shovel that was of more ornament than use. After my sixteenth pailful my back ached, my arms felt as though they were being torn from their sockets and my 'funny bones' as though they had been beaten repeatedly with hammers; yet we had made little or no impression on that glistening black mound. Fenziedly we filled and carried, constantly glancing behind us at the line of water creeping inexorably nearer. All the time we worked my landlady discoursed on such subjects as the wisdom of teaching young girls mathematics; juvenile delinquency (a police friend in Glasgow

35

had told her that 'galvanised delinquency had reached terrible propulsions these days'); and, inevitably, politics. I soon learned that Morag was an enthusiastic Tory; and by the time the last pail of coal had been tipped into the shed she was convinced that I was equally enthusiastic. The truth being that I had no breath to express any opinion save a grunt.

By the light of a hurricane lantern firmly planted on the top of the wall and with the sea washing around our ankles, we scooped up the last pailfuls from among the shingle. When daylight came we found that we had scooped up a fair amount of shingle too, but by lamplight wet, black pebbles look remarkably like wet, black coal.

'My, but I'll be fallin' asleep in church tomorrow I'm that tired,' said Morag as we plodded wearily up to the house.

'So you go to church?' I asked.

'Why, yes indeed,' she replied in shocked tones. 'I go whenever the missionary's there to take the service.'

(Missionary?—I recalled the words of my doctor, 'people tell me they're only half civilised up there'— but missionaries?)

'I thought you said in your letter that you had a minister,' I said.

'Surely, there's a minister for marryin' and buryin' and such, but he's too busy to be takin' services here, there and everywhere. He has missionaries to do that for him.'

'The missionary's not a minister then?'

'No, no, indeed!' She turned a pair of soulful blue eyes on me. 'Sure the missionary's wages aren't as big as the minister's, for he doesna' feel the call of God till he retires from work and finds his pension won't keep him,' she explained with startling irreverence. 'But the minister now, he's a true man of God. He starts earnin' when he's quite a young man.'

After her piety of the night before, her guileless sarcasm shocked me.

The next morning, my landlady, sober of mien and attire, placed my breakfast before me. The weather, in direct contrast to the coal merchant's prediction, showed a distinct improvement, but the atmosphere was heavily Sabbatarian. When I offered to take the food to the hens Morag merely nodded and thanked me meekly. Outside I was relieved to find that the hens still had their weekday appetite and scrambled eagerly for their food.

'Will you give a bitty to the cockerel under the creel yonder?' requested my landlady in a sepulchral call.

I went to the henhouse where she pointed and there discovered an upturned peat creel from which a cockerel's head was thrust disconsolately forward. Having dropped plenty of food through a gap in the wickerwork I returned to the house.

'Why is the cockerel under the creel?' I asked. 'Is he sick?'

'It's the Sabbath,' Morag assured me piously, as though I was not already well aware of it.

'Yes,' I agreed doubtfully, 'but do you always put the cockerel under a creel on Sundays?'

'Yes I do!' she burst out, 'but there's plenty here as don't. Churchgoin' folks too, and all they do on the Sabbath is to tether their cockerels with a piece of string.' Her eyes were flashing as she continued. 'I say if you live up to your religion then you must do the job properly and close him up altogether. Tetherin's only hippinocrasy,' she added severely.

I listened to her outburst with a show of concern, but was glad when a bubbling kettle compelled her to return to her own room.

Church service, it transpired, was held at the convenience of the missionary, not the congregation, and Morag asked me if I would prefer a late lunch or an early one. I plumped for a late meal and accordingly, a little before one o'clock, we set out; Morag garbed in

37

black and wearing low shoes that revealed a pair of sturdy ankles. The church, she told me, was on the high road. I thought it strange that I had not noticed it on my stroll to the post office but I put it down to the mistiness of the morning, or perhaps to the counter-attraction of the bedsteads. Slowly and quietly we walked, as befitted the Sabbath, and at varying distances in front of us and behind us other figures in groups of twos and threes marched at the same devout pace. The men and the elderly folk were clad uniformly in sombre black; the young women and girls flaunted the excruciating blues and reds so beloved of the countrywoman, whatever her complexion.

It was not until we were picking our way along a muddy and refuse-strewn path that I realised from the subdued knot of people at its door that the ugly iron shed we were approaching was in fact the church.

'Why on earth don't they clean up the path?' I said to Morag.

'Aye, well, d'you see, the man who has this piece of land is of a different religion altogether and it just pleases him to make his dung heap in the path of them he calls the "unrighteous".'

At the church door we were greeted by a scissor-shaped man in an old-fashioned black suit.

'The precentor,' Morag said as he took my hand. Having previously been under the impression that a precentor was some sort of miniature organ I was quite interested to shake hands with a flesh-and-blood one, even though the flesh and blood were limp and chilly. His whispered welcome was scarcely audible. Around and about us the other worshippers also whispered, the fierce sibilance rushing and eddying through the tin church like wind through the tree tops. My own words acknowledging the introductions fell into their midst like thunderbolts.

A young man came forward in response to a nod from Morag.

'This is Lachy,' my landlady introduced him in a whisper, adding, 'the other half of the boat.'

I shook hands with a young man whose stocky, muscular figure was constrained by a tight navy-blue suit. His neck was disfigured by a large goitre which appeared to contend with an exceedingly tight collar for the privilege of choking him. Lachy, with punctilious politeness, and much to Morag's surprise, escorted us to our seats; and, having seen us settled, promptly sat himself down on the form in front. A couple of minutes later a vile-smelling woman nodded familiarly at the two of us and took the seat beside me.

I stared around the interior of the church, which was as uninspiring as the exterior, being furnished with several backless wooden benches on which numerous people slouched in impious attitudes. The place was disgustingly dirty; toffee papers littered the concrete floor; cobwebs festooned the beams of the iron roof; the plain glass windows were obscured by dirt, and, as there was no heating arrangement of any sort, it was evident that the fervour of the worship was expected to overcome the frigidity of the atmosphere. A small drunken-looking table, carved all over with initials, stood at the far end of the room and on its dusty top reposed a mouldering Bible. An ordinary kitchen chair and two tarnished brass oil-lamps completed the furnishings of the most squalid little House of God it has ever been my misfortune to enter.

From outside there came the noise of a motor followed by the slam of a car door.

'Here's the missionary,' whispered Morag.

Footsteps thudded up the muddy path and a few moments later an obese, pale-faced figure entered the church alone. He too was garbed in black, but more expensively so than the parishioners, and as he strode along the central aisle he had so much the air of a star performer appearing on the stage that I had to stifle a desire to applaud. Restrained hissings and obsequious flutterings echoed through the church but ceased abruptly as the missionary, reaching the table, turned to stare long and superciliously at the congregation. He spoke a few words which I could not understand, but as Morag prodded my waist and rose I stood up obediently.

The missionary, with legs widely straddled, one arm hidden behind his back and his eyes turned virtuously to the roof beams, began a prayer. Morag had intimated that it was to be a prayer, otherwise I should have thought it was the sermon, so long did it last. Colder and colder grew my feet, momently more agonising became the crick in my neck, and still the vehement supplication and exhortation continued. I became aware of the sound of rustling paper behind me, then to the right of me, to the left of me and also in front. Morag thrust a bag of peppermints under my nose, thus adding her own particular rustle to what had by this time become a general one. Soon the rustling was replaced by a steady sucking which resounded from every corner of the building. I was sure that the missionary must be deaf if he could not hear it. At last the long prayer finished and we were able to sit down, whereupon the vile-smelling woman seized my hand, thrust two damp, warm peppermints into my palm and instructed me in a hoarse whisper to pass one of them on to Morag. I nodded and obligingly passed on both sweets.

The precentor now stood and, there being no organ or other instrument in the church, began to intone the paraphrase in a shaky tenor voice while the congregation, still seated, joined in demurely, their lips barely moving, their eyes fixed vacantly in front of them. Impressive as were the prayer and the paraphrase, the sermon which followed was even more so.

It began with the missionary standing very still behind the little table and treating the congregation to a prolonged combative stare. His eyes bulged; his lips pouted. He continued to stare silently for a while and then without the slightest warning he raised his fleshy fist and brought it crashing down upon the frail little table. The congregation flinched perceptibly.

'Someone has been here!' the missionary bellowed accusingly, and thirty or forty pairs of eyes stared in awed consternation.

Again he raised his fist above his head and brought it crashing down. Some of the women present appeared to shudder in sympathy with the table.

'Someone has been here!' he repeated in even louder tones.

I accepted another peppermint from Morag's proffered bag. For the third time table and fist met and now the voice rose to a thunderous roar:

'Someone has been here!'

There followed a significant pause and the walls of the church seemed to echo his words with tinny accusation. Clutching the table with fat, white hands, one of which was now ringed with grey dust, he dropped his voice to a gentle, sorrowful whisper.

'The Devil has been here,' he lamented. 'The Devil! The Devil, I say, has been here!'

The repetition was irritating and was hardly complimentary to the previous Sunday's preacher. Furtively the missionary ran his tongue over thick lips; tears glistened in his eyes, and as he opened his mouth to speak again he almost lost the peppermint he was sucking.

'Don't ask me how I know.' His voice was rising again. 'Don't ask me how I know,' he repeated. 'But I know! I know! I know!' The sentence culminated in an ecstatic shout and, letting go the table which rocked unsteadily, his hands flayed the air like those of a man who has suddenly had the support snatched from beneath his feet. I wondered if he was holding the Devil responsible for all those toffee papers.

His brow was moist with perspiration; the tears had started to trickle down his cheeks; both his hands were by now exceedingly dirty and I was much relieved to see him produce a clean handkerchief; but instead of using it as I expected he held it in front of his mouth, disgorged the remainder of his peppermint, and bundled it back into his pocket. The tears were allowed to flow unchecked.

'Ahhhhhh,' he breathed sadly. 'It is easy to smell the Devil amongst you.'

I almost giggled as the melodramatic words ran through my head like a play title: *The Devil smells of Peppermint*.

'Beware of the Devil in your hearts and in your homes,' he adjured us. 'Beware of the Devil who calls you out on Friday nights to listen to his luring music.'

A man whom Morag had pointed out as being the gamekeeper and the village piping enthusiast looked suddenly startled and a guilty flush suffused his face and neck.

'Beware of the Devil that teaches you to dance cheek to cheek, belly to belly, with strangers,' continued the missionary.

There was an aromatic gasp from the congregation, and the missionary, enamoured of his theme, licked his lips appreciatively. (Morag explained to me afterwards that the denunciation was occasioned by the introduction of the fox-trot and the one-step to the Island dance hall.)

Dumbfounded, I fixed my gaze on the shoulders of 'the other half of the boat' and was astonished to see that they were heaving with mirth. I blinked rapidly but as my incredulous eyes travelled along the row of dark-clothed backs in front of me I perceived that several pairs of shoulders were shaking uncontrollably. I looked at the women. They all appeared to be staring piously into their laps, their mouths exaggeratedly prim. Catching an oblique glance from my landlady I saw that her eyes were merry as a child's. In fact the whole congregation, except for one obvious half-wit who sat tense and horror-stricken on the edge of a front pew, seemed

42

to be nearly exploding with laughter. I stared steadily at the dirty floor.

At length the harangue ceased and the collection began. If the service had struck me as being crazy I was equally shaken by the manner of the collection. Two of the older members of the congregation produced little black velvet bags and made with what I thought to be irreverent haste towards the back seats, jostling and striving as one tried to outdo the other. Money dropped and rolled and was struggled for on the concrete floor, the collectors rising grey and dusty from between each row of seats. I dropped my contribution into the first bag thrust under my nose and received a savage glare from the bearer of the rival bag.

As soon as the collection was over the service was concluded and the worshippers shuffled out with dreadful solemnity. After the histrionic display we had just witnessed I felt that our exit could very appropriately have been accompanied by the slam of tip-up seats and a band playing the National Anthem. Outside the church chattering groups formed; they seemed to be waiting for something. They were.

The two collectors came outside and stood facing each other, their faces red and angry. Behind his back each held his full collection bag. Simultaneously each extended a hand towards the other and demanded: 'Give me that bag!'

'What on earth is the matter with them?' I whispered.

'Well, it's the joint service that does it,' said Morag. 'They shouldn't give permission for joint services, for they always lead to trouble.'

It appeared that there was only one church in Bruach which had to be shared by two rival denominations. Everything went smoothly except for the collections. 'Last time they were after goin' round the back of the church and fightin' for it.'

'But surely the missionary . . .' I began.

'Ach,' said Morag, 'he'll not come out of the church till one of them goes back with the money.'

The combatants were becoming angrier, staring at each other defiantly. There seemed to be little prospect of ending the tension.

'They ought to toss for it,' I said flippantly.

Morag looked at me with admiration and then spoke out. 'Miss Peckwitt says you'd best toss for it,' she told them.

Miss Peckwitt wanted at that moment to become invisible; but I was surprised to find myself the centre of approbation.

'That's right! That's what they should do,' said the precentor, and everyone echoed his words, including the rival collectors. He extracted a penny from one of the bags.

'It was Miss Peckwitt that suggested it and as she belongs to neither side I think she should toss it,' he said. Meekly I took the penny.

'Now call out,' said the precentor. 'Which side will you have, the head or the man with the hayfork?'

They called; I tossed.

'Which side is it, Miss Peckwitt?' demanded the precentor.

'The man with the hayfork,' I said tremulously.

The scene was over; the loser handed over his bag with good grace and the winner disappeared into the church. Gradually the worshippers dispersed.

The sky was becoming overcast as we hurried home.

'What did you think of the service?' asked my landlady.

'That missionary of yours is just a witch doctor,' I said.

'Aye,' she admitted, 'but yon fellow's always the one for a good laugh.'

'Is that why people here go to church?' I enquired ironically.

Morag chuckled guiltily. 'Ach, no, it's no like that at

all really,' she denied. 'It's just that man, the rest aren't like that at all. They say he's had too much religion. You know, one of these religious mannequins.'

It was dusk before we had finished our meal, so while my landlady rushed off to milk the cows I prepared the food for the hens.

'Don't forget the cockerel,' she reminded me as she disappeared with her milk pail.

I knew I should never forget the cockerel.

3

Of Fare and Fishing

My stay in Bruach lengthened from weeks to months and looked as though it might continue indefinitely, for the attractions of the Hebrides are indisputable and compelling; there were times when I felt I could not wish to forsake them for whatever England might offer in recompense. I soon surprised myself by becoming interested in agriculture generally and surprised my neighbours by my zeal in learning to milk, to plant and hoe potatoes, to make hay and even to scythe and to cut and carry peats.

The transition from town to croft life was accomplished without too much difficulty, though it was certainly not without its humorous side. Despite Morag's expert instruction, my early efforts were amateurish in the extreme: my haycocks, however painstakingly built, were wont to collapse; my corn-stooks curtsied; potatoes habitually impaled themselves on the tines of my fork; my scything was erratic to the point of danger—('You'll be hoppin' around on one feet if you thrust yourself about like that,' Morag continually warned.) However, perseverance brought some measure of skill and in time my offers of voluntary labour came to be accepted by the villagers with something akin to eagerness instead of sly mirth.

My own unfamiliarity with country folk and their habits was, if anything, outrivalled by the Bruachites' ignorance of English people, for Bruach was extremely isolated and, apart from a meagre sprinkling of tourists

46

who came and went during the summer months, it was only the indefatigable researchers into crofting conditions who ever succeeded in negotiating the steadily worsening roads and penetrating the quiet seclusion.

The general impression seemed to be that 'the Englishman is a fool but his money is good,' and during the whole of my Hebridean sojourn I doubt if I gave the Islanders cause to alter that opinion. I must admit that at first it comes as a shock to the egotism to realise how far one is discounted merely because of being English, though one eventually grows accustomed to it; so that I was not more than ordinarily surprised when Morag, after telling me that a certain woman had been married twice, replied, in answer to my observation that I had heard the woman had been married three times: 'Aye, my dear, so she has rightly, but the first one was an Englishman.'

The phenomenon of an Englishwoman actually resident among them—and an uninquisitive Englishwoman at that—was enough to arouse the curiosity of the crofters to fever pitch, and my movements were followed by the populace as eagerly as the movements of Royalty are followed by the Press. Trifling incidents which befell me during my walks were already known to Morag before I returned home, and inevitably her greeting would be some comment on the day's adventures, such as: 'I'm hearing you met so-and-so by such and such a place today,' or: 'They're after tellin' me that you near got caught by the tide and had to paddle.'

This constant prying on my activities was naturally a little irksome, but I assured myself that the interest was only temporary and soon I should be able to enjoy my leisure without feeling myself to be the cynosure of all eyes. As I have said, I knew practically nothing about country folk!

Some of the stories concerning my initiation into Island life are still told in Bruach today, and will, I am sure, continue to be told for years to come. The story for instance of how, after volunteering to collect a broody hen for my landlady, I struggled the whole length of the village, one hand clutching one leg of a vociferously outraged bird which flapped wildly above my head, the other hand shielding my eyes from I knew not what. Morag, striving to compose her features, met me outside the house.

'What fool gave you that?' she asked.

I explained with some irritation that the lady of the house had been out and that the ancient grandfather and myself had chosen this hen because it happened to be the only one sitting down at the time.

'Why, a broody hen should sit under your arm as quiet as a lamb,' she told me, 'but that rascal you have there will no sit on an egg supposin' you set a haystack on top of her.'

My spirits sank on learning that my errand had been in vain. 'What shall I do with her then?' I demanded, for the hen's struggling and clamouring showed no signs of decreasing.

'Let go of her leg,' counselled Morag, adding optimistically, 'she'll likely find her own way home.' I let go the leg and the hen, still squawking, flew heavily towards the sea.

'That's no a broody hen at all,' said my landlady. 'You can always tell a broody hen by her clockin'.'

A few days after this episode, I was passing a neighbour's garden when I happened to notice a sulky, bedraggled-looking hen which was being cold-shouldered by its companions. It looked distressingly familiar. I was sure in this case that Morag's optimism had not been justified and that it was up to me to do something about it, so sidling over the wall, in a manner that was fast becoming second nature, I cautiously approached the bird.

'Chuck, chuck,' I called seductively.

The hen appeared to have recognised me and, with a frenzied squawk which immediately stirred the rest of the hens into a screaming cacophony of terror, she took wing, scattering stray feathers as she flew, and disappeared behind a distant byre. I never saw her again. I doubt if her owner did either.

They tell too the story of the pet sheep.

It happened that I had taken a picnic lunch and had spent a long day exploring the moors. Evening was coming on by the time I started on the homeward road and I had not gone far when I heard a forlorn 'baa' and looking round saw a lone sheep hurrying towards me.

'Hello,' I greeted it, and as it 'baad' and rubbed itself against me in an ecstasy of recognition I knew it to be a motherless lamb which Ruari had brought home from the hill for his wife to bottle feed. The lamb had, not unnaturally, become the pampered pet of the household, cropping the grass of the park and running in and out of the kitchen like a frisky child. When it had grown into a fat and sturdy 'wether' it had become rather a problem and had to be banned from the house. Unfortunately, this did not discourage its devotion and it rarely ventured far afield, except to follow Ruari or Bella whenever they went to the well.

How the sheep had managed to stray so many miles from home I was at a loss to understand. Whether it really knew me or whether it would have thrown itself on the mercy of any passing human I could not be sure, but there was no escaping the fact that it was lost and that it was delighted to see me. I was certain Ruari would be missing the beast and wondering what had happened to it. Doubtless at this moment he would be out looking for it. With this in mind I unwound the scarf from my neck and tied it around the wether; then, feeling rather like the Good Shepherd and anticipating Ruari's gratefulness for having restored the lost sheep to the fold, I led the animal homeward. It was eager enough to be led and trotted obediently beside me all the way until, as we neared Ruari's house, I slipped my scarf from its neck and waited to see what would happen.

49

Rushing forward delightedly, the wether bounded through the gate and, running up to the door of the house, commenced butting it with its horns, 'baaing' happily.

The door opened quickly and Ruari, obviously interrupted in the ritual of shaving, appeared on the threshold. I was just congratulating myself on my good deed when I was shocked to hear Ruari utter a curse which made me flinch and to see him put his boot against the thick fleece of the former pet and push it roughly away. He then embarked on an ear-stinging recital of the poor beast's pedigree, during which he got right down to fundamentals. Turning, he saw me.

'Look!' he commanded exasperatedly. 'Fourteen miles and more I trudged yesterday with that beast. Fourteen miles I took him to try would I lose him, and here he is back at my own doorstep within twenty-four hours!' A resentful oath bubbled again in his throat. 'Would you believe it, Miss Peckwitt, that a beast would know its way home from fourteen miles away?'

I replied feebly that I should have great difficulty in believing it, and Ruari, still muttering, drove the unhappy animal towards the byre.

With ears still singing I slunk away home where Morag awaited me. Almost the first words she said were: 'You'd best give me your scarf and let me wash it. It'll be smellin' awful strong of sheep likely?'

Before I had been long in the village I discovered that one of the essential differences between the English and the Hebrideans is that, in general, the former 'live to eat' and the latter 'eat to live'. There is a vast difference. The crofters ate sporadically, alternately gorging and fasting, while their eating habits made those of savages seem relatively elegant. As a consequence one saw otherwise healthy people looking as wishy-washy as a bowl of gruel; swallowing spoonful after spoonful of baking-soda or patent stomach powder, and if they were 'educated' punctuating their conversation with so many 'excuse-me's' that listening to them was like listening to the playing of a badly cracked gramophone record. In all my years in Bruach I never once met a crofter who regularly enjoyed his food. 'Sore stomachs' were such a frequent complaint that the job of the doctor must have been as monotonous as working at a factory bench, so busy was he kept cutting out identical pieces from an interminable procession of stomachs.

The fare was plain and shockingly lacking in variety. Except for the ubiquitous turnip, vegetables were practically unknown, the average crofter having as little inclination for the eating of vegetables as he has for the growing of them. So much is he in the thrall of his own fatalism that he will stand beside a plot of good cabbages and placidly assert that 'cabbages will not grow hereabouts'. So hypnotic are his mellow pathetic tones that the inexperienced are inclined to accept the truth of this astonishing statement despite the evidence of their own eyes.

In many ways my landlady, having been employed in the laird's kitchen 'till lately' (twenty-five years since!), was far superior to her neighbours both in the preparation and serving of meals, a circumstance for which I was ineffably grateful. She had even progressed far enough to boil mint along with new potatoes, which she did, she said, 'because new potatoes is poisonous and the mint sucks the poison to itself'. However, the laird's menus struck me as having boasted scarcely more variety than those of his tenants, and I had some difficulty in persuading Morag that there were puddings other than rice and custard, and that there were more palatable ways of cooking young chicken than boiling it in a pot along with chunks of ancient turnip. She was always very anxious to please and accept my suggestions without rancour, though she was inclined to dismiss the idea of serving a separately cooked vegetable each day of the week as eccentricity or, as she put it, 'city swank'.

Quite soon after I had arrived in Bruach Morag's own

small stock of turnips had become exhausted and as we were then without vegetables she suggested that I should pay a visit to 'Old Mac', who, at the age of eighty-four, had decided that it was time he started to save up in readiness for his old age. With this object in view he was reputed to have begun experimenting with the novel idea of growing vegetables for sale to hotels on the mainland.

I set out for old Mac's one chilly January morning. The moors were grizzled with hoar frost and the heather roots crisp under foot. A biting easterly wind frisked and rippled through the shaggy coats of the Highland cattle which grazed desultorily, one eye on the sparse grass, the other on the fence which barred them from the clustering buildings below, whence they were expecting their owners to appear bringing them filling bundles of hay. As I passed they lifted their heads hopefully and then, disappointed, returned to the task of filling their enormous bellies.

Dropping down the hillside I came upon Old Mac's croft, which was rush-grown and mossy, and decidedly unpromising-looking even to my inexperienced eye. The house itself huddled low into the hillside and from the single podgy chimney which pierced its grey thatched roof sprouted a wavering plume of peat smoke. I knocked on the door, over which drooped a dark moustache of battered ivy, and the old man's niece, a virago of about forty who also sported a dark moustache, appeared in answer to my summons. I acquainted her with my mission and, all smiles, she led me towards a small thatched shed where her uncle, white-bearded and as podgy as the chimney pot, sat—'marrying his potatoes', the niece explained. I thought I must have heard incorrectly but there the old man was, a heap of potatoes on either side of him. With serious concentration he took a potato from each heap, cut them into the required shapes with a meticulousness which would have been obscene in anyone less primitive, and then tied them together tightly with string. He hoped, he told me, to

52

produce by this method a new variety which he intended to call 'Mac's Victory'.

Like Ruari, old Mac was rather deaf but, unlike Ruari, his speaking voice was inclined to be low and confidential. When the necessary civilities were over and the virago had departed to put on the kettle I repeated my errand. Mac shook his head.

'Turnips?' he said; 'it's no good tryin' for to grow turnips here.'

'Too sour?' I asked politely.

Mac glanced quickly towards the door from which came the sound of his niece's receding footsteps. He put a warning finger to his lips.

'Yes,' he agreed fervently. 'She's been like that ever since her operation. I don't know what's come over her.'

I had an uneasy feeling that the footsteps had paused.

'I mean the soil,' I put in hurriedly.

'Oh aye,' agreed Mac. 'Can't grow turnips.' He sighed deeply. 'The doctor said it might be her glands. I don't know . . . ever since her operation. . . .'

'Did you ever try to grow turnips?' I persisted desperately in unnecessarily loud tones. To my relief the footsteps recommenced and then died away.

'Yes indeed! I grew turnips here one year and they was just like my fist.' He clunched a gnarled hand expressively.

I nodded.

'And I grew them again the next year and they was like . . .' He glanced impatiently about the shed but his eye lit on nothing suitable for demonstration and he continued: 'They was the size of my two fists together.' He hurled his knife into the potatoes and clenched his two fists together.

I smiled encouragement.

'And the third year I grew them, and they was just like my head,' he went on.

A cursory glance at his head showed me that it was certainly not lacking in size.

'Just like my head they was,' he repeated; 'but when I cut them open what did I find?'

He leaned forward earnestly and I rewarded him with a doubtful shake of my head.

'Well then, they was all rotten and maggoty inside,' he said disgustedly.

'Even more like your head,' I murmured jocularly. He stared at me, a quizzical frown between his eyes.

'Beg pardon?' he asked, grunting as he levered himself up from the potatoes to escort me to the house to drink tea.

'I just said it was a pity about the turnips,' I dissembled.

His finger went again to his lips. 'Yes,' he began, 'ever since her operation. . . . I don't know . . .'

We were almost at the door of the cottage.

'Come away in!' called the virago hospitably. She fixed me with a resolute smile, and I retaliated with equal determination.

I said goodbye to Old Mac and his niece after listening to the recital of a list of vegetables which included all I'd ever heard of and more besides, and which were bound to be failures on the Island because of the ravages of sun; rain; wind; mist; snow; hail; dogs; cows; sheep; horses; rabbits; deer; hens; blight; disease and tourists. From the way the old man referred to them I should have bracketed the last three together. It seemed that the growing of vegetables was an extremely hazardous business, and that Old Mac would be old indeed before he achieved his nest egg.

On my return home I wrote ordering a sack of carrots and one of turnips from a supplier on the mainland, and with these we managed tolerably well throughout the winter months. By the time spring came round I was heartily sick of both vegetables and an S O S was despatched to Mary, which resulted in the welcome arrival of a parcel containing peas, radishes, lettuce, cabbage, french beans and onions. ('I get funny with the smell of them,' Morag observed, pointing to the onions.)

The preparation of the vegetables Morag accomplished quite successfully with the exception of the beans and radishes, which items must have been strangers to the laird's kitchen. The beans she painstakingly shelled, cooking only the sparse brown seeds and throwing the pods to the hens, exclaiming contemptuously as she put them before me in an egg-cup instead of the usual vegetable dish: 'Sure they silly little peas is enough to crack the nails off a body.' The radishes were laboriously stripped of their colourful outer rind and served as a wan accompaniment to the lettuce. When I explained that they needed only washing, she commented: 'My, my! And I believe they'd be fine and comical if you can do that with them just.'

Due no doubt to the invigorating air of Bruach my own appetite soon became prodigious. My taste in food had always been catholic and I was able to enjoy the novelty and simplicity of the traditional Island delicacies. Porridge, which in town I had eschewed as being too heating, now appeared regularly on the breakfast table—and as regularly disappeared! Dulse soup, carragheen pudding (both seaweeds), I found fairly agreeable and also such things as boiled cormorant ('skart' as it was known locally) and many other kinds of sea fowl, though in some cases I must confess there was decided evidence of their marine habitat. Salt herring, which is the staple food of the crofters, sent me, after my first cautious mouthful, to the water bucket, where I drank more water in less time than I can remember ever having drunk before or since. The taste for salt herring, I venture to suggest, is rarely acquired. Indeed I maintain that to be able to enjoy salt herring one must first be able to speak the Gaelic, or, alternatively, to speak the Gaelic one must first have eaten plenty of salt herring. Which acts as the better throat abrasive I am not qualified to say, but before eating salt herring I think my voice would have been classified as 'soprano'. After I had eaten it my voice sounded to my own ears more like 'basso-profundo'.

Winkles, which during the winter months Morag picked for the London market, I managed to swallow after they had been boiled, but the prospect of letting them wriggle down my throat raw as Morag and Ruari did was too revolting to contemplate. Crabs, very much alive and wriggling, were put into the hot embers of the peat fire for about twenty minutes and then taken out and pulled to pieces with the fingers—a poker being used for all necessary tool-work. I soon became very partial to crab suppers and with practice grew adept at wielding the poker.

'Crowdie', a soft sour milk cheese, was very good when well made, though I could not fancy it served as a pudding with jam and cream; nor could I cultivate a taste for sugar instead of salt with my boiled eggs, which was the way the Bruachites relished them.

Sour milk was much drunk locally, but I had the townswoman's distaste for milk which is even slightly on the turn.

'I canna' understand you,' said Ruari one day, after I had watched him tilt a jugful of thick sour curds to his lips and suck them greedily down his throat. 'You town-folk now, you'd never think to eat a plum or an apple before it was ripe? Then why would you be drinkin' milk before it's ripe?'

I admitted that I had never thought of it in that way.

'Why, when I was for a time in England during the last war,' went on Ruari, 'I never saw a drop of ripe milk but except it was fed to the pigs. Everyone wanted this unripe new stuff straight from the cow. Ach, there's no good in that, except for the tea, and no as much taste in it as in a drink of water.'

During the summer months, when milk was plentiful and rich, Morag made butter—and such butter! In town I would have complained that it was rancid, but though its 'ripeness' stung my throat and I might have to swallow two or three times to every mouthful, I came to enjoy it as I had never enjoyed butter before. Morag's butter churn was a large sweetie jar with a hole in the lid. Through this hole went a rod about three feet long, at the bottom of which was a circle of wood with three or four holes in it. To make the butter Morag would sit on the edge of her chair, the jar, which would be about half full of cream, gripped firmly between her knees; then she would grasp the plunger and jerk it furiously up and down until the butter came. She reminded me of a jockey crouched grimly on the neck of his mount, his eyes fixed on the winning-post, while the illusion was intensified by the spatters of cream from the churn which spotted and streaked her face and hair, like the flecks of foam from a hard-ridden horse. The process some-times lasted for hours and neighbours dropping in would obligingly take a turn at churning while Morag made tea. If she tired, my landlady would go to bed and re-sume her butter-making the next day or even the day after, and sometimes I would hear the 'plop! plop!' of the churn as a background to my dreams. It was a slap-dash way of butter-making—slap-dash in every sense of the word—but we nearly always got the butter, and it usually took longer to make than it did to eat!

Mushrooms in season grew abundantly on the moors and when the villagers heard of my fondness for them they persisted in bringing me all they could find. Day after day the mushrooms arrived, in milk-pails, in jam-jars, in dirty handkerchiefs and even dirtier caps. I ate mushrooms fried for breakfast; I ate them in soups; I concocted mushroom savouries; I experimented with the idea of drying them, but still I could not use all the mushrooms they so generously bestowed upon me. I was touched by the thoughtfulness of my new friends until disillusionment came with the discovery of their ineradicable belief that all mushrooms were deadly poison!

There were of course the dumplings.

There appears to be a tradition that a Scotch dumpling shall weigh at least ten pounds when cooked, no matter what size the household may be. It is fruity and spicy and is a noble sight when it is lifted from the pan in which it has been bubbling away for several hours and turned out on to the largest meat dish. Morag always used one of her old woollen vests, well floured, for a dumpling cloth as this produced a pleasing lacy effect on the outside. Ten pounds of rich fruit dumpling is a formidable quantity for two women to eat their way through unaided and whenever I saw one in preparation I knew I could look forward to a prolonged bout of indigestion. No scrap of it was ever wasted. The first day we ate it in steaming wedges hot from the pan and it was wonderful; on the following days we sliced it cold with a sharp knife and ate it either as cake or heated in the frying-pan for pudding. It was still good. Towards the end, when the pattern of Morag's vest began to take on a decidedly angora-like quality, we hewed the last craggy pieces, soaked them in custard and made them into a trifle. And that was the dumpling finished. I would heave a sigh of mingled regret and relief and put away my magnesia tablets—until the next time.

Fish, naturally, were there for the catching, but though when in England I had glibly prophesied to Mary that I should soon be doing my own fishing, I had never really expected the opportunity to arise. Fishing as a sport did not attract me in any way; I had not even held a fishing-rod in my hand. But 'Needs must when the Devil drives', and to my dismay there came a day when the butcher's meat 'went bad on him' and Morag, having developed a stomach ache, suggested that I should borrow a rod from Ruari and try my luck at catching a fish or two for the evening meal. She seemed to be so sure I could manage the task that, after a moment's hesitation, I decided that fishing might be as pleasant and profitable a way as any of spending an afternoon.

I went to see deaf Ruari, who by this time had become a very good friend of mine—if friendship can be said to exist between two individuals who resemble one another about as closely as a blast furnace resembles a candle. Ruari's powerful voice may at times have been an asset, but a few minutes conversation with him left me feeling bruised all over. It was said of Ruari, and I could well believe it, that his call for his stick and his dog was enough to put to flight the sheep on the far side of the hill. It was said that the cattle on the neighbouring island ceased their grazing and stared apprehensively about them when Ruari called home his own beasts. His dog, having had orders bawled at him since he was a puppy, would obey no command given in an ordinary voice, though he obviously possessed acute hearing. Ruari's voice was unique in my experience, and his habit of 'whispering' confidential asides was a source of embarrassment to everyone within earshot. On Sundays he was repeatedly adjured by both his wife and his sister to 'keep his mouth quiet' lest he should desecrate the Sabbath, and I had no doubt whatever that if Morag could have had her way her brother would have been banished to the creel along with the cockerel. But Ruari was a big man, and a determined one. His blue eyes topped by belligerent tufts of white eyebrows could be very fierce on occasion and when roused from his normal stolid good humour his red face beneath its feathering of white down would deepen to the colour of an over-ripe plum. He certainly would never be dominated by any woman.

This particular afternoon I found Ruari sitting on a kitchen chair in front of his house, his head supported by the ample stomach of the grocer-cum-barber, a cherubic octogenarian, who stood with wide-straddled legs in front of the chair and wielded a pair of scissors menacingly over Ruari's thin white hair. Against the wall of the house squatted a queue of patient but critical 'customers' of all ages and sizes, all alike in their indolence and shock-headedness.

I was greeted courteously and at considerable length, and when the subject of the weather had been completely exhausted and a polite interval had passed I collared Ruari's ear and made my request known. The waiting group concealed their smiles with difficulty. Women have for so long been nonentities in the islands that the idea of any woman, particularly a townswoman, going fishing appeared to them highly ludicrous. Ruari's voluble acquiescence was only slightly muffled by the barber's paunch, which shuddered visibly so that he stepped back a pace with the hurt look of a man who has received a low punch.

Ruari's wife Bella, having heard my voice, appeared in the doorway of the house and beckoned. Bella was pleasant and rubicund and had the shy, foolish look of the woman of seventy who had remained a virgin until she was sixty-five, for she and Ruari had married late in life. She accompanied me to the calf shed where Ruari's rods were kept, so that I might choose one for myself. The door of the shed stood wide open and inside a tousle-headed young boy sat on a log of wood, reading a comic which he held awkwardly in one hand. The other hand grasped a battered pail. I recognised the boy, chiefly by his insignificant nose, to be one of the clan of 'the other half of the boat.'

'Johnny here is waitin' on the calf to watter,' explained Bella with a bashful smile and in answer to my look of enquiry continued, 'He's awful sick with the red watter.' I was not at all sure which of the two occupants of the calf shed had the 'red watter' until Bella went on to tell me that red water fever was a very common ailment of young calves and that the only remedy was to 'make him drink his own watter'. This they intended to do and young Johnny was now engaged in earning a sixpence by waiting, pail in hand, for the calf to perform.

The boy's hopes of his sixpence were apparently fast receding when we arrived on the scene, for so engrossed had he become in his comic that the calf had already foiled him twice. At our entrance, however, the beast woke from its torpor and almost before Bella had finished explaining it rose to its feet; there was a shout, and Johnny leaped forward and at last the precious medicine was safely in the pail.

'There now,' gloated Bella, 'you've brought him good luck; so soon as Ruari's finished with his hairs we'll give him the dose.' She took the pail and put it in a safe place.

I chose my fishing-rod under Johnny's careful supervision. It was of hazel and resembled a young sapling, to one end of which was attached a length of gut and a hook. I carried it outside into the sunshine and looked at it dubiously.

'Have you got any bait?' called the barber jovially.

I admitted that I had no bait and knew nothing about getting bait, or using it if I should get it.

'I'll come and get you bait,' offered Johnny, who evidently had not forgotten my help in the earning of the sixpence.

'Thank you,' I said. 'But aren't you waiting to get your hair cut?'

'Ach, they'll no be finished for a while yet,' he said, as he fell into step beside me.

I called my thanks to Ruari and Bella and, conscious of the surreptitious smiles of the onlookers, balanced the rod carefully over my shoulder and set off down the lane.

'I doubt she'll bring home a shark,' Ruari's 'aside' echoed down the lane and Johnny glanced anxiously at my face. I walked on indifferent, my companion padding silent and barefoot a yard or two to the side of me, wisely keeping his distance, for I was inclined to hurry, causing the fishing-rod to thrash around wildly.

We made our way to a rocky part of the shore and

61

here my young friend pointed out a suicidal boulder which overhung the water, insisting, in spite of my protests, that it was the only good fishing place along the whole length of the shore. It began slowly to dawn upon me that, for the sake of his own reputation, Johnny intended me to catch some fish that day. I yielded hesitantly and with a good deal of trepidation climbed, skated and tottered to the top of the boulder, glad that my residence in Bruach had accustomed me to such exercise. Had I refused to go my youthful friend would doubtless have commandeered the fishing-rod for himself and I should have been relegated to the position of bait-seeker.

Meanwhile the boy was industriously investigating the deep pools among the rocks, grunting and wheezing the whole time like a man nine times his age.

'What is happening?' I called.

'Ahhh!' He gave a grunt which sounded more satisfied than the previous ones and held up a lively, wriggling crab. I felt a little nauseated when he wrenched off its legs and threw them into the sea, but the nausea was nothing to what I experienced when I saw him apply his mouth to the soft underpart of the body and dig his teeth so deeply into it that the shell almost sliced off a portion of his rudimentary nose.

'You'll die!' I gasped.

'I've been dead plenty times then,' he replied seriously.

I almost believed him.

For a few moments Johnny chewed with gusto and then, spitting out the conglomerate mass, divided it into equal portions, which he laid carefully on a flat rock. I had just begun to wonder what on earth had given me the idea that fishing might be a pleasant way to spend an afternoon when the boy whipped out some dirty grey stuff from his pocket and commenced to work it about in his hands.

'What is that?' I asked.

'Fleece,' he answered shortly and, commanding me to watch so that I could learn to do it by myself, he took my rod and proceeded to attach one of the disgusting little morsels of chewed crab to the hook and then to wrap it carefully with the sheep's wool.

'Goodness!' I ejaculated with a smile. 'Do fish need food and clothing then?'

He treated my remark with the contempt it deserved and handed me the rod.

'Now what do I do?' I asked.

'Put it out as far as you can,' he enjoined me.

Gingerly I stepped to the edge of the rock and prepared to do as my tutor advised. In vain I tried to recollect some angling photographs which might give me an idea how to cast; but perversely I could only recall a series of pictorial instructions on how to achieve a good golfing stance. I compromised by holding my rod as though it was a bayonet and I was about to charge.

Having always had the notion that anglers spent their time as Constable depicted them, sitting comfortably beside quiet, tree-shaded rivers, lazily swatting the occasional bothersome fly and carefully unhooking the occasional fish, I was totally unprepared for the rough and laborious business which I had undertaken. My rod was so long and heavy I felt I stood more chance of spiking my fish as it lay on the bottom of the sea than of hooking it near the surface. My feet were threatening at any moment to slip from under me and if this happened the slimy, seaweed-covered rocks would jettison me into the water like a helter-skelter.

'Throw it out,' insisted Johnny impatiently.

'I'm much too afraid I might follow it,' I argued.

'Ach, that's because you have shoes on,' he said with a scornful glance at my very good brogues.

Resignedly I laid down the rod and took off my shoes. Thank goodness I was not wearing stockings. 'The fish round here are very particular,' I remarked peevishly.

'Dinna talk of the fish to their faces,' wailed Johnny in agonised tones. 'You'll never catch a fish if you talk of them by name.'

Groaning inwardly I took up the burden of rod again and as my glance rested on the water I glimpsed a swift iridescent shape in the depths.

'There's a fish!' I yelled shrilly. 'A fish! Look!' I turned excitedly to my companion. His expression was one of extreme anguish.

'There now!' he said sadly; 'You've gone and pointed at the fish, and surely it's that bad luck to point at a fish I'm thinkin' we may just as well go home.'

'Well I'm sorry,' I apologised; 'but you'll have to forgive me. I had no idea the fish were so self-conscious.'

He turned his back on me and went seeking another crab. 'You'll never catch a fish with your rod on dry land,' he threw at me over his shoulder.

Resolutely I lowered the rod.

'Ach, that's no good at all. It's in the sea itself the fish are, not in the air.'

Johnny's continual reprimands began to get on my nerves. 'It is in the sea,' I retorted. 'Come and see for yourself.'

He came, and agreed that the hook was in the sea—just.

'Then you do it,' I said. He relented and taking the rod from my unresisting hands, he brandished it and sent the line out over the water. He then allowed me to take over. Nothing happened except that my rod became momentarily heavier and more difficult to handle; but there was some compensation in that I was able to admire a view of the village which I had not previously seen. The hills away to the right were dark and sombre, their peaks lost in the lowering clouds; the moors were dust coloured and by contrast the crofts looked richly green. In the distance I could see the roof of Morag's house and the gable end of what I decided must be Ruari's barn. Behind me, close to the shore, was a regular row of houses, only a few yards between each. 'Beach Terrace' I mused, and even as I watched a figure came out from one of the houses and waved. I waved back, a foolish action which very nearly caused me to meet the fishes in their own element. There was an audible titter from behind me and I concentrated again on my rod, which by now seemed to have grown from a sapling into a tree trunk. I remembered Ruari's jocose 'aside' and felt that it might yet turn out to be a prophecy. Certainly I seemed to have the right tool for the job.

'How shall I know when there's a fish on the line?' I called.

Johnny, who had got another crab and was busily preparing it, disgorged it into his palm. 'You can never mistake that.'

I invariably mistake the unmistakable. 'I might hook some seaweed,' I hazarded.

'Seaweed doesn't pull and wriggle,' he replied.

Seeing that I was standing on a carpet of the stuff I was immeasurably thankful that what he said was true.

As though Johnny's word had been a sign, I felt almost immediately a sudden twitching of the rod which it was impossible even for a novice to doubt. I forgot the self-consciousness of the fish.

'A fish! A fish!' I cried. 'I have one here.'

'Bring him in then,' ordered Johnny, running towards me. 'Up with the rod.'

In the bustle of those few moments I was not quite sure what happened, but with a sudden onrush of strength I jerked at the rod, which came up in the air, the line flying like a kite behind it; I sat down heavily on a wet and glutinous cushion, aware as I did so that a silvery writhing missile was flying over my head and towards the houses beside the shore.

'Why, you'd be throwin' him right across the Island

and into the sea the other side,' grumbled Johnny irritably.

'Was it really a fish?' I demanded.

'It was indeed,' he assured me. 'but if I don't get it quick it'll likely be hen food!' and skipped away in the direction in which the fish had disappeared.

'See if you can bait yon hook now,' he called. I looked at the hook; I looked at the bait; I looked at the sea, and decided that in this case, ignorance was bliss.

Standing up again I saw that in the garden of one of the houses two figures darted here and there as though seeking something. I had no doubt at all that one of the figures was Johnny, and in a few minutes he returned bearing proudly on the flat of his palm a silver-bellied fish of pathetic size.

'It's no a bad one at all,' he complimented me, caressing the fish gently with his other hand.

I asked him what sort of fish it was and he gave me the name in Gaelic. It sounded rather like 'brickbat'.

'What is it in English?'

'Ach now, I haven't the English for it.'

'Can one eat those sort of fish?' I asked him.

'Indeed you can. They're good. You should have it for your supper supposin' you get no more.'

I thought that might be quite a good idea.

'Where did you find it?'

'Under the gooseberry bush, just beside the manure heap in Kirsty McKinnon's garden,' Johnny said.

'Oh!' I said, abandoning the idea of a fish supper.

I offered the fish to Johnny. He refused politely, saying that they had 'plenty fish' and telling me that by the time I got home I would have an appetite for all the fish I could catch. I did not contradict him and, with one glance at the neat piles of chewed crab and then at the empty hook, he set about the task of re-baiting without further comment.

Thus in partnership we continued fishing for some

time, I manœuvring the heavy rod while Johhny fielded very efficiently in the rear. It was at the moment of retrieving my third 'brickbat' that we noticed one of my shoes was missing. Together we searched, but in vain, and it became obvious that in the excitement of landing the fish one of my shoes had been kicked into the sea.

'Bother!' I said. 'If I've got to walk home barefoot I shan't have time for any more fishing.'

'Kirsty'll lend you a pair of her own shoes,' Johnny consoled me.

Remembering the size and more particularly the shape of Kirsty's feet I rejected the suggestion, feeling that my own would suffer less by going unshod than by being subjected to the torture of having the toes turned up very nearly at right-angles.

Slowly Johnny and I toiled homewards, he carrying the fish and the rod, and I, optimistically, carrying my remaining shoe. It took nearly two hours to cover the distance we had earlier covered in half an hour, and at times I felt that even Kirsty's turn-ups would have been preferable to the grazes and cuts I sustained as a result of encounters with limpet-covered rocks and over-familiarity with shell-strewn shingle.

'What sort of fish d'you like best?' asked Johnny abruptly.

'Plaice, sole, any sort of flat fish,' I replied.

He thought for a moment and then offered: 'I could show you how to flounder next week.'

'I've no doubt you could,' I replied with a forced laugh.

'Will I do that then?'

I glanced at his face. It was quite serious.

'What do you mean?' I asked.

'The flounders. They're good,' he replied. 'Flat fish they are and all you have to do is paddle out into the water when the tide's comin' in and wriggle your toes in the sand.'

'But how do you know when you find a flounder?'

'Ach, you can soon tell, for it's smooth and slippery, and you just bend down quick and whip it up.'

'How deep is the water?'

'Not more than this.' He indicated a line well up on his thigh.

'I don't think I should take to floundering, but I'll give you a sixpence for every one you bring me,' I told him, and saw by the gleam in his eyes that I had said exactly the right thing.

After an absence of about four hours we reached Ruari's house again and I was relieved to find that Johnny was in plenty of time to get his hair cut. The knot of men, no longer shock-headed and indolent, but shorn and alert-looking, still hung about and they had been joined now by 'the other half of the boat'.

'Where's your shoe?' queried the barber, glancing from my bleeding feet to the one shoe which dangled from my hand.

'She's used it for bait,' chuckled Lachy, and was in no way quelled by my withering glance.

I received much congratulation on my catch and even more commiseration on the loss of my shoe.

'But you'll know better next time, and maybe you'll get better fishing.'

'If there is a next time,' I said doubtfully, but they mistook my meaning. (In point of fact there never was a next time.)

'Surely the tide will be right again tomorrow and the day after that too if the weather holds,' someone said as I turned to go.

'Sure the weather will be good.' One of the men spat with the air of making a profound announcement. The Bruachites put more animation into their spitting than they ever allowed to come into their speech. They spat expressively and with consummate skill.

'No it won't then,' someone contradicted him. 'Occasional showers with patches of smoke, that's exactly what the wireless says.'

'Ach, what do they know about the weather?' retorted the seer contemptuously. 'They have no influence on it at all. No influence whatever.'

I left them arguing and limped home where Morag awaited me on the doorstep.

'Ah, mo ghaoil,' she greeted me solicitously, 'what for are you dancin' around in your bare feets at this time of the evening'?'

I assured her that I had never felt less like dancing, bare feet or otherwise, and held up the one shoe for inspection. 'I don't know why I bothered to bring it home,' I said.

'Ach, but you never know what treasure the watter might yield up in time,' she remarked, wagging her head mysteriously. 'It's just as well you brought it for what the sea takes away here it gives up there,' and strangely enough my shoe was eventually washed ashore, about a mile from where I had lost it.

I presented Morag with my catch. They were rather warm and limp, doubtless because Johnny, proud of the success of his pupil, had seized every opportunity to display them, with many tender caresses, as he expatiated on their virtues to me and to everyone we had met.

It appeared that the fish were considered a delicacy in Bruach and my landlady expressed pleasure at the sight of them. 'In the Gaelic,' she told me, 'we have a sayin' that this fish is so good that the daughter is not expected to give it up even to her own mother.'

I decided not to relate the adventures of at least one of my catch.

'And how is your pain now?' I asked.

'Me, I'm just fine,' she replied, 'but you'll need to bathe your feets, my dear, or some of them cuts might go turnin' antiseptic.'

The next morning at breakfast I was confronted by a reproachful one-eyed glare from my share of the 'brick-

bats'. I glared back seeing not the fish but the mouthfuls
of chewed bait; the seeking figures near the dung heap
and Johnny's hot, grimy hands nursing the catch all the
way home.

I said that I would prefer a boiled egg.

4

The Funeral

During the whole of my first year in Bruach there occurred no birth, marriage or death to disturb or enliven the leisurely amble of our lives. With the coming of the second autumn each of the three events came to pass, though not in that specific order.

The birth excited little interest beyond a sporadic procession of female visitors to criticise and admire the baby. The wedding was an insipid affair, the ceremony having taken place in a Glasgow register office, and, except for a complaint from the postman when he was called upon to deliver almost a mailbag full of sanguinary 'wee wee pokes of cake crumbs', it passed practically unnoticed. The death was easily the most impressive event of the year for due to the frequency of inter-marriage everyone was related in some degree to everyone else. As a result the funeral necessitated the attendance of the community *en masse* and the occasion became virtually a general holiday. Now the Gael in holiday mood is irrepressible and, as he arrays himself in exactly the same 'best' clothes whether he is to attend a funeral or a festivity, it is perhaps not surprising that he shows a tendency to combine the two.

The news of the death of Ian Mor, the old fisherman, came one dull October morning when Morag brought in my breakfast tray. Ian Mor had lived with his two sisters in one of the houses which I had dubbed 'Beach Terrace', and, as he had always been a strong, healthy-looking man, his 'being changed' had come as rather a

71

shock to everyone in the village. To everyone, that is, except myself; I could feel little surprise at the death of a man who had passed the allotted span by at least nine years. Rather was I inclined to wonder how the villagers, in view of their seeming disregard for their physical well-being, managed to live so long.

'And he was such a fine man,' Morag lamented tear-fully. 'A good Christian and a good fisherman.' She wiped the sleeve of her cardigan across her brimming eyes.

It was the custom, my landlady went on to tell me, for everyone to pay their respects to the corpse and, though I was loth to do so, she eventually prevailed upon me to accompany her on a visit of condolence to the be-reaved sisters. Thus it was that in the twilight of the evening before the funeral we set out for the house in 'Beach Terrace'. The melancholy of the occasion was increased by the fact that it was raining; the steady relentless rain that makes the grass and the trees and even the sea itself look tired and defeated. Morag had donned her largest oilskin and with it a cloak of intense piety which effectively prevented her from being her usual voluble self. For some time we plodded heavily and silently across squelching crofts and along boggy footpaths until, irritated by the solemnity, I tried to draw out my companion by asking about the deceased fisherman's youth. The experiment was successful.

'Indeed he was very fond of myself at one time,' she confided, a trace of coyness in her voice. 'Why, he'd even made a song for me.' (In Bruach the 'making of a song' for one's sweetheart was of far more importance than the giving of an engagement ring!) Love's ardour had cooled, however, when Ian had learned that Morag's father was not going to be particularly generous in the matter of a dowry for his daughter, and the final break had come when Ian had called one evening to 'do his wee bitty courtin' ', and Morag, instead of sitting beside him on the bench, had set him to carrying manure for the potatoes.

'He was that vexed because I put too much manure in his creel that he never came near me again, and that was the end of it.' The resigned sigh which followed this recital was expressive of my landlady's conviction of the fickleness of all sweethearts.

'Whatever came over him, I don't know,' she continued sadly, 'but he started to get religion. I always used to comfort myself afterwards that maybe I spoiled him with too much manure, but he came near to spoilin' me with too much religion.'

The subject of Ian Mor was summarily dismissed from the conversation as a figure approached us from the opposite direction, doubtless returning from the same errand as that on which we were bound.

'Who on earth can this be without a waterproof on an evening like this?' I asked.

Morag made a noise approximating to a snort.

'Sure it's yon fool Dugan Ruag. He'd be the only one to care naught for rain such as this,' she replied.

Dugan Ruag, hands in the pockets of his tweed jacket, paused as we drew closer and I had no difficulty in recognising the 'precentor'.

'Here, Dugan,' Morag greeted him. 'It's a wonder you're not under the ground yourself, man, with no coat on and a day like this.' The threat combined with the allusion to the prospective funeral made the man spit contemptuously.

'Me? I've been wet since the day I was born near enough, and never taken no harm,' he replied.

'I've seen him in a coat but once in his life,' Morag admitted to me.

'You have once? Then if you've seen me in a coat she must have been blowin' a gale on us. Man! I'd wear a coat for the wind, but the rain!' He spat again and glanced confidently at the leaden sky. 'The rain itself would no hurt me.'

73

'I'm no so sure,' called Morag over her shoulder as Dugan, with elbows pressed close against his body and chin tucked well down, continued on his way. To me she remarked: 'In all the years I've known that man, and there must be over sixty of them, there's few have seen him in a coat, and yet he's never needed a doctor in his life.'

I wondered if peat smoke has an effect on the human skin like tanning on a cow hide, for there was no doubt that many of the Bruachites seemed to be well-nigh impervious to rain.

We reached the house of the late Ian Mor and pushed open the door of the kitchen to receive a restrained welcome from the two sisters, who immediately set about preparing a strupak. While the tea was brewing Morag followed the younger sister upstairs to view the corpse but, though invited to go with them, I shook my head, electing to stay in the kitchen with the elder sister to whom I proceeded to offer my condolences.

'Indeed it was spiteful of him to go and die on us like that,' she replied, with a touch of asperity in her voice.

I reminded the old lady that her brother had lived to a good old age.

'Old age, indeed!' she expostulated with some bitterness, 'he could have been looking after us for ten years and more yet. There's plenty does.'

'He certainly looked very fit the last time I saw him,' I said.

'Aye, aye,' she agreed, 'and who'd have thought now that a little thing like pleurisy could have killed him; and him as strong as a bull.'

'Yes, he did look strong,' I conceded.

'Indeed, that's true enough, but ach! that doctor!' She expressed her contempt for the doctor by a vindictive poke at the fire. 'If I could have got the vet to him instead of that doctor,' she continued to my amazement, 'I truly believe he would have been alive and out fishin'' at this minute, instead of lyin' up there senseless in his bed.'

'Do you really think so?' I asked, too much taken aback to think of anything else to say.

'Yes I do,' she replied with an emphatic nod. 'Why, when our old cow had pleurisy didn't the vet cure her of it in no time at all? And she after havin' a calf regular each year since?' She glared at me intimidatingly as she continued: 'And if he could do that for our cow then I'm no doubtin' but what he could have done the same for our brother.'

I suggested, somewhat diffidently, that the two cases were not identical.

'That's what the vet said when I sent him the telegram,' she answered.

'Of course it would be quite different,' I began, but she silenced me with a peremptory flourish of the dish cloth.

'Same cause, same cure,' she observed epigrammatically. She swabbed the table top vigorously for some minutes before saying with biting scorn: 'I'm tellin' you that doctor couldna' cure a corn on your toe without cutting off your foot and if he cut off your foot and buried it, likely as not it would grow into a poisonous weed.'

I was saved from further confidences by the re-entry of Morag and the other sister who were closely followed by Johnny the bus-driver and Lachy of the boat. Presently the two sisters led the men upstairs, while Morag and I remained in the kitchen. From the room above came the sound of heavy footsteps.

'Johnny and Lachy have come to take Ian down to the sofa in the parlour,' my landlady explained.

'Doesn't the undertaker do that on the day of the funeral?' I asked.

'Well, he would likely,' she replied, her voice dropping to a whisper, 'but d'you see the coffin won't go up these narrow stairs, and the undertaker doesna' care one bit. He just takes hold of the corpus by the feet and

75

drags it bump, bump, bump down the stairs whichever way it'll come best.' She illustrated her words horrifically with a fist on the table.

'Oh no!' I protested.

'Ach, indeed he does, and folks doesn't like it, you know.'

'I should think not!'

'No, they don't,' she repeated; 'they say they never seem to get the noise of it out of their ears for weeks afterwards. That's why the men try to get them down before yon fellow can lay his hands on them.'

At that moment the door of the kitchen opened and the two sisters came inside. They closed the door firmly behind them. The noises in the bedroom above increased, and were followed by the sound of slow, halting footsteps on the stairs, and the scuff of garments against the wooden walls. I tried hard not to listen.

'The weather seems to be improving,' I said desperately.

My companions merely nodded, their whole attention being riveted on the performance without.

'Steady there!' That was Lachy's voice, respectful and quiet.

'Up your end a bit.' That was Johnny, purposeful and businesslike. 'Now over this way a bit.'

Suddenly there was a choking gurgling sound followed by a fit of violent coughing, which caused the four of us in the kitchen to stare questioningly at the door and then at one another.

Johnny's voice, now plaintive, filled the passage: 'Lachy, you damn fool! Lower your end a bit; that was his big toe nearly halfway down my throat.'

From the stairs came Lachy's voice raised in remonstrance:

'For God's sake let him down a minute!'

There was a significant pause and then the ominous noises began again. This time, except for a suspicious-sounding thud, there was apparently no mishap, and a few minutes later Lachy and Johnny burst into the kitchen. Both were inhaling deeply at the cigarettes in their mouths. Johnny made a beeline for the water-pail, helped himself to a ladleful and tilting it to his lips drank deeply.

'Did you manage him all right?' asked one of the sisters unnecessarily.

'Aye, so we did,' exploded Johnny, panting and shaking his head like a swimmer after a cold plunge. 'By God I'm tellin' you that many's the corpse I've carried, but that's the first time I've been forced to swallow one.' He banged down the ladle heavily. 'Bah! What a taste!'

'Whisht!' said one of the sisters, while the other repeated: 'Oh God! Oh God!' over and over again, but whether as an imprecation or an invocation I could not guess.

Johnny and Lachy, after drinking the tea which had been awaiting them, were armed with the gift of a bottle of whisky and departed to dig the grave. They reassured the anxious sisters, one of whom was worried 'in case they should get Ian taken all that way and then find no hole to put him in', that with the stimulus of a bottle of whisky there was bound to be plenty of labour.

'I'm after takin' the bus anyway,' said Johnny; 'so there's plenty will come along just for the ride.'

Other people began to arrive and Morag and I prepared to take our leave.

'It's funny Old Farquhar hasn't been near since Ian died,' said the sister who saw us to the door. 'I don't believe he can have heard yet.'

Thus obliquely she suggested that we should take upon ourselves the task of acquainting Farquhar with the news of Ian's demise and, as the rain had stopped, bringing a bright starry sky with a full moon on the point of rising, we readily agreed.

Old Farquhar was the tatterdemalion of the village, who passed a hermit-like existence in a secluded little corrie a couple of miles away from the nearest habitation. I had seen him infrequently, and then always hurrying awkwardly in the opposite direction. I was hearing of him constantly, for in addition to his being something of a bard he was reputed to possess the 'second sight', but I had not yet met him and, as his was a character obviously worth investigation, I was not averse to taking this opportunity of doing so.

To reach Farquhar's house we had to pass by the graveyard. The empty bus stood outside and we could not help being aware that somewhere beyond the trees an extremely merry party of grave-diggers were already engaged upon their task.

'Dig first and drink after!' called Morag, with a hand cupped to her mouth, but there was no response and the sounds of merriment continued unabated.

Farquhar's cottage when we reached it appeared to be nothing more than a dilapidated barn, and, in spite of Morag's reiteration, I could not at first believe that it was actually occupied by a human being. It was stone built and thatched, but the latter was black with age and part of the house seemed to have fallen away altogether. A space in the wall which had at some time been a window was now partly blocked with a barrel, from the chinks around which there eddied drifts of peat smoke.

Morag called out and then opened the door. Hesitantly I followed her into a room where an old man sat at a table slicing a loaf with a large clasp knife. He looked up as we entered and, brandishing the knife in welcome, bade us be seated. My companion lowered herself on to a plank supported by two more barrels and introduced me to Farquhar, a scarecrow of a man whose clothes hung raggedly on his gaunt, bony frame. As he shook my hand his blue eyes gazed at me with quick intelligence from deep in his lean, dark face, the skin of which was fissured and brown as the bark of an ancient oak.

Morag and our host immediately started to compare reminiscences of Ian Mor and, as their conversation lapsed into the Gaelic, I was at leisure to examine my surroundings. The room, though rude, was surprisingly warm with the heat from an enormous peat fire which glowed on an open hearth; the smoke curled upwards to be caught by yet another barrel suspended from a beam and guided through a hole in the thatch. By no means all the smoke escaped this way; quite a lot still eddied about the room, but peat smoke can be thick indeed before it becomes unpleasant. Apart from the table and the plank upon which we were sitting, the only furniture was the barrel on which Farquhar himself was seated when we arrived. The floor was a jig-saw pattern of driftwood of all shapes and sizes, and in all stages of decay. There was no sign of a bed and I wondered if there could possibly be another room in which Farquhar slept, or if he slept on the plank we now occupied. Illumination was provided by a candle which stood, supported by a cake of its own grease, in the centre of the table. Beside the loaf of bread was a jar of jam, a paper of butter, some oatcakes and a saucer of crowdie. Evidently we had interrupted Farquhar at his evening meal but, in no way put out, he gestured enthusiastically towards the oatcakes and jam, telling us as though it was a recommendation that he had made the former himself; he was already wiping a horny finger round the inside of two handle-less cups 'to chase out the dust' before Morag, noticing my frantic signals, managed to convince him that we could not possibly drink another cup of tea or eat one mouthful of food. He was sorely disappointed at our refusal and obviously considered that he was being slighted; but I felt that I had gone through enough for one night. For the life of me I could not have swallowed food in that house.

As Farquhar talked animatedly I noticed that he continued to cut and butter slices of bread, until he had sliced up the whole loaf. It seemed an enormous meal for one old man but, before he resumed his own repast, he deliberately placed one of the buttered rounds at each corner of the table farthest away from him. I had by that time become accustomed to the eccentricities of some of the older crofters but, as Morag had distinctly told me that Farquhar had always lived alone since he was capable of doing so, I rejected the idea that the rounds were set there for a brace of memorable family ghosts. My thoughts were busily engaged in seeking a reasonable explanation for his action when I glimpsed a stealthy movement and, turning, saw two beady eyes followed by the head and body of a large rat appear over the corner of the table. Stifling a scream I jumped up on to the plank.

'There's a rat!' I gabbled hysterically. 'A rat! A rat! He's taken your bread!'

Morag pulled at my skirts; Farquhar stopped eating and stared at me; only the rat remained completely self-possessed.

'Surely,' answered Farquhar mildly. ''Tis for him that I'm after puttin' it there.'

'You put it there for a rat?' I stammered in awed incredulity. 'Is it poisoned then?'

'Indeed no,' replied Farquhar, 'but I always put something out for him when I take my own food and he knows it well.'

'Why?' I asked weakly.

'Because if I didn't he would come up here and pinch mine,' answered the old man philosophically.

I gripped Morag's arm as a second rat appeared at the opposite corner and took away the remaining slice of bread.

'That's his wife.' Farquhar explained, but I was too upset even to pretend an interest in rodent relationships.

'Is it just two pets you have?' I asked, gingerly lowering myself to the seat.

'Ach indeed no!' Morag answered for him. 'Sure all the rats in the village is welcome in Farquhar's house.' She turned to the old man. 'I hope the rest are as well trained as those two.'

Farquhar shook his head in sorrowful denial.

I made desperate signs that I wished to go home, but courtesy forbade brief partings and so it was some agonising minutes before I made for the door with what Morag afterwards referred to as 'indigent haste'.

'Come again any time, Miss Peckwitt,' Farquhar called; 'and don't be afraid of the rats,' he chuckled. 'Rats is all right. I always know what to expect from a rat, and that's more than I can say of any other body in this village.'

'What did you think of that now?' queried Morag when we were a safe distance from the house.

I made no reply.

Morag laughed. 'He's got some sense though has old Farquhar,' she said.

'That's not my impression of him,' I retorted.

It was now past midnight; the sky had cleared completely and a brilliantly full moon sailed placidly on an indigo sea. The distant hills were crested with silver and away to our right Rhuna Island appeared like a handful of crushed black velvet dropped carelessly on the water. We walked quickly, for the night was cold. A rabbit darted across my path and I jumped as though shot.

'It's no a rat,' comforted Morag. I guessed that Miss Peckwitt and the rats would soon be making a good ceilidh story.

As we neared the burial ground we saw that the bus still stood outside.

'Good,' said my landlady; 'maybe we'll be able to get a lift home.'

A murmur of voices reached us and turning into the ill-kept graveyard we went towards them, picking our way through tufts of weed and evading the cluttering branches.

Suddenly Morag pulled me to a stop.

'Listen!' she commanded.

I listened with a quaking heart, uneasy among the

shadowed grey tombstones and the sibilant rustling of trees. The voices became distinct.

'My, you near had that one.'

With relief I recognised Lachy's voice, for the second time that evening.

'Try again.' That was undoubtedly Johnny. 'Maybe you'll get it this time.'

There was a sound as of a pebble falling, followed by an exclamation of disgust, and then Lachy's voice again: 'Your turn, Angus.'

Morag held my arm tightly.

'What on earth can they be doing?' I whispered fiercely.

Cautiously edging our way between drunken tombstones and avoiding innumerable rabbit burrows, we moved forward, guided by a strong aroma of whisky which had completely overcome the customary dank and musty smell of the graves, to come upon a spectacle as macabre as that of the graveyard scene from *Hamlet*. Lachy, Johnny and Angus were crouched together in a devout-enough-looking group and were staring as though hypnotised at a wooden cross about ten yards in front of them. I too stared at the cross, for spiked carelessly on top of it was a widely grinning human skull.

'Throw!' Johnny's voice broke out imperiously into the temporary silence.

Angus drew back his arm, a pebble hit the skull, and Lachy, going forward to inspect the target, gave a shout of admiration: 'Good for you, man! That's only five teeth he has left now.'

'Good-oh!' ejaculated Johnny. 'We'll finish him off tonight yet.'

To come across three grave-diggers playing Aunt Sally in the moonlight with a human skull as a target was a shattering enough experience, but I had yet to appreciate the full horror of the situation. Morag stepped forward bristling with indignation.

'Why! Johnny. Lachy, Angus!' she addressed them

with withering scorn. 'I'm ashamed of you! Grown men like yourselves, and nothin' better to do when you're supposed to be diggin' a grave for a poor man, than be playin' games with a corpus.'

The three men looked sheepish, but only for a moment.

'We've finished diggin' the grave,' Lachy replied pertly.

'Show me, then,' demanded Morag.

We followed them towards a clump of bushes a few yards away and looked down at a grave which was no more than two feet deep. Beside it lay a large sod of turf which had been rolled around a tree-trunk, Swiss roll fashion.

'Surely if you don't put him deeper than that the dogs will have him out by the mornin'!' Morag reprimanded, throwing out her hands in a gesture of despair.

'He'll be all right there,' said Johnny brusquely.

'He will not,' answered Morag; 'why did you no put him over there where there's more soil?'

'Because it's so boggy over there now that the first shower of rain will float him out,' replied the undaunted Lachy.

'It's only one bottle of whisky we got and it's only one grave we're diggin',' put in Angus.

Morag sighed heavily.

'Anyway,' continued Lachy, 'even diggin' that far we've dug up one body, so it must be plenty deep enough.'

'Who would that be?' asked Morag with sudden interest.

'You remember yon fellow who was drowned in England about twenty years ago, and they did somethin' to his body and sent him up here?'

'So I do,' replied Morag; 'Euan Beag that was surely?'

'Aye, well it was him.'

'Indeed.' Morag sucked in her breath impressively.

'And what has he kept like?' she asked, curiosity over-coming indignation.

'He was just as good as new,' answered Johnny, and the other two echoed his words.

'And you had to bury him again?' pursued Morag.

'No, we didn't yet.'

'You didn't? Then what did you do with him?'

'Ach, he's just there,' answered Lachy, pointing; 'in the bushes there behind where Miss Peckwitt is standin'.'

Miss Peckwitt moved very quickly away from the bushes.

'He's kept so well all these years, he'll keep a good while longer, so we'll put Ian Mor in and then put Euan Beag on top of him. That's the best way to keep the dogs out.'

The logic of Lachy's argument seemed to appeal to Morag, but she was a little disturbed in case someone might find the body under the bushes.

'Ach, stop frettin',' Angus chided her; 'we covered him over well with bracken and twigs, and there's no-body will find him there unless they tread on him first.'

I followed very closely on the heels of my com-panions.

'Who's that?' Morag stopped and pointed to a mound that was conspicuous by its neatness.

'That's Donachan, that was,' said Lachy in words strangely reminiscent of a famous petrol advertisement.

When we returned to the site of the Aunt Sally Morag went straight up to the skull and, taking it down from its perch, examined it critically.

'Where did you get this?' she enquired.

'Same grave,' said Lachy nonchalantly. 'We found three of them altogether. That one was on the top.'

With renewed indignation Morag turned on the bus driver.

'Why, Johnny! This is your poor great-grandfather, and indeed if he'd been alive this day, I'm tellin' you, you'd no be darin' to play skittles with his teeths.'

This statement was received in a contrite silence which lasted perhaps three seconds.

'Well, I wish I'd inherited his teeth,' said Johnny with unseemly levity.

Morag looked at the skull affectionately, turning it round in her hands as a fond mother might display a pretty doll to a child.

'There's not a mite of him you've inherited,' said Morag tartly. 'You're no half, no, not a quarter the man he was.'

Johnny shuffled uncomfortably from one foot to the other.

'Where's the rest of him?' Morag demanded.

Johnny pointed and Morag handed him the skull with the injunction that he must put it back with the rest of his great-grandfather.

'Not till we've finished our game,' insisted Johnny. 'I've got twenty cigarettes on it, and he canna' feel anythin' now.'

Morag clucked despairingly.

'You shouldn't make people dig graves if you don't like what we do here,' began Lachy argumentatively.

'Why, people must die and graves must be dug,' Morag interposed regretfully.

'Why shouldn't we just burn them?' asked Angus.

'D'you mean we should all be incriminated?' Morag's voice rose shrilly.

'Aye indeed.'

'Angus Mor Ruari! May the Good Lord forgive you for your words,' prayed Morag with infinite pathos. 'I hope nobody will have the wickedness to incriminate me when I die, or I'll haunt them sure as I'm here.' With this threat she drew herself up stiffly. 'Why,' she taunted them as she turned to go, 'to incriminate anybody is as wicked as murderin' them.'

I followed her out of the graveyard, after one hasty glance over my shoulder which showed me the target being replaced and the men preparing to take up their positions. Morag evidently saw it too, for she paused and shouted warningly: 'Johnny! See and don't leave your great-grandfather lyin' around or the seagulls will have him for sure.'

The next day, which was cold and blustery, we gathered at the house on the shore to see Ian Mor on his last journey.

'It'll be the minister himself to bury him,' said Morag; 'the missionary is laid aside.'

'He's dead d'you mean?' I asked.

'No, no, he's just laid aside through illness.'

By the time we arrived the coffin had already been brought from the house and had been placed on two kitchen chairs in front of the door. I recognised in the black-clad, bowler-hatted undertaker my friend the taxi-driver. He was moving with solemn decorum among the cluster of mourners, shaking hands, muttering greetings, and, to judge from the expressions of some of the people, indulging in some pretty humorous wisecracking at the same time.

The minister, wearing a black overcoat and hat, a striking canary-yellow muffler and brown boots, arrived in due course and insisted upon shaking hands with everyone lengthily and boisterously. The preliminaries over, he took up his station behind the coffin, and the men, except for those not directly under the minister's eye, doused their cigarettes and bowed their heads reverently, though only the undertaker removed his hat. The women began to leak out of the house to congregate in a colourful knot in the doorway. They commenced to knuckle their eyes with hard, work-coarsened hands and to sigh and moan, faintly at first and then louder, but their grief, despite quite genuine tears, seemed almost mechanical. Their expressions remained alert and watchful; their eyes, darting here and there, missed nothing of what was going on. Shortly after the service had begun, two latecomers—young girls dressed in blatant reds and blues—came galloping up, their faces glowing with the exercise and excitement. Without ceremony they pushed their way through the crowd of men and insinuated themselves into the huddled group in the doorway. They turned to face the coffin and miraculously their faces had become composed into masks of condolence.

It was sometimes difficult to hear the words of the service above the rustle of wind in the trees, the plashing of waves on the shingle, the wailing of the women and the mocking chorus of the seagulls as they hovered and wheeled above us. There was a glut of herring in the loch and the presence of the seagulls caused much discomfiture to the mourners who, from time to time, lifted irreverent heads to glare with savage apprehension at the offenders. Imperturbably the minister droned on, though when he came to the words 'and the years of our age are threescore and ten' I got the impression, both from his tone and his countenance, that he was feeling rather cross with Ian Mor for having cheated him out of a job for nine years.

The service over, the men began to form themselves into a long double line. The first six grasped the handles of the coffin and, with the nearest male relative of the deceased man to lead the coffin by a silken cord, the procession moved off at a leisured pace. The minister, after bidding everyone a cheerful farewell, jumped into his car, which, after a preliminary grumble of its engine, leaped forward impatiently to envelop the mourners in a cloud of smoke before it disappeared into the distance. Some of the women remained to comfort the bereaved relatives and to fortify themselves with cups of tea; others chose to follow the cortège at a discreet distance. Morag suggested that we should take a short cut to the burial ground and thus save ourselves the fatigue of following the winding road. This we did but though we were separated from the funeral procession by some distance it was not too far to disguise the fact that for such a procession it was decidedly hilarious. There was not, as I had been led to believe by some writers on the Highlands, anything in the nature of a quarrel or a fight at any time, either in progress or even brewing. On the contrary, joviality was the keynote of the day. The men, even those carrying the coffin, puffed unconcernedly at cigarettes and laughed and chatted as they walked; stopping at every telegraph pole to change bearers. At one time, when only a drystone wall was between us and the road, I heard one of the mourners call out: 'Lachy Murdy says he's cold.' Instantly the reply came: 'Let's take out the corpse and put Lachy Murdy in—he'll be warm enough in there I doubt.'

Loud laughter rippled along the line, Lachy Murdy himself laughing louder than anyone.

At the graveside there was no prayer or service whatever. The coffin was stripped of its ornaments by the undertaker and earth was thrown on top of it by any man who could find a spade. It was all done with as little ceremony as a dog inters a bone, and those not actively engaged in shovelling attended desultorily to the graves of their kinsmen, uprooting weeds and throwing them indifferently on to the surrounding graves. Old men, pipes in mouths, shambled among the tombstones, spitting recklessly.

As the earth shovelling progressed I heard Lachy call a halt and point towards the clump of bushes beside which I had stood the previous night. I glanced at Morag. Her eye was fixed steadily on Johnny whom we had observed to pause once or twice and to cast furtive glances about him. I wondered if he had mislaid his great-grandfather.

'Let's go now,' I implored my landlady.

She turned a distasteful glance on the rest of the women who were hanging round the grave like voracious seagulls round a fish pier.

'There, look at that!' she said. 'Ian Mor was a bachelor and there's more women at his funeral than ever I seen before. Indeed,' she went on pointedly, 'they've been chasin' him all his life and now they've chased him to his grave.' The promptness with which she agreed to my suggestion that we return home made it plain that she herself was not going to be accused of such forward behaviour.

That night both Lachy and Johnny were among those who dropped in at Morag's house to ceilidh. Naturally funerals were the main topic of the conversation.

'Come, Morag,' said Lachy, pulling out a bottle of whisky from his pocket. 'Give us some tots and we'll have a drink.'

'What'll we drink to?' someone asked.

'We'll drink to the hope that the rest of the people to die here from now on will have been ailin' for three months or so before they go.'

'That's a terrible thing to wish for,' I ejaculated. 'Surely you yourself would not care to be ill all that time?'

'Indeed but I would,' retorted Lachy.

'But why?' I asked.

'Because I know fine how heavy folks are when they die suddenly,' said Lachy candidly. 'It's no fair on the folks who have to carry when a corpse hasn't lost a bit of weight first. Just look at Ian Mor,' he continued, warming to his subject. 'Seventeen stone that man was and ill less than a week. It's no right I'm tellin' you. It near killed some of us today the weight of him.'

'That's right enough,' agreed Johnny fervently, and his words were echoed with approbation by every other man present.

'You sounded as though you were being killed,' I said drily.

'We ought to have a bier that can be drawn by a horse in this place,' said Lachy, ignoring my sarcasm.

'A what?' demanded Ruari, a hand to his ear.

'A bier—a horse bier,' vociferated Lachy.

'There's no enough beer for the men in this place without givin' it to the horses indeed,' roared Ruari amid laughter.

Morag changed the subject. 'Miss Peckwitt was tellin'
me she was awful shocked that none of you men took off
his hat when the service was on,' she told them, her lips
quirking faintly.

Several pairs of astonished eyes were turned on me.

'Take off our hats?' repeated Lachy foolishly. 'Why
now would we do that? Our heads were not hot!'

'The undertaker took off his hat, I noticed,' put in
someone.

'Aye,' answered another, 'tryin' to shame us folk
into followin' suit so that we'd catch our death of cold
and make plenty of work for him I doubt. Ach, but
we're too wise here for that sort of caper.'

They were indeed too wise altogether.

5

The Cattle Sale

'If I'm spared,' remarked Morag one hazy morning in early spring, 'I'll be after puttin' the stirk to the sale on Friday. Will you be comin' with me?'

'I will,' I replied promptly as I spooned thick yellow cream on to my steaming porridge. 'But where is the sale and how do we get there?'

Morag poured out two cups of tea from the pot and taking one for herself sat down on the edge of the sofa.

'The cattle float will be takin' him on Thursday evenin',' she explained, 'and we'll folly by bus on Friday mornin'.'

I was infinitely relieved that the few shreds of dignity I had managed to retain were sufficient to prevent there being any suggestion that I might occupy a spare stall in the cattle float.

'But I thought you had only one stirk and surely you said that was a female?' I said.

'So I did,' elucidated Morag, 'and so he will be when she's older you understand?'

I nodded wisely, accepting the fact that it was not nature but the Gaelic language which was responsible for the beast's being temporarily an hermaphrodite.

'You'll need good boots to your feets and a good stick to your hand,' warned my landlady seriously. 'Why, there's some of them beasts that wild, they'd be ridin' you round the ring on their horns for nothin' at all.'

I put down my cup and stared at Morag. The sight of the most placidly grazing cow had always been sufficient to fill me with trepidation; the prospect of horn riding I viewed with complete terror.

'Then count me out,' I said decisively. 'I've neither the figure nor the inclination to become a toreador.'

'Ach, you can always stay out of the field if you've a mind,' cajoled Morag, who loathed going anywhere at all without a companion.

I relented, though not without misgivings, but stressed most emphatically that I had a mind.

'In that case,' went on my landlady nimbly, 'will you 'phone for me from the new kosk to tell the cattle float to come.'

Morag claimed to be 'feart to death' of the 'phone, so, after giving a hand with the breakfast dishes, I went up the road towards the post office beside which stood the new telephone kiosk. This was a very recent arrival in Bruach and its installation had naturally excited a good deal of interest. Almost immediately it had become a popular evening rendezvous for the youth of the neighbourhood and, within a few days, or even hours, countless people were to be observed busily popping in and out, lifting the receiver, dialling numbers and indulging in prolonged and apparently cordial conversations with unseen friends; all regardless of the fact that the 'phone was as yet connected to nothing more responsive than the outside of the post office wall.

Though on arrival the kiosk had been an unimpressive pink, Lachy, who was by way of being the village odd job man, had soon transformed its pallidness into a vivid and arresting red. It was perhaps regrettable that for such odd jobs as Lachy deigned to undertake he would accept no payment but whisky; and as he always insisted on drinking the wages before commencing the work the results of his labours were frequently somewhat startling. On this occasion Lachy excelled himself, and even Bruach had been astonished when, next morning, unsuspecting crofters opened pillar-box red doors to discover striped sheep, cows with fiery

92

horns and hens that looked as though they had been crossed with flamingoes. Lachy had succeeded in 'painting the town red' with a vengeance. But though Bruach was surprised, it was in no way dismayed. The escapade was dismissed with a philosophical shrug of the shoulders, sometimes with a smile, and in nearly every case it was left to the weather to remove, or at least modify, the damage. Only two of the villagers showed distinct signs of wrath. One was Kirsty, the gaunt and prim-mouthed spinster of 'Beach Terrace', who had had the misfortune to leave a pair of combinations and a chaste white nightgown hanging on the clothes line overnight, with disastrous results.

'When I came to gather them in, Miss Peckwitt,' she told me, with tears of indignation in her eyes, 'I fell down on my knees on the grass, for I thought the Lord Himself had struck at me for wearin' such fancy under-wear.'

The other was the over-sized, over-aged schoolmis-tress who was seen the next morning in full pursuit of the miscreant, furiously pelting him with threats, with insults, and with cauliflowers from her carefully tended garden—cauliflowers which had overnight exchanged their blonde heads for red ones.

As to the success of the actual 'odd job', one could perhaps best judge from the following notice which appeared a day or two later in the window of the post office:

WANTED: Boy *under sixteen* to scrape paint off
glass in kiosk

It was some weeks now since everything had been made ship-shape and Bruach had been connected with the outside world. To all but the excessively righteous it was a welcome link, and though the latter professed to regard it as an implement of the Devil their con-

93

demnation did not extend to their being rung up by friends.

As I came in sight of the kiosk, an old man, leaning heavily on two sticks, shuffled with laborious haste from one of the low-roofed cottages and along the road in front of me. Reaching the flamboyant red door, he managed with some difficulty to pull it open, and with even more difficulty to insert himself inside. I sighed. Old men of the Bruach variety were not as a rule adept in the use of modern inventions like the telephone and I realised that it might be some time before I could contact the owner of the cattle float. I had by now acquired the Hebridean brand of patience so, lighting a cigarette, I settled myself contemplatively on the lichen-blotched stump of an old gate-post to watch the mist, like a grey vagabond, ragging itself across the hills and sending groping fingers down into the hidden corries. Every few minutes I glanced behind to watch progress in the kiosk. The old man appeared to be an extraordinarily restless conversationalist. My first glimpse showed him to be writhing convulsively from side to side in a manner suggestive of a hula-hula dancer. Another time he seemed to be embracing the telephone so closely that it looked as though he must be attempting either to swing from it or to wrest it from the wall. I was of course perfectly well aware that men are much inclined to strike attitudes when using the 'phone, but this old man had hardly progressed far enough to achieve such poise. On the other hand, even the most agonising rheumatic pains could surely not account for his contortions? I waited and waited; my watch ticked on; I threw away the butt of my third cigarette; the wraith-like mist crept inexorably nearer, yet still the performance in the kiosk continued.

Feeling rather puzzled, I got up and moved closer. The old man, catching sight of me, waved a bland greeting and I saw that he had not yet lifted the receiver. I answered his wave with a friendly smile, hoping that he might thus be encouraged to enlist my help in his difficulty, which was probably nothing more serious than the inability to find the correct number in the directory. The smile had its effect and, grunting and sighing noisily, he pushed open the door, collected his sticks, manœuvred himself carefully through and hobbled a few steps towards me.

'Excuse me, Miss Peckwitt,' he began with bashful humility, 'but can you tell me if it's true that I haff a spot of green paint on the side of my face and under my chin?' He turned the left side of his face towards me, tilted his chin, and awaited my comments. I examined his face critically, and was able to assure him that so far as I could see there was not the slightest trace of greeness about him.

'Ach, they was just haffin' me on then up at the house,' he said ruefully. 'Just after haffin' me on they was, the rascals: and me haffin' to come all this way for to see.' He grunted again gustily. 'And what a job I'm after haffin' with my rheumatics to try would I get to see under my chin.'

'Aren't you going to use the 'phone then?' I asked him.

'Me?' he asked with pained surprise. 'Me? Why indeed, I couldna' use that thing to save my life.'

After again bemoaning the cruelty of his family in forcing him to such exertions, just because he 'was after makin' a bitty mess paintin' the house door green again', he lumbered off home, and I was able to take his place in the kiosk. I did not realise until I was inside that in addition to the telephone it was fitted with a small mirror—a luxury which so many crofter homes lacked. At last I understood the reason for all those one-sided telephone conversations.

For several hours on the Thursday evening preceding the sale, the rain came down in torrents, but by Friday morning there seemed to be a faint prospect of the day developing into a reasonably fine one. The ditches on either side of the road still gushed exhilaratedly as Morag and I, clad in waterproofs and armed with stout sticks, hastened towards the bus-driver's house. The hills loomed darkly through a billowing mantle of cloud; behind us the tawny washed moors stretched interminably, and a chill eddying breeze whispered terse messages to the trembling bog cotton.

The bus was due to leave at 7.30 a.m. and at 7.25 a.m. my companion and I were comfortably settled on one of the front seats, watching the grey blanket of sky being swept northwards to reveal elusive shafts of sunlight which patterned the dark water with pools of silver. At a quarter to eight we still sat, or rather I still sat, no longer enraptured by the swift changing panorama, but thinking yearningly of the extra cup of tea I should have had time for if only I could have known that the bus-driver was going to lie so long abed. Morag had gone on a reconnoitring tour but now she appeared at the door of the bus.

'He's no out of his bed yet, the scamp,' she said. 'I think we'd best give him a shout.'

I alighted from the bus and stood with Morag in the road.

'Johnny!' Morag called as she would call a cow three miles distant.

'JOHNNY! JOHNNY!' We called in unison, but the house remained still and silent. We called repeatedly.

'We could do with our own Ruari here now,' sighed Morag.

I felt a twinge of pity for Johnny and climbing aboard the bus I found the horn and pressed it several times. The strident hoot should have awakened the dead, but Johnny must have been more than dead. We were wondering how next to proceed when a loud hail from down the road made us turn in that direction and we saw Padruig, the old road-mender, labouring up the hill towards us on his way to an eight o'clock start.

'Why, surely the man's no sleepin' through all that noise?' he greeted us querulously. 'I could hear you bletherin' away down at my own house there.'

'Call yourself then,' commanded Morag as he paused beside us. Padruig, thus invited, threw back his head and gathered himself for the effort.

'JOHNNY!'. His stentorian shout shamed us into silence, but was as little productive as our own efforts had been. He tried again, but with the same result.

'Well now, what d'you think of that?' he asked, turning to us in amazement. 'Indeed I've a good mind to drive off the bus myself and give him a good fright,' he added threateningly.

'You canna' drive,' jeered Morag.

'I can so,' argued Padruig with some vehemence.

'You can no,' insisted Morag. 'You canna' drive a bus anyway.'

'And why not?' demanded Padruig.

'Because,' said Morag crushingly, 'you havena' got a public convenience licence and you canna' drive a bus without one.'

Padruig opened his mouth to repeat his shouts but as though struck by some sudden suspicion turned to gape foolishly at Morag for some seconds.

'JOHNNY!' This time Padruig's voice was augmented by a handful of flints which he hurled vindictively against the bedroom window. The combination had the desired effect, and instantly the window was thrown open and a stream of Gaelic issued forth. I gathered, from Morag's anxious glance towards me, that it was mainly maledictory.

'Get you out of that, man,' Padruig cut short Johnny's diatribe. 'It's gone eight o'clock.'

'Eight!' Johnny's voice was incredulous. 'Whose time is that? God's time, Government time or daft time?'

'Daft time,' answered Padruig evenly, 'and isn't it daft time the mails are goin' by anyway.'

'Oh my God!' gasped Johnny. (I should perhaps explain that locally 'God's time' was Greenwich time; 'Government time' was British Summer time, and 'Daft time' was the scornful designation for British Double Summer time.)

'You'd best bring your bed with you, you're that fond of it,' chided Padruig mercilessly as he stumped off along the road to his work.

Johnny, ignoring the insult, addressed Morag, 'Go you into the kitchen and get the kettle on, Morag,' he said peremptorily; and as his dark head disappeared through the window Morag and I hurried to the back door of the house, which opened unresistingly. Together we set about lighting the Primus stove.

Johnny, in shirt sleeves, his braces hanging down the back of his trousers and his shoes unlaced, came clattering down the stairs, seeming in no way ashamed of his *déshabillé* or disturbed by the fact that two of his intending passengers were busily preparing his breakfast half an hour after the bus should have left. Hastily he poured some of the hot water from the already steaming kettle into a cup and commenced shaving at reckless speed. Morag brewed tea with the remainder of the water while I searched in a cupboard for something to eat. I found a couple of oatcakes and fed them to Johnny as he fastened his braces with one hand and dabbed a towel over his face with the other.

'You've cut yourself,' I told him as he wiped a smear of blood across his cheek.

'Damn!' he muttered and held a handkerchief to the cut.

'Sticking plaster?' I suggested helpfully.

'Ach, there'd be none,' said Johnny with disgust. 'There never is in this place.'

'A stamp?' put in Morag. Johnny indicated the wallet in his jacket pocket, from which Morag extracted a twopenny stamp and, after licking it, carefully stuck it over the cut.

'You'll do fine,' she told him.

I thought it an appropriate treatment for a mail carrier and extremely effective in both senses of the word.

We waited only while Johnny swallowed two or three mouthfuls of scalding tea, then hurrying outside we clambered again on to the bus. Almost immediately it leaped forward as Johnny, not giving the engine a moment to warm up, let in the clutch. At last we were off, forty minutes late it is true but Johnny was, through experience, an expert at catching up on lost time.

There were several halts along the road, where we loaded up with parcels, mailbags and impatient passengers, and with such careless abandon were all these stowed aboard that Morag complained a little fretfully that, 'You didna' know if it was a pillar-box or somebody's grandfather would be landin' in your lap next.'

Some of the passengers were at first inclined to testy remonstrance regarding the lateness of the bus, but Johnny, with his foot hard down on the accelerator, soon put them in their places both literally and figuratively speaking, and before we had covered more than a few yards even the most wrathful of them seemed to have lost either the desire or the ability to argue. Like some mad demon the bus pounded, rocked, bumped and thundered along the road. My insides felt as though they were being pulverised and for the first time that morning I ceased to yearn for that missed cup of tea.

We reached the post office with only two minutes to spare, and here the passengers, their peevishness forgotten, entered gleefully into the spirit of the affair. Tumbling out of the bus they rushed the sacks of mail into the sorting office, where, anxious to ensure the utmost celerity, they stood menacingly over the harassed sorters. Astonishingly the task was completed just as the clock finished striking the hour and, though the postmaster's baleful glare should have annihilated Johnny, the latter remained sublimely indifferent. He stood,

99

hands in pockets, whistling tunelessly, his stamped face looking remarkably at home in such a setting.

'You'd best lace up your shoes,' said Morag in an undertone as we passed near him on our way out.

Johnny treated us to a benevolent smile.

Still slightly breathless, Morag and I made in the direction of the sale yard, which was situated, as were most things of importance in the Island, in close proximity to a public bar; a fact which no doubt accounted for there being no sign of the presence of humans, though many sheep and cattle were tied to stakes around the low wall of the field.

Together my landlady and I leaned on the wall, each examining with an anxious eye the qualities of the various beasts. Morag's interest was for the comparative condition and therefore likely price of her own stirk; mine arose purely from cowardice.

An old car rattled to a stop in front of the entrance to the field, and a couple of men with the brisk air of those who are intent only on making money stepped from it. Simultaneously groups of flushed crofters began to emerge from the adjacent bar, and without preliminaries, as far as I could see, prices were being called and business had begun.

I left them to their bargaining, and wishing to look for specimens of wild flowers I wandered along the road towards a promising-looking clump of trees. They proved on investigation to be mostly hazel, though here and there a rowan waved its exquisite fronds in the capricious breeze. Beneath them the celandines grew in profusion and a gleam of sunlight catching the wet grass transformed it into a shimmering carpet of diamonds. Leaving the trees I ambled slowly across the road to sit on a large stone which, in Morag's youth, had been used for weight-lifting contests by the Bruach males on their way homeward after a sale. It was a pleasant spot for meditation and I lingered some time watching the burn below tearing its swift, loquacious way towards the sea.

Above me a pair of buzzards circled with superb grace, their plaintive mews mingling with the liquid notes of the curlews which echoed eerily among the desolate hills.

Suddenly from the distance there came a loud shouting and, glancing uneasily over my shoulder, I saw with horror that a distracted bull or cow was careering madly along the road in my direction. It ran erratically, weaving from side to side, and making wild sweeps with its enormous horns at two furiously snapping sheep dogs which raced on either side. Some way behind the cow but obviously in pursuit tore a frantically gesticulating figure whose shouting had attracted my attention. As the figure perceived me the shouting and gesticulating were intensified.

For one awful moment I was transfixed with fear but the realisation that I was being warned to run for my life galvanised me into action. I do not believe it would be any exaggeration to say that in spite of my heavy gumboots I was across the road in one bound and into the wood, and in another I was up in the top of the most dependable-looking hazel tree I could see. Certainly I could recollect afterwards a sensation of flying more than of climbing, and I felt I might more reasonably claim to be an ex-mate of Tarzan than an ex-school-marm. Quaking with fear, I clung to my perch while the noise of hooves and the incessant altercation of the dogs drew nearer, passed, and faded into the distance. I was shakily descending the tree when a voice assailed me in voluble Gaelic and I espied the elderly pursuer of the cow advancing, red-faced and truculent, towards me. My boots touched earth, but so formidable was the old man's countenance that I was tempted to repeat the climb. Without preamble he began to address me elo-quently and though he spoke in Gaelic I had the un-comfortable feeling that much of the eloquence was vituperative.

'Please say what you have to say in English,' I told him with as much hauteur as I could command.

At once he became confused and apologetic.

'Ah, my, my, you have no Gaelic is it? Indeed and I'm after mistakin' you for one hereabouts. Ach, but you've no Gaelic.' He looked at me pityingly.

'What were you saying to me then?' I asked.

'I was just sayin' if only you would have stood still in front of the cow and waved your arms at her she'd have taken fright at you and would have turned back likely.'

I pondered the compliment carefully.

'Now d'you see,' he continued, his voice full of pathos, 'I'll never turn her before she gets home, and it's fourteen miles the day already I've driven the beast.'

I condoled with him suitably, but had to admit that I was afraid the cow might have tossed me if I had stayed within reach. My excuse seemed to puzzle him for he blinked thoughtfully for a few seconds.

'I don't believe she would have,' he said seriously, 'but even supposin' she had tossed you there would have been no malice in it—no malice at all. She's not a cross cow by rights.'

I was wondering if it felt any different to be tossed by an unmalicious cow than by a malicious one when the old man spoke again.

'What a pity you had not the Gaelic,' he said mournfully. 'I could just as well have shouted to you in English, and then maybe I wouldn't have had all this trouble for nothin'.'

We commiserated with each other at some length on our joint misfortunes before he could bring himself to continue his forlorn trek homeward.

'What were you up the tree for?' he rounded on me just as I was hoping I was rid of him and, strange as it may seem, I could not think on the spur of the moment of a plausible reason why a middle-aged woman should be up in the top of a tree, for I was not willing to confess the full extent of my cowardice. Providentially the man went on to answer his own question.

'Lookin' for nuts were you?'

I grasped at the straw and nodded affirmation.

'Ach!' he burst out derisively, 'there'll be no nuts there till September or after.'

At my affectation of surprise he permitted himself a short bark of laughter. 'No, no,' he repeated. 'Not till September, so you've started climbin' a few months too soon.'

Pleased with his joke he plodded off down the road in the wake of the recalcitrant cow.

Deciding that it was time for me to go in search of Morag, I returned to the sale yard and there found my landlady. She was in high spirits, her stirk having sold at a good price.

'Didn't you say something about there being sheep-dog trials here today after the sale?' I asked.

'So there was to be,' replied Morag, 'but they tell me they've been cancelled.'

'Why is that?'

'All I heard was that the sheep had broke out of the pen and they'd been chasin' the dogs all over the place. They must have been a wild lot of sheep that, and the poor dogs have had an awful time with them.'

There was very little activity at the sale yard by now: most of the beasts had been disposed of and the knots of arguing men—an inevitable occurrence whenever Gaels fraternise—were already beginning to move off. I noticed the butcher, an immense man, leading a tiny calf by a tiny piece of rope. He reminded me of a portly matron airing her Pekingese.

Morag was eager to hurry me off to the hotel for lunch and there we ate our meal in the kitchen with the cook who was a good friend of hers. The hospitality of the Islanders is proverbial, and it is, or seems to be, accepted that their hospitality extends beyond their own larders to those of their employers, so the excellent meal cost us nothing.

As we sat sipping our after-lunch cups of tea, the cook rose and opened a door which gave on to a small passage. Through this passage was the bar and it was possible both to see and hear the barman serving drinks to the assembled crowd. The cook considered this excellent entertainment and assuring us that it was 'as good as a concert', she settled herself in a chair placed as near the door as possible.

Most of the male population of Bruach were present in the bar along with many others I did not know and all were in good trim; full of beer and whisky and, to begin with, bonhomie. Gradually as more whisky was consumed the voices became first argumentative and then threatening. One or two were heard soothing or cajoling, while every now and then the barman himself intervened on a note of warning. In the midst of a particularly noisy dispute the outside door of the bar was flung violently open and for a moment every voice was hushed. Then the clamour broke out afresh as the newcomer was recognised. But this time it sounded to be congratulatory. From my position I could not see who had entered, but the cook whispered excitedly:

'My, my, if yon isn't Hamish Mor himself.'

'It is so?' gushed Morag ecstatically.

'It is so,' reiterated the cook.

Edging forward I saw that the cause of all the acclamation was a tall well-made man with fiery red hair peeping from under his cloth cap. Like a conquering hero he strode up to the bar counter while on all sides people pressed about him effusively, shaking his hand vigorously, and interspersing their salutations with commands to the barman to ply the newcomer with drinks. Only an odd one or two of the customers, seeming to find their own drinks suddenly distasteful, slunk towards the door and sliding round it disappeared unobtrusively. Meanwhile Hamish Mor, utterly unperturbed, was downing drinks as fast as his friends could pay for them. I asked Morag why he should be so popular.

'Ach, you'll no be knowin' him,' she told me. 'He's no from the village at all.' Her tone was like a rebuff.

'They're making a great fuss of him,' I observed.

'Aye indeed, and so they might, for a better man never lived,' breathed the cook reverently.

'Do they always treat him like this?' I persisted.

'No,' replied Morag guardedly.

'Then why today?' I asked. 'Is it his birthday or has he won a medal or something?'

Morag sighed. 'No,' she said, 'but today he's just come out of prison.'

'Prison?' I echoed incredulously.

'Aye, prison,' she confirmed.

'What was he convicted of?' I asked.

'Assault,' interposed the cook shortly.

'Assault? Who did he assault?'

'He threw the barman out of the window there,' the cook replied with a languid gesture towards the bar.

'Which barman?'

'Why, the one that you see there now,' said the cook with a touch of impatience.

I ventured a further peep round the door. The barman appeared to me to be a dissolute-looking fellow of the type that makes a woman's flesh creep and a man's fists tingle, but even so the behaviour of the crowd seemed too cruel. I watched carefully as with impassive countenance he served drink after drink to his assaulter, every drink paid for by the admiring company, who continued to jostle one another for the privilege of patting Hamish Mor on the back and wishing him, rather pointedly: 'Better luck next time!'

'Sure Hamish was for killin' that barman, was he not, Morag?' said the cook with a tinge of regret in her voice.

'I suppose that is why the wretches are wishing him better luck next time,' I retorted drily.

'Aye, I'm thinkin' Hamish will be killin' that barman one of these days yet,' asseverated Morag and added hurriedly, 'that is if the Lord spares him.'

The cook and Morag continued to discuss Hamish and his perfections while I listened with one ear to their gossip and with the other to the tragi-comedy of the bar.

'D'you mind that summer Hamish signed the pledge?' asked the cook with a chuckle.

'Aye, I mind fine,' replied Morag.

'Three days he kept off the whisky,' said the cook reminiscently.

'Three days? Three weeks it was more like,' corrected Morag.

'Three days it was,' maintained the cook stoutly.

'What happened then?' I interposed.

'Why, Hamish was lyin' in his bed that night when he hears the thrush singin' outside. "Drink well, Hamish, drink well, Hamish," says the thrush, "drink all the time." '

The two women laughed together.

'And bless me,' went on the cook, 'but Hamish jumps up. "To Hell with the missionary!" says he. "When the birds in the trees are tellin' a man to drink it canna' be wrong." So he comes here—two o'clock in the mornin' it was—and he knocks us up and tells us what he'll do to us if he doesn't get a bottle or two of whisky there and then.' The cook lifted the corner of her apron to wipe the tears of laughter from her eyes.

Hamish's message seemed to me to be an odd interpretation of the call of the thrush, but then I remembered that the bird, unlike myself, would be fortunate enough to have the Gaelic.

'D'you mind that time the artist told Hamish he wanted to paint him?' asked Morag of the cook.

'No, I don't mind that at all,' replied the other. 'Indeed I never heard of that.'

'He was only a poor wee soul,' said Morag, 'and Hamish looked down at him. "Wee mannie," says he, "if you dare to lay a brush on me I'll kick the pants off you." '

The sound of our laughter attracted the attention of the bar customers. Quickly the cook pushed the door. 'We'll just keep it shut while we finish our strupak,' she said, 'or they'll be wantin' in here with their drink.'

When the door was opened again, Hamish had left and with him the merriest of the drinkers. The atmosphere now was decidedly less convivial. Of the remaining occupants of the bar, I had no difficulty in spotting Lachy's red, flushed face and also the pale cadaverous one of Alistair the shepherd. There appeared to be some sort of argument in progress between the two.

'Lachy, my lad,' I heard Alistair say with complete amiability, 'if you say that to me again, I'll throw you out the door.'

'Alistair, my boy,' replied Lachy with equal affability, 'I'll say it to you again, and if you don't like it I'll smash your head through the counter.'

The argument terminated in a brief but cyclonic disturbance among the lounging figures; the barman shouted and the amazed crowd parted to reveal a dazed and vanquished shepherd pulling splinters of the bar counter from his hair. Lachy bent and solicitously assisted his victim to rise.

'Lachy, my boy,' began the shepherd respectfully, 'you kept your word, man, and I'm one as respects a man who can keep his word.' He turned to the barman. 'Two doubles quick now, and we'll feel the better for it,' he commanded.

Soon the erstwhile combatants were tossing off two doubles, topping them with another two, and, with arms entwined about each other's shoulders, were already proceeding into the next stage of the argument which, according to the cook's experience, they would not be long in reaching.

'Goodness! Here it is three o'clock in the evenin' and

time we were makin' for home,' broke in Morag, as she caught sight of the clock.

'My, how the clock runs away with the time,' said the cook politely.

We said goodbye, and were shortly being ushered through the main doorway of the hotel as though we were honoured guests, I trying hard to look as though I had paid for my dinner.

We had to pass by the public bar entrance where I saw on the road several scraps of material of different colours. Morag, seeing the direction of my glance, bent down and picked up one of them.

'Aye, but it's always like this after a sale,' she said.

'It's the neckband of a shirt, isn't it?' I asked.

'It is so,' agreed Morag, 'and I've a good idea this one belongs to our Ruari.'

'But how on earth?' I began, when my question was cut short by a commotion inside the bar; the door burst open and out tumbled Lachy and Alistair, fighting mad once again. Lachy flung off his coat; Alistair had already discarded his. For a moment or two the men glared at one another ferociously and then each, with one swift movement that could only have been achieved with practice, pulled his clean cotton shirt up and over his head, leaving the tight cuffs around his wrists and the neckband around his neck. There was no need to finish my question.

'Come on!' said Morag, oblivious of the fact that I was already a few yards ahead of her. 'Best leave them to fight it out.'

We had agreed that our best plan was to walk on homeward until we were picked up by the bus. In this way we should avoid being crowded and also miss most of the drunks, who, according to Morag's reckoning, would by that time have been dropped off, knocked out or put to sleep in the rear. Also it would save us having to wait about for the bus as the time of its departure even on normal days was wellnigh unpredictable. We set off at a brisk pace and had not gone far before we overtook Donald Beag, one of the crofters, shepherding in front of him an unusually docile black-faced ewe and her two tiny lambs. Now I must admit that there had been a time when the sight of curly little lambs provoked in me a sentimental leaning towards vegetarianism, but after a year or so of heather-fed mutton I am afraid the sight of them merely made my mouth water. Donald was glad of our company and so that he might keep pace with us he urged on the sheep by beating his side with his artificial arm, the gleaming hook of which aroused memories of Barrie's infamous captain. The Great War which had deprived Donald of his arm had in recompense provided him with a fund of stories of his experiences, which he was always ready to relate, but now he listened avidly while I recounted the story of the runaway cow.

'My, my,' he exclaimed as I finished, 'you mean to tell me you havena' the Gaelic yet then?'

I told him that my knowledge of Gaelic was limited to such phrases as 'Kamera-ha' and 'Ha-goo-ma'.

'Indeed and it's surprising how far that bit itself will take you supposin' you have no other words of the language,' said Donald, with a wisely reminiscent smile, and embarked on a war anecdote to illustrate his words.

He was once, he told us, in a trench with a couple of dozen other soldiers when a shell came over and not one but himself was left alive. He picked himself up and started to walk away from the trench, but though he walked and walked he met with no living soul. He walked until dusk and then, espying the ruins of a house, he made towards them. Just as he reached them a figure jumped from behind a wall, held up its arms and shouted, '*Kamerad, Kamerad.*'

'Ach, well,' continued Donald. 'There was a good few Gaelic speakers in our regiment at that time, so I just holds out my hand and says, "Ha-goo-ma". As soon as I'd said it we both stared at each other and then we both turned and ran like blazes in opposite directions.'

Donald chuckled at the memory. 'Ach, but I was sorry enough afterwards I can tell you,' he went on. 'For I'd sooner have had a German to talk to than nobody at all, and I daresay that with the Gaelic we might have understood each other pretty well.'

As Donald's story came to an end we were drawing level with an elderly man who was making repeated attempts to drive an emaciated cow before him. It was fortunate that he had not far to go or he would have stood little chance of getting the beast home.

'What on earth came over the man to buy himself a beast like that?' muttered Morag under her breath. 'It looks as though it started to shiver when the frost came and it's still frozen into its shiver.'

I thought it an apt description, but Donald was not to be outdone.

'You need to get a rope on that cow quickly,' he shouted to the owner.

'A rope?' The old man looked bewildered. 'Why, she's that quiet she has no need of a rope.'

'It's no to quiet her she's needin' it,' said Donald with brutal candour, 'it's to keep her from fallin' to pieces.'

The man glowered in reply and as the sheep were in better condition than the cow we soon left him behind. Some distance in front of us we could see a knot of people and animals progressing slowly along the road. I have never been able to determine whether the crofters walk slowly so as not to distress the animals they herd, or whether the animals walk slowly out of consideration for the crofters they lead. Whichever way it was I had learned that, short of brutality, it was impossible to hurry either a crofter or his cow. As we drew abreast of them we were hailed delightedly by the jovial red-faced

110

drovers, many of whom I remembered having seen quite recently in the bar. They were decidedly merry and seemed quite unconcerned whether they reached home that night or the next day. Bottles were soon being extricated from jacket pockets and proffered confidentially. Had glasses been obtainable Morag and I would have had great difficulty in refusing their generosity but fortunately they accepted the fact that bottles were for the privileged, or not so particular, menfolk.

Much interest was focused on Murdoch, a white-haired old bachelor, who was riding a horse purchased at the sale.

'Why did you buy a new horse?' asked Donald. 'Was your other one not good enough?'

'No,' replied Murdoch, 'she wasn't very good at the ploughin' this year.'

Morag was quick to defend the old horse. 'Well, she was gettin' old,' she scolded Murdoch, 'and you must expect horses to disintegrate with age.'

No one seemed to think this characteristic of old horses in the least peculiar, and I waited in vain for Donald to offer his suggestion of a rope.

'Your own horse is gettin' old at that,' Murdoch told Donald.

'Indeed she is not,' retorted Donald indignantly. 'My horse put in three bags of potatoes for me only last week.'

'Did you see yon cow Ian Tearlaich had bought?' asked someone in reference to the bag of bones we had lately passed.

'So we did,' replied Morag, 'just one big bellyache that beast is and nothin' more.'

The train of men and beasts strung itself out along the road; cows bellowed and from time to time calves tried vainly to elude their new owners.

'We'll just stay and wait here for the bus,' suggested Morag, and as we had already covered a good distance I willingly agreed.

At that moment one of the drovers treated us to a conspiratorial wink.

'Why is Angus givin' us the wingéd eye?' whispered my companion.

Angus pointed gleefully at Murdoch, who sat with unshakable confidence astride his surprisingly quiet horse. The old man's back was comfortably rounded, his hands were deep in his pockets and his outsize feet swung loosely on either side. Angus went alongside and put his hand on the saddle.

'Sure, Murdoch, it's yourself that's havin' the nice ride home now, is it not?' he teased.

'So I am,' agreed Murdoch cordially. 'She's a nice quiet horse indeed for an old man like myself.'

'And you with the biggest flat feet in the place to take you home too,' went on Angus.

Murdoch laughed self-consciously.

Before I realised what was happening Angus had stealthily lifted the saddle, placed his lighted cigarette under and dodged quickly away. Instantly the horse reared, pawed the air desperately for a few seconds and then, to the delight of the wildly cheering drovers, galloped madly along the road with Murdoch clinging to its mane like grim death and swearing comprehensively. The startled cattle scattered to right and left.

'You fool!' I flung at Angus as I took off in the wake of the runaway, feeling certain that the old man would come to some harm. I ran quickly but not having had the same incentive my performance was much less impressive than that of the horse.

Rounding a bend I was in time to see Murdoch being flung, or flinging himself, from the back of his mount on to the grassy verge of the road and some minutes later, closely followed by the gamekeeper, I came upon his prostrate body. Murdoch lay quite still and though I could see no blood I was quite sure that he was injured in some way. Gingerly I began to examine him. By this time the rest of the men had left their cattle to look after

112

themselves and had arrived on the scene. They stood watching in a subdued silence while Morag, who had come panting in their rear, prodded exploratively at the prone figure.

'He's no dead but I believe he's unconscience,' she pronounced.

'D'you hear that now?' The gamekeeper turned on Angus with simulated rage.

'Ach, you couldna' kill that one without shootin' him first,' rejoined Angus lightly; 'and supposin' you shot him dead you'd still have to go and knock him down afterwards, his feet are that flat.'

A gust of relieved laughter swept the onlookers.

'It was a crazy thing to do,' I cut in tartly. My rebuke brought a completely unrepentant smile to Angus's ruddy face.

The gamekeeper tried again: 'It was a fool thing to do,' he stressed reproachfully; 'and you're lucky he's only been knocked unconscious. He could easily have been hurt badly.'

After that inane observation I gave up trying to bestir in them any feelings of remorse.

Someone bethought himself to go and catch the horse, which by now had rid itself of the cigarette and was grazing quietly, utterly indifferent to the fate of its owner.

The bus opportunely arrived at that moment and Murdoch was deposited on the top of a snoring pile of inebriates who were in turn bedded on a mattress of bulging mailbags. His condition was the cause of much levity and even when, still unconscious, he was being carried home by four of the more sober of the Bruachites it seemed to have occurred to no one but myself that the man might have sustained serious injury. As it was quite possible that the four carriers would tire of their burden before they reached Murdoch's house and that the invalid, like the old woman with the pig, would 'never get home that night', I insisted on accompanying them.

Morag came too and we were present to see Murdoch taken off to bed by indifferent relatives who seemed in no way surprised to see their kinsman being brought home insensible. I gathered that it was the rule rather than the exception for Murdoch to be in this condition after a sale, and my proposal that a doctor be sent for was received with icy disdain.

After taking a welcome cup of tea, Morag and I set off home. The night was patchily dark and there was again a threat of rain in the scudding clouds through which a fugitive moon peeped anxiously. I remembered I had a torch and had just retrieved it from the bottom of my handbag when a savage scream rent the stillness of the night, and out from one of the cottages a white shape staggered. My companion and I stopped still and in the beam of the torch saw a middle-aged woman clad only in a nightgown. The woman's eyes were sunken and staring, her grey unkempt hair fell in wisps over her dirt-streaked face. Her hands tore convulsively at her breast and her mouth moved soundlessly.

'It's Barbac,' whispered Morag, but I had already recognised the figure, despite the fact that when I had first met her she had been a plump and pleasant little woman, with only a slight inclination to neurosis. A long illness coupled with careless nursing had affected her brain, and now here she was, a wasted gibbering lunatic. Her plight was shocking but at this moment the sight of her made me shudder.

'Go back to your bed, Barbac,' Morag entreated softly, 'go back to your bed.'

A man appeared and, taking the unresisting woman by the arm, led her back to the cottage with silent resignation. The incident had shaken Morag nearly as much as myself, and it was not until we were on our own doorstep that she spoke again.

'Indeed it's a pity when people go like that,' she said sadly.

I agreed wholeheartedly.

'Sure,' she went on, 'I would sooner lose my hearin' or my sight than I would lose my sanitation. I believe to lose one's sanitation would be the end of everythin'.'

The following day I called at Murdoch's house to ask how he fared, for I was still the only one who was in the least worried by his mishap. I was assured that he was 'fine except for a sore head', and this was apparently of such frequent occurrence that I realised my enquiry was not tactful. On the contrary, my concern was regarded as a reflection on Murdoch's capacity to hold his drink.

Later I called at Lachy's home to collect some wool for Morag. Lachy was there, his jaw much swollen. He also complained of a 'sore head'—a 'sale head', interpreted his mother pithily. It was not long before we heard the voice of Alistair the shepherd and Lachy was quick to invite his recent opponent to come in for a strupak. Both Alistair's eyes were black and he had a cut on his nose.

'Lachy, my boy, they tell me we was fightin' like bulls yesterday,' said the shepherd contritely.

'We was?' asked Lachy, tenderly feeling his jaw.

'Aye, it's true they're sayin'.'

Lachy inspected his knuckles critically.

'Ach, if we was fightin' it was no us fightin',' expounded the shepherd.

'No?' queried Lachy.

'No, 'twas the drink inside us that was fightin',' said the shepherd importantly.

Their heads nodded in unison as each studied the other's wounds, and then Lachy let out a self-satisfied chuckle.

'Well, Alistair, my boy, I'd say from the look of you that my whisky was stronger than your whisky.' He gave me an audacious wink. 'D'you not think so?' he asked me.

I declined to give an opinion and after politely refusing the invitation of Lachy's mother to stay and 'take a drink of milk from the cattles', left them to their raillery. At several of the houses I passed on my way home a solitary shirt hung limply on the clothes line. Each shirt was devoid of cuffs and neckband!

6

Patients and Patience

The paralysing effect of an influenza epidemic which swept the village was the means of my obtaining a far deeper insight into the customs and living conditions of the inhabitants than I could possibly have obtained in ordinary circumstances. The epidemic temporarily incapacitated the nurse and deluged the doctor with work; so daily Morag and I, who were lucky enough to escape infection, sallied forth to make beds, to wash dishes, and in some cases, where the illness had struck most severely, to do a good deal of the house and croft work besides. It was fortunate that I had by this time learned to milk, but, though most of the women exclaimed favourably at the degree of skill I had acquired, most of the cows expressed grave doubts as to my ability; doubts which often resulted in the milk-pail being a much different shape at the end of the milking than at the beginning!

During this period of ministration to the sick I discovered that Morag's mother had been regarded as the 'medicine woman' of the village, and, as the daughter was expected to have acquired much of the mother's skill or 'magic', my landlady's remedies were often much in demand. It soon became evident to me that her advice and instructions were adhered to far more conscientiously than were those of the doctor. The latter, who was by no means unaware of the attitude of the crofters towards his profession, accepted the position with amused tolerance and between the amateur and the professional there existed a friendly rivalry which neither the one nor

the other would allow to be affected by the continuous
badinage of their patients. Naturally, we saw a good
deal of the doctor at this time; constantly encountering
him in and out of sick rooms; and though in me he expected to find an ally, I was already too conscious of
the efficacy of Morag's prescriptions in contrast to his
own to prove a particularly staunch one. Indeed I was
inclined to suspect that he himself had more faith in the
simple traditional remedies than in his own involved
treatments, especially so when I overheard him asking
my landlady what she recommended for rheumatism.

'Thicker soles on your boots, boy,' she advised him,
with a disapproving glance at his dressy town shoes.

'I cannot get strong shoes on my feet they're so swollen,' countered the doctor.

'The swellin' would come down if you rubbed your
feets with eel fat a time or two,' said Morag, and though
the doctor pretended scepticism he insisted on driving
us home, where, after allowing himself to be persuaded
to take a 'wee strupak', he offhandedly reintroduced
the subject of rheumatism. Morag, taking the hint,
searched in the cupboard and then brought out a small
bottle of yellowish-brown oily stuff which she handed
to the doctor. There was a contemptuous smile on his
lips as he accepted it, but nevertheless the alacrity with
which he pocketed the bottle convinced me that a good
deal of his manner was assumed purely for my benefit.

Though in the opinion of the crofters the doctor's
medical skill was negligible, his presence in the sick
room was as welcome as it was at the ceilidh. He drank
their tea, capped their jokes and criticised their cattle—
he was generally considered to be a better vet than doctor—and probably his camaraderie contributed as much
to the recovery of his patients as anything he might give
them from a bottle. Personally I found the doctor re-
freshing, for, whatever his faults may have been, he had
at least retained a character. He was clever and he knew
it; he liked whisky and he drank it—in quantity; he ate

118

his food with more gusto than grace and the evidence of it could be seen all down the front of his waistcoat. His sense of humour was puckish, and his contempt for the English, despite the fact that he had married an English-woman, permeated much of his conversation; before I had been acquainted with him for half an hour, he had embarked on a story of his student days in which he claimed to have got the better of a supercilious Englishman.

It was during the university vacation, he told me, and the doctor was roaming the hills herding his father's cattle, when two tourists, a man and a woman, approached him. The doctor was barefooted and bareheaded and was clad, as he himself put it, 'in a well-ventilated pair of breeks and a shirt with more front than back in it'.

'Hello, young fellow!' said the Englishman condescendingly.

'Good afternoon,' answered the doctor politely.

'And do you live around here?' asked the man archly.

'I do,' replied the doctor.

'And do you go to school?'

'Sometimes I go,' the doctor admitted.

'I see you have a book under your arm. Can you read?'

'A little,' said the doctor hesitantly, though the book happened to be an advanced medical textbook.

'Ah!' The man turned and conferred in low tones with his companion and then addressed the doctor once more. 'And can you count?' he asked.

'Er, yes,' faltered the doctor.

'Very good!' exclaimed the man. 'How much can you count?'

The doctor looked puzzled.

'Tell me, my boy, how many people there are here just at this moment. You, myself and my wife. How many is that?'

'One hundred,' answered the doctor after a struggle.

The man and his wife laughed derisively. 'Come,

come, my boy. How do you make that out?' they remonstrated.

'Well,' explained the doctor, turning to go, 'there's myself, that's one.'

'Yes?' the couple waited in amused expectancy.

'And there's yourself and your wife—you're the two nothings. Good day to you both.'

Never before or since, it seemed, had the hill been so strangely quiet as it was in the following moments. Whether or not the story was true I cannot say, but I do know that the doctor possessed an enviable gift for disconcerting people whom he regarded as being impudent, and I am forced to admit that my countrymen seem to regard themselves as having the right to interrogate the Islanders much as a policeman might interrogate a suspicious character.

Of all the intractable patients that we helped to nurse during the epidemic, Murdoch was by far the most difficult. He was by turns haughty, mischievous, crafty and ingenuous. One day he would decide he was at death's door and would be amenable to every suggestion; the next he would not only be out of bed, but visiting a neighbour's house to read the newspaper. When he had exhausted the news he would crawl back to his own home and would again make rapid strides towards death's door, where, moaning piteously, he would remain until the time for delivery of the next newspaper. Why Murdoch would never go to the length of buying his own paper I do not know, but then many of the crofters' little economies are entirely incomprehensible to the outsider.

Murdoch's two elderly sisters had also been taken ill with the influenza at the same time as himself, but they were all three fairly well on the road to recovery when I called one day to milk their cow and to make their tea. As soon as I pushed open the kitchen door I could hear voices coming from Murdoch's room, one of which belonged to the doctor. After a word to the sisters I set about preparing the tea-trays and was engaged on this task when the door leading from Murdoch's room was opened and the doctor, winking furiously, beckoned me to accompany him. His expression prepared me for some sort of joke and as I followed him through to the bedroom I wondered what it could be.

'Well, Murdoch,' said the doctor, 'I'll be away now as Miss Beckwith's come to make your tea.'

Murdoch lay back on his pillows and greeted me with a benign smile.

'Just you see and keep on taking your medicine,' the doctor told him.

'Aye, that I will, Doctor. I feel the better of that medicine indeed,' replied Murdoch earnestly.

'Did you take it in the morning?' asked the doctor.

'Aye, I did,' said the old man.

'And after your tea?'

'To be sure I did.'

'And did you take it last night after supper?'

'Certainly I did,' nodded Murdoch solemnly.

'Murdoch!' accused the doctor suddenly, 'you're a b—— liar!'

Murdoch sat bolt upright and fixed the doctor with a pair of startled eyes.

'Doctor,' he declared with touching dignity, 'wouldn't I swear before God I did as you said. I'm tellin' you I took it three times yesterday and twice this day already, and there's no more than half the bottle left now. I swear it indeed.'

Murdoch lifted up his hand as though taking the oath and I was sure that even the doctor would be convinced that the old man was telling the truth.

'Murdoch,' repeated the doctor sternly, 'I'm telling you you're a liar.' He produced a bag of peppermints, offered it to me and then popped one into his own mouth. Murdoch scrutinised the doctor's face.

'Am I indeed a liar?' he asked, an unrepentant smile beginning to touch his lips and eyes.

The doctor extracted a bottle of medicine from his bulging jacket pocket and set it on the table beside the bed. 'There now,' he announced triumphantly, 'though I brought your medicine along with me on Tuesday, I forgot to leave it for you, and when I got back home I found it still in my pocket. You old rascal, you didn't even miss the stuff so I know fine you're a liar.' He folded his arms across his chest and stood smiling down impishly at his patient's discomfiture which was brief indeed.

'Why then I must be a liar,' admitted Murdoch equably. 'But fancy me been suckin' at an empty bottle these three or four times. It just shows how poorly I've been.'

'Empty bottle!' exploded the doctor with feigned wrath. 'You old bodach, you've never sucked at an empty bottle in your life. I'll guarantee that any bottle you've sucked was more than half full; but, you devil, you'd sooner take your medicine from the barman than from the doctor.'

Murdoch chuckled appreciatively. 'I'd take the medicine all right if you'd dose me with the right stuff,' he retaliated.

The doctor grunted non-committally. 'If you're quite comfortable I'll be on my way,' he said.

'Comfortable!' echoed Murdoch. 'I'm comfortable enough except for my feets.'

'What's wrong with your feet?'

'Indeed my feets and my legs is as red as the dove's with the cold,' the old man said plaintively. 'I canna' seem to keep the warmth in them.'

'You must be dyin' from the feet upwards then,' retorted the doctor callously.

'That wouldn't be true now would it?' pleaded the old man.

'And why not?' asked the doctor, indifferent to Murdoch's sudden woebegone expression. 'It's well over seventy you are, isn't it?'

'Just a year or two over,' muttered the patient with a sidelong glance at me.

'Ah well, maybe a hot-water bottle will save you this time,' said the doctor with a laugh. I laughed too, but more with the desire to comfort, and Murdoch, taking courage, joined in wholeheartedly.

After seeing the doctor to the door and collecting the tray from the kitchen, I returned to the invalid to find him eyeing the bottle of medicine distastefully. 'I wonder what's in that?' he asked me.

'You'll soon find out,' I told him.

He removed the cork, sniffed once or twice and then, carefully replacing the cork, offered the bottle to me, in case I should catch the influenzy and be in need of a dose. Upon my refusal he respectfully bade me to throw the bottle in the sea on my way home.

'But you should take it,' I argued, 'it will do you good, otherwise the doctor wouldn't give it to you.'

'Ach, that joker!' Murdoch said scornfully. 'It was for my sisters I had to send for him rightly, they was that bad with the influenzy; and if they'd gone and died on me, and me not after havin' the doctor to them, they'd have been grumbling at me for the rest of their lives.'

He reached for his pipe. 'Whisky's the stuff for me,' he resumed. 'I'd be dead many times over if it wasn't for the wee dram I take every night of my life.'

I did as much as I could for Murdoch and his household and was on my way home when Morag's voice hailed me from a neighbouring cottage.

'Can you give me a hand in here?' she beseeched. 'There's all of them sick and not a body to do a hand's turn.'

I followed her into the cottage and into the one and only bedroom where 'all of them'—father, mother, nine children and the daughter-in-law—were compressed into three beds. The father and mother along with two of the younger children occupied one of the double beds; the other was shared by three girls and three boys, head to tail, while the married son and his pregnant wife looked almost comfortable in the comparative spaciousness of a single bed. All the beds were littered with paper-back novelettes and tattered comics, which some of the occupants had been reading avidly as we entered, despite the fact that there was little light filtering through the deep, yellow, lace-screened window. The room was sickeningly hot, for it was impossible to open the window and Morag had a big peat fire blazing in the grate. By the time we had tidied the beds and I had collected several bruises from the iron bedsteads I was feeling that I should soon be in need of attention myself.

'Why d'you cramp yourselves like this?' asked Morag. 'Why are you no usin' the recess bed in the kitchen?'

'But it's more fun when we're all together,' the mother replied evenly. 'It's kind of lonely for those in the kitchen.'

'Fun' seemed a strange description of their plight, but those who were not too ill to appreciate it were obviously quite content.

I was glad when Morag suggested that I should make some tea, and escaped thankfully to the relative coolness of the kitchen, where, as I buttered scones already baked by Morag and waited for the kettle to boil, I marvelled at the crofter's ability to endure discomfort, which is as often due to choice as circumstance.

I was in the act of setting the teapot to warm when a shout took me back to the bedroom. One of the younger invalids wanted to vomit and while Morag held the child away from the bed I was requested to seek the necessary receptacle. Going down on my knees I drew from under the bed what I imagined was the chamber, only to discover it to be a tightly packed bowl of salt herring—part of the family's winter supply. A burst of hysterical laughter greeted its appearance and, pushing back the bowl, I tried again. Gingerly I slid out another bowl of a slightly

124

different shape. This was the cause for further merriment.

'That's the milk settin' for the cream,' shrieked the lady of the house joyously. 'Annie promised she'd come and make butter for us tomorrow.'

I replaced the bowl of milk and again poked warily under the bed; my explorations being accompanied by gusts of unrestrained laughter from the beds. My fingers touched a bundle of clothes, a small barrel, some wood, a pile of books and then, thank heaven! earthenware. This proved to be the utensil I was seeking and drawing it forth with a flourish I thrust it towards Morag. But the pantomime of my attempts to find it had reduced the small invalid to such a state of helpless mirth that all thoughts of being sick had been banished.

'My, that was as good as a tonic,' gasped the patients feebly as they wiped away tears of laughter with the edges of blankets.

An hour or two later, after we had made our happy family as comfortable as we could, Morag and I set about for the home of 'Padruig the daftie'. The word 'daftie' in the islands covered a multitude of mentalities. It was applied to the repulsive, misshapen imbeciles who were capable of nothing but vice, but also included the innocuous souls like Padruig who, if his income had been five thousand pounds a year instead of five thousand pence, might have been classed as merely eccentric. My acquaintance with Padruig was slight, for, though I had at various times noticed him shambling in and out of the houses of the neighbours, he was very shy and reserved and had seen to it that we never came within speaking distance. I knew, of course, that he lived in a tiny two-roomed cottage which he shared with his half-wit brother Euan. I knew that until three months previously they had been looked after by their very attractive sister but, on her marriage, she had left them to fend for themselves. Padruig was reputed to be immensely strong and to do those jobs which he was capable of doing remarkably well. Despite his simplicity he was well behaved and was, except in moments of excitement, an upright and devout Christian.

His brother Euan was a different character altogether, for, on the death of his parents, he had had the misfortune to be sent to live with a reprobate old uncle who had taught the boy nothing except a comprehensive vocabulary of vulgar abuse and profanity. The uncle had possessed such a violent temper that no one had felt inclined to interfere, and thus it was that Euan acquired a language peculiarly his own. For instance he referred to a man quite inoffensively as a 'he-bugger', a woman as a 'she-bugger', a dog as a 'hairy-bugger', and a bird as a 'feathery-bugger', and so on. After the death of his uncle Euan returned home and Padruig, whose vocabulary was extensive enough when occasion demanded, set himself the task of thrashing the evil out of his poor brother. So effective was his punishment that Euan, instead of refraining from the use of oaths, found it easier to refrain from speaking. This he did whenever possible, substituting a rapid blinking of the eyes for the words he did not utter.

Morag nudged my arm as we stumbled along the tortuous little path that led to Padruig's cottage. 'He talks awful wild sometimes,' she warned, 'but don't be laughin' at him to his face or you'll upset him.'

I promised not to laugh.

'And don't talk to Euan at all if you can help it,' continued Morag. 'If he was to swear in front of you, the Lord knows what Padruig would do to him.'

Reaching the cottage my companion pushed open the door and entered. I was about to follow, ducking my head to save banging it against the low roof, but recoiled as a dreadful stench assailed my nostrils.

'Padruid, Padruig,' Morag chided the unseen occupants. 'You and your ferrets! The smell of them is near knockin' Miss Peckwitt over backwards.'

Cautiously I started forward again, circumnavigating

the large wooden chests which impeded the entrance both
of people and of light. Morag motioned towards the
chests. 'Ferrets,' she explained in a whisper, but I had
already discovered four of the little horrors for myself.

'And you're feelin' better today, are you, Padruig my
boy?' asked my landlady brightly as she crossed the
kitchen. The room was incredibly dark and smoky and
at first I could make out nothing but the dim glow of a
fire, though there was still ample daylight outside.

A man's voice answered hoarse and low: 'I'm better
now. I'm for gettin' myself up tomorrow.'

'You are not!' contradicted Morag flatly.

'I am so,' maintained the voice firmly. 'I got to sweep
the chimbly.' Morag accepted the announcement with a
sigh.

'Here, I've brought Miss Peckwitt to see you,' she
said, adroitly changing the subject.

With difficulty I groped my way across the kitchen;
past a wooden bench on which I was just able to discern
the figure of Euan sitting motionless as a statue; past a
large barrel on top of which stood a water-pail, and as
my eyes became accustomed to the gloom I managed to
make out the shape of a recess bed in the corner where
Padruig himself reclined. His horny hand grasped mine
and shook it lengthily.

'I'm goin' to light the lamp,' said Morag in a busi-
ness-like tone and turning to Euan she commanded him
to blow up the fire so that she could make a wee oatcake or two for their tea. Euan jumped up instantly, but
instead of taking a pair of bellows, as I expected him to,
he dropped down on his knees, puffed out his cheeks
and commenced to blow on the fire with such prodigious
gusts that his eyes threatened to start out of his head at
any moment. The dim glow showered sparks and blos-
somed gradually into a flickering flame which in contrast to Euan's madder-hued cheeks looked positively
anaemic.

'It's that dark in here I canna' see if you're well or

dyin',' grumbled Morag as she put a spill to the wick of a miniature oil-lamp. 'Sure if you don't throw them ferrets in the sea soon, they'll be takin' the bed from under you,' she admonished Padruig.

I smiled at Padruig and his gentle brown eyes smiled back at me shyly.

'Are you hearin' from Lexy?' Morag enquired as she set the lamp on the mantelpiece and, taking a basin from the meagrely equipped dresser, scooped up some oatmeal from the barrel.

Padruig nodded.

'Did you get someone to read it for you?' asked Morag.

Again Padruig nodded and, pointing to the mantelpiece, asked Morag to hand him an envelope which was hiding demurely behind a glass net float. Holding the envelope in his hand he pointed eagerly to the stamp.

'All the waitresses in Glasgow has them little caps on their heads,' he told me, indicating the tiara worn by the Queen.

'Do they?' I asked stoically.

'Turn up that lamp a bitty, Euan,' Morag's voice interrupted, 'I canna' see whether it's my hands or my feets I'm stirrin' with.' Euan did as he was told and then returned to his seat on the bench.

Padruig spoke again. 'It's darker than this in Buckram Pàlace,' he said.

'In Buckingham Palace? Is it really?' I asked in astonishment.

'Yes,' he asserted, nodding his dark bullet head emphatically. I nodded wonderingly in return.

'I been to England once,' Padruig continued, watching my face intently.

'You did?' I asked, giving him nod for nod as well as I was able. 'How nice that must have been. Did you enjoy yourself?'

'Yes, yes.' His own nodding was becoming extraordinarily vigorous. I doubted if I could keep pace.

'I went to Buckram Palace to see the Queen.'

Helplessly I glanced at Morag, but she was busily occupied in pouring melted fat into the bowl of oatmeal.

'You did? You were very lucky,' I said faintly.

'Yes, up lots and lots of steps I been.' Padruig was still staring at me with concentrated attention and I risked a sober nod.

'Ever so many steps,' he continued. 'Up, up, up.' He demonstrated on the blanket with two of his stubby fingers how he had laboured up the steps of 'Buckram Palace', pausing every now and then to ensure by an anxious glance that I understood him.

'Just give me a hand with this,' Morag broke peremptorily into a brief but awed silence. Thankfully I moved over to the table. She put a finger to her lips and frowned expressively: and, guessing that she was again imploring me not to laugh, I shook my head reassuringly, for I was not so much amused as amazed by the tale. On the bed Padruig was still engrossed in climbing the innumerable steps of 'Buckram Palace', while from the bench the almost toothless Euan watched him with wide, fascinated eyes.

'We get to top.' Padruig waved an expressive arm above his head, and out of the corner of my eye I saw Euan ogle the rafters.

'And what did you find then?' I asked him, feeling rather like the inquisitor of the pussy cat who went to London.

'Chairs!' burst out Padruig. 'Chairs!' he repeated, 'hundreds and hundreds of little red armchairs all in rows. As true as I'm here.' He leaned earnestly towards me as though doubting my credulity.

'Really?' I murmured politely. 'And the Queen? Where did you see the Queen?'

'The Queen,' echoed Padruig rapturously. 'My, my, beautiful she was. Beautiful just.' He sighed lingeringly. 'But it was so dark in Buckram Palace,' he went on, 'that the Queen herself had to run in front of everybody with a little torch, and show people which was their seats.'

'Really!' I quavered.

'And what did you take for your breakfast, Padruig, my boy?' My landlady's voice broke opportunely into the recital and, giving Padruig no chance to reply, she pushed a cup of tea and two or three hot buttered oatcakes into his hand.

I subsided on to the bench beside Euan, refusing the tea Morag had proffered, which I was quite sure would be ferret flavoured. Suddenly Euan uttered an exclamation and jumping to his feet he charged recklessly through the outer door, muttering under his breath words which sounded suspiciously maledictory. I wondered what I had done and looked questioningly at Morag.

'It's his ducks,' she told me. 'He has one duck and one drake and he thinks the world of them just. But they plague the life out of him, always gettin' into the wee bit garden Padruig takes so much care of, and if Padruig catches them there he'll be for killin' them. Is that not right, Padruig?'

Padruig, his mouth crammed to capacity with oatcake, grumbled confirmation.

'Sure,' continued Morag, 'Euan spends most of his time chasin' them ducks away from Padruig's garden, and when he's chased them far enough he has to go and seek for them for fear they'll run away on him.'

As Morag was speaking she was rinsing soiled dishes in the remainder of the hot water from the kettle and, taking a cloth which was grey with age, I dried them and put them back on the dresser. Morag then started to tidy up but as the room was so austerely furnished the amount of actual tidying needed was negligible. The house may, as Morag claimed, have been spotlessly clean —if one excepted the ferrets—but there was so little illumination, either natural or artificial, that it was impossible for the casual observer like myself to tell whether it was clean or filthy.

Before we went I pointed to an extremely handsome bird-cage which was suspended from the ceiling on the far side of the room. It was a beautiful cage, shining and clean, its ornate brassy decorations gleaming like gold, but to me the thought of a creature so sun- and freedom-loving as a bird incarcerated in such gloom was distressing.

'Your bird is very quiet,' I observed.

Morag prodded me hastily. 'He has no bird,' she told me, hurrying me out of the house.

Outside there was still enough daylight for us to see Euan returning to the byre, shepherding in front of him two plump, waddling, quacking ducks. He stood and smiled at us vacuously.

'Fine ducks,' I commented.

'Bloody fine ducks,' Euan agreed blissfully.

'Euan!' interposed Morag in tones that shrivelled the half-wit into abjectness.

'What do you feed them on?' I enquired.

'Duck eggs, Missed,' the reply came with prompt servility. (Euan had never made up his mind whether to address me as 'Miss' or 'Mistress', but his compromise of 'Missed' was, I suppose, as apt a designation as any other for a middle-aged spinster.)

'Duck eggs?' I echoed foolishly. 'Where do you get them?'

Euan bestowed on Morag a look that was eloquent with pity. 'The ducks lays eggs,' he elucidated. 'Best Bl—— Best food for ducks, Missed.'

'Yes, of course,' I agreed wanly, faced with the eternal problem of which came first.

We were well out of range of the house before I asked Morag why she had nudged me at the mention of the bird-cage. She told me that Padruig had seen the cage at an auction sale some years ago and had fallen so much in love with it that he had insisted on buying it.

'There's nothin' in the whole of the village that gets a quarter of the care that cage gets; if he isna' paintin' it he's polishin' it, and if he's no polishin' it he's tattin' with it some way or another.'

'I wonder he doesn't want a bird to keep in it,' I said.

'Indeed if a bird set foot in that cage Padruig would wring its neck,' replied Morag seriously.

The next day Padruig kept to his intention of leaving his bed and when Lachy and I passed the house in the early afternoon we saw him preparing to sweep the chimney by means of a large bunch of heather and a stone which were tied to one end of a rope.

'He ought not to be doing that,' I told Lachy. 'He hasn't really recovered from his flu.'

'Ach, we'll just keep behind the dyke here and see he doesn't come to any harm.'

We watched Padruig, who may have been feeling as dizzy as he looked, climb with the aid of a flimsy ladder on to the roof and fling his arms passionately around the single chimney pot. After clinging desperately for a few minutes he decided it was safe to let go with one hand with which he began to manipulate the rope.

'How does he sweep the chimney with that arrangement?' I asked Lachy, who explained that the stone was lowered down the chimney and was then removed by a confederate inside the house. The confederate then pulled on the end of the rope until the man on the roof shouted the signal to stop; the cleaning being accomplished by each man hauling on the rope in turn, thus causing the bunch of heather to scrape up and down the chimney and dislodge the soot.

'Ready!' We heard Padruig's stentorian shout, but unfortunately Euan, who should have been ready to remove the stone and pull, had just noticed that his ducks were bent on entering Padruig's beloved garden and had rushed off after them, hurling murderous-looking boulders and colourful abuse. Padruig, discovering the desertion of his accomplice, pulled furiously on the rope, climbed wrathfully down from the chimney and also gave chase. His abuse was equally colourful and the boulders he threw looked just as murderous. It was only the target that was different!

A few minutes later Padruig returned dragging a crestfallen Euan by the scruff of the neck. Again he ascended the roof and again, with the deliberateness of a star performer in a play, he made his preparations.

'Right!' he bawled down the chimney, but the recalcitrant ducks had grown impatient for their feed and were already engaged on their investigation of the garden. With a stream of curses and an utter disregard for Padruig's instructions, Euan chased the two ducks down towards the burn. Padruig's language as he descended from the roof a second time and took off after his errant brother outrivalled Euan's worst.

Lachy and I made our presence known.

'I'm goin' to tie him to the end of the rope when I get him, and jiggle him up and down the chimney,' Padruig panted as he passed us at a vengeful trot.

'I believe he means it, too,' laughed Lachy.

By what means Padruig eventually completed the chimney sweeping I have no idea, for I had to be on my way, but when I returned later that afternoon a sinuous column of blue smoke was ascending serenely from the chimney, and the satisfying fragrance of burning peat lingered warmly in the chill air. I caught sight of Euan, who, with many furtive glances at the house, was shooing his duck and drake towards their evening quarters in the cow byre.

'He Breeah!' I called.

With a guilty start he whisked round to return my greeting. He looked very chastened—and very black!

It was about a month or so later when I met Euan again. He was staying alone in the house, Padruig having gone to spend a holiday with his newly married sister on the other side of the Island.

'Well, and how are your ducks?' I asked him, after I had made the necessary enquiries as to his brother's health.

'Bugger died on me,' he replied despondently.

I was suitably astonished. 'When was that?' I asked.

'Soon,' he answered with a lachrymose nod.

I wanted to commiserate but was at a loss to know which tense to commiserate in.

'But you still have your drake?' I said.

'Yes, yes.' He started off towards the house, obviously expecting me to follow, but I was slightly surprised when, beckoning to me eagerly, he disappeared into its dark depths. I wondered if, in Padruig's absence, the drake had ousted one of the ferrets, and after taking some deep breaths of fresh air and doing some rapid eye-blinking I warily poked my head and shoulders round the door into the kitchen. Immediately a frenzied quacking and hissing broke out in the gloom of the far corner and even before I could make out the wildly swinging cage and the outline of its occupant's head darting and feinting in all directions, I guessed that Padruig's cherished toy had become the new refuge for Euan's equally cherished drake. Recalling Morag's prophecy I hoped for the sake of both Euan and his bird that Padruig would not return without due warning.

I had taken my leave of Euan before remembering that I had omitted to ask after the health of his recently married sister. I turned to him with the enquiry.

'Her buggered, Missed.' The profane affability of the reply made me wince.

'Whatever is the matter?' I asked.

Euan lifted his shoulders in a prolonged fatalistic shrug. 'He-bugger, she-bugger, quick come little-bugger,' he informed me with remarkable frankness.

I walked for some distance before I permitted myself to consider his extraordinary statement, which persisted in running through my head like an oft-repeated formula. I was shocked to find myself walking in time to the words just as one unwittingly walks in time to a band playing in a city street. I shook myself and changed step resolutely.

I had to change step three or four times before I finally reached home.

7

Seagull

Seagull, which was the name of the boat shared by Lachy
and Ruari, was used for inshore fishing, lobster creeling
and for the occasional tourist trade. She was slow and
heavy and, like a Cheshire beauty, broad in the beam.
Her insides were spangled with fish scales which, though
decorative, were inclined to be somewhat odorous; her
engine was capricious but only slightly more so than
her crew; her name was inapt, for she looked as much
out of her element on the water as would a bedroom
slipper floating on a bathtub.

The frequent invitations I received from Ruari and
Lachy to accompany them on their trips were flattering
in the extreme, though I must frankly admit that, once
aboard, neither of the men seemed to be aware of my
presence. They addressed me seldom and left me more
or less to my own devices, and I was perfectly content
that it should be so. Seasickness never troubled me in
Seagull, nor did I ever reach the stage which Morag
described as being 'sick of the sea but not sick in it'.
Sometimes I would take a darra and lower it hopefully
into the cool, green water, and was thrilled when it came
in again, as it sometimes did, with half a dozen or so
rainbow-hued mackerel writhing on its hooks. Sometimes I would help haul in the creels but was always
careful to retire to a safe distance while Lachy tied the
vicious claws of their occupants. Invariably I dragged
a spinner after the boat and, to the amazement of the
crew, who thought they knew everything there was to be

known about fishing, hooked all kinds of fish ranging from dogfish to salmon. The latter of course we always threw back into the sea as the law demands. By what method we managed to obey the law and still have the salmon for supper is nobody's business.

Though Ruari and Lachy could reasonably be described as intrepid sailors there was an underlying nervousness about them which revealed itself in the altercation between them which continued incessantly. If Ruari saw a cormorant, Lachy swore it was a porpoise. If Lachy saw a rock, Ruari contended that it was a seal and on more than one occasion *Seagull*'s keel was scraping against the back of a 'shark' before one or the other would give way and admit that that particular shark had been marked on the Admiralty chart for the past twenty-five years.

It was one bright morning in early spring that Morag limped into my room having, as she said, 'gone off her anchor' the night before when looking for the cow.

'Ruari's after takin' a great lump of them jolly gees to the hills and then he'll be after collectin' some cattle from Rhuna and he's sayin' you'll get with them if you've a mind,' she informed me. (Morag always expressed quantity in 'lumps', whether she was speaking of manure, cheese or humanity.) Messages from Ruari reached me via his sister, for, though my company was not despised, it was beneath the male dignity to issue invitations to non-Gaelic-speaking females. I accepted with alacrity even though, as I told Morag, I had no idea what 'jolly gees' might be.

'Jolly gees? Why, they're yon fellows who hammer little bits off the hills and then fancy they can tell the Lord Himself how the earth was made,' Morag replied.

'Geologists!' I exclaimed. She nodded.

'It's awfully good of Ruari to take me,' I remarked as my landlady was about to signal my acceptance.

'You should see the size of the stones he'll need to

put into the stern for ballast if he doesna' take you,' she replied with devastating candour.

I felt momentarily deflated, but even deputising for a few stones acted as no damper to my enthusiasm for the trip. Rhuna, shaped like a crumbly brown bread sandwich with a bite taken out of it, had always fascinated me, and though I had hinted many times to Ruari that I should like to visit it he had so far fobbed me off with one excuse or another. I was swallowing breakfast as quickly as I could when Morag came back into my room.

'There they go,' she muttered resentfully, pointing through the window at the straggling party of men, each armed with a capacious rucksack, who were picking their way down to the shore.

'Don't you like them?' I asked carelessly.

'Like them? Indeed I do not!' she replied with unaccustomed vehemence. 'Climbin' like spiders all over the hills and tap, tap, tappin' with they little hammers. One of these days we'll wake up in the mornin' and find no hills left.' She snapped her fingers expressively and went out of the room, leaving me to wrestle with the remains of a tough kipper and an imagination that tried to picture an army of 'jolly gees' engaged on their gargantuan task. I finally abandoned the kipper and, pulling on a warm coat, started off for the shore. Before I was halfway I was arrested by an affronted bellow from Ruari.

'Six legs I had last night! Six legs I had and none but two have I got this mornin'. Who's taken my legs? How am I goin' to manage without my other four legs now?' he declaimed.

Ruari was as yet invisible to me and so also was the recipient of the tirade.

'Taken and chopped them up for firewood I'll be bound!' His bludgeoning voice apprised the world in general of the probable fate of his four spare legs.

Arriving, a little breathless, at the shore, I found an enraged Ruari holding aloft two 'legs'—small logs of

138

wood used for hauling the dinghy over the rough shingle —for the bewildered survey of the party of geologists who, I felt certain, were less impressed by the substance of the complaint than by the volume of it. Actually, when the time came, Ruari and Lachy managed very well without the four missing legs and soon they and myself and the geologists had been rowed out to where *Seagull* lay wallowing gently at her moorings. We stowed ourselves aboard and the engine, after resisting the power of Lachy's muscles for a time, yielded suddenly to the power of Ruari's vocabulary and, overcoming a slight preliminary fretfulness, settled down to the task of propelling us to our destination.

The hills for which we were bound looked cold and remote, their wintry peaks appearing to jostle one another for a glimpse of the morning sun, which transformed the sky into a rippling canopy of blue and gold. The geologists stared towards them speculatively, their minds no doubt occupied with formations and faults, bridging the gap of millions of years. I stared reflectively, dwelling only on the past hundred years of their history. Ruari and Lachy stared at them indifferently, merely as an object in the course they were setting; and bickered eternally.

We passed a dilapidated old boat, swinging sluggishly at her mooring; a seagull poised, aloof and graceful, on her masthead.

'She'd be the better of a coat of paint,' I observed, using the Bruach idiom.

'If he leaves her there much longer the seagulls will soon paint her white for him,' retorted Lachy meaningly.

Except for the fact that the weather was rather cold it was a perfect day for our sail. I enjoyed the feel of the engine labouring beneath my feet; the sight of the bow cleaving its way through the water which curled and splashed on either side. I liked to try to identify the different sea-birds as they bobbed and ducked in the ripples, and to watch the seals or porpoises or even a venturesome otter.

All too soon we reached the tiny jetty where the geologists were to be put ashore and, after arranging to pick them up at six o'clock in the evening, Ruari headed the boat seaward and set course for the island of Rhuna.

'It's deep watter all the way,' Ruari told me. 'Would you like to try your hand at steerin'?'

'Certainly I should,' I replied and grasped the tiller confidently.

'Just fix your eye on that end of the island and steer straight for it,' he instructed. It looked child's play, and I sat with one arm thrown negligently over the tiller, adopting Ruari's own habitual attitude when steering. The two men, thus released from duty, went to the forepeak of the boat and were soon occupied in inspecting tackle. I fixed my eyes on the point indicated by Ruari and concentrated on steering a straight course, which is infinitely more difficult than it looks. The boat chugged steadily, but only the water falling away on either side of the bow showed that we were not at anchor, for Rhuna seemed to be coming no nearer. The scenery was breathtakingly beautiful even for the eyes that had feasted long on such glory. The Bruach hills and moors, hardly yet aware of the tentative prodding of spring's green fingers, offered an intricate patchwork of browns and greys. Rhuna and her companion isles, which a loitering winter had left sprinkled with snow, reposed lightly on the strangely still water, looking as fragile as meringues on a baking board, needing only a palette knife slipping under them to lift them cleanly from their calm, blue base.

A lacerating 'aside' from Ruari brought me back to reality with a bump.

'She steers a course as crooked as a dog pissin' in the snow,' he confided to Lachy.

Stunned by the criticism, I stared at the two men. Lachy's face crimsoned with embarrassment and from the awkward position of his elbow I judged that he had just dealt Ruari a vigorous dig in the ribs. The latter, looking slightly sheepish, became absorbed in the complications of rope splicing. I turned round to see for myself the narrow lane of bubbles which marked *Seagull*'s wake and though I had to accept the veracity of Ruari's statement it was not until the following winter that I was able to appreciate the aptness of his simile.

Somewhere about one o'clock in the afternoon we crept into the sequestered bay of Rhuna. The island was dotted here and there with ruined habitations, outside which lounged their equally ruined inhabitants. On the shore awaiting us were Murdoch and Angus, who had rowed over in a big, flat-bottomed barge of a boat early that morning and who now stood guard over half a dozen or so uneasy-looking cattle. Murdoch regarded himself as the 'big' cattle man and, as none of the official buyers ever crossed to Rhuna, he looked upon it as his own private gold mine, buying cattle there cheaply, ferrying them over to Bruach and thence to the mainland sale yard, where he usually reckoned to make a hundred per cent profit.

A young boy appeared from one of the cottages and whispered a few words to Murdoch who translated them into an invitation to come ashore and take a 'wee strupak'. There were a few feet of water between *Seagull* and the shore and Angus, wading out in thigh-boots, offered me a piggy-back. I refused, for the water looked shallow enough and Angus's propensity for practical joking was too well known for me to be taking risks. I slipped off my boots and stockings and climbed over the side. The water was shockingly cold and of course much deeper than it had appeared; the shingle was slippery and the gunwale of the boat was a long way off, but willing hands grasped my shoulders and I was soon hauled ashore, my legs pink and tingling and my dress sodden only as far as the waist. I smothered the impulse to race to the cottage and toast myself in front of the fire,

141

remembering that the Bruachites always spoke of the inhabitants of Rhuna as being 'mad as I don't know what', a description which was in no way reassuring to one cognisant of the very moderate degree of sanity in Bruach itself. I therefore matched my pace to that of the men, which for me necessitated a rigorous exercise of muscle control, their walk being as deliberate and meticulous as a slow-motion film. One foot was put forward and then, after separately relaxing each muscle of the calf, it was slowly lowered to the ground heel first. When it was certain that the ground was flat enough and safe enough for the whole foot, it was trusted with the man's weight and the process repeated with the other foot. In heavy thigh-boots or hill-boots the ritual might have been both prudent and necessary; with bare wet limbs and an empty stomach it was excruciating.

After what seemed an interminable time we reached the house to which we had been invited and were greeted with the utmost cordiality by a grey-haired crone of incredible age, who then presented her mother, another grey-haired crone of even more incredible age. Suspecting that the introductions might continue *ad infinitum* I glanced covertly into the shadowy recesses of the room, wondering what vision of decrepitude I might be confronted with next. Fortunately the introductions ended there and 'mother', with many smiles, suggested I should come away in and dry myself through. Taking the chair she drew forward I proceeded to carry out her suggestion. The younger crone, with pursed lips, and eyes darting here and there, busied herself brewing tea while the elder jabbed a knife viciously into a jar of jam, spread the confection lavishly on thick slices of bread and butter and ship biscuits; then seized the delicacies with sticky, dirt-ingrained fingers and urged them upon us. The young boy who had brought us the invitation was, in an agony of shyness, trying to insert his stocky little body into the crevice between the dresser and the wall, his limpid brown eyes watching my every move-

142

ment as though I were a creature from another world, as perhaps I was. I wondered if he could possibly be the son of the less incredible of the crones, for my stay in the Hebrides had already taught me that it was not impossible for the recipient of the old age pension to use it for the purchasing of a layette!

While I munched and drank and my clothes steamed, I examined the room, which was reasonably clean. It boasted no ceiling except for the rafters over which lay the dark thatch and from which hung various species of dried, salt fish, a bundle of rabbit skins, a herring net and an iron girdle. The fireplace was of rough stone and the peat fire burned upon the flat hearth. A chimney pot saved it from being what is known as a 'black house', but so inadequate was the tiny window that the designation was merited. The furniture was a replica of what I now expected to see in the homes of the crofters who did not cater for tourists, namely a bench, table, dresser and the one wooden chair upon which I was now sitting. A long blue curtain covered an alcove in which was probably a recess bed. There was no clue to the number of people in the household. It might have been only the three I had met or it might have been a dozen.

The men, having finished their tea, put down their cups and stumped outside to begin the task of loading the protesting cattle into the likewise protesting boat. I too stood up and thanked my hostesses for their hospitality, but as the loading looked like taking some time they pressed me to stay and steam my skirts for a little longer in front of the fire. The mother questioned me courteously about my stay in Bruach, plainly disbelieving that I found the remoteness to my liking. They were both astounded when I told them I actually enjoyed the wild weather and was in no hurry to go back to England. Though they gave every appearance of accepting my statements I got the impression that they could imagine only two reasons why a woman should choose to settle down in Bruach: either that she was running away from

143

the police, or escaping from a lurid past. My plain homely features probably inclined them to the former belief.

In my turn I questioned them about their own lives. Did they differ much from those of the Bruachites? It seemed not.

'You haven't many places to cayley,' I said. They admitted there was little of what could be called 'good cayleying'.

'I suppose you have lots and lots of books here,' I began, resolving that in return for their kindness I could perhaps send them some.

Mother drew herself up haughtily.

'No indeed!' she answered frigidly. 'None at all.'

'No books? You don't like them. How strange!' I said.

'It's no strange at all.' The daughter's denial cut witheringly into an atmosphere that had changed suddenly from the cordial to the antipathetic. I puzzled as to what on earth I had said to upset them.

'I should have thought you would have had plenty of books,' I began, but the mother cut me short.

'Forty-five years I've lived in this house and never a bug did I see in it yet,' she asserted indignantly.

'Good heavens no!' I expostulated, glancing round fruitlessly to see if there was a book of any sort I might use as an illustration. 'Books,' I repeated desperately. 'Printed pages, magazines, reading books.' My cheeks burned; I was mortified that they should think I would repay their generosity by making such an aspersion.

To my immense relief the two women relaxed simultaneously and indulged in quite genuine laughter.

'I thought for a minute you must be one of them social women we used to get comin' round askin' questions about bugs and childrens and things.'

'Do they really do that?' I enquired mirthfully.

'Aye, indeed they do,' nodded the old mother. 'One

144

comes to me and she says she'll tell me how to bring up my thirteen childrens.'

'You have thirteen children?' I asked.

'Aye, so I had,' admitted the old woman proudly.

The daughter giggled. 'Tell Miss Peckwitt what you told the woman,' she implored her mother, and the latter continued the story eagerly.

'Says she to me, "How many childrens?" "Thirteen," says I. "How many have you?" She looks at me surprised. "Why, none at all," says she. "Well," says I, "go you away and have fourteen and then maybe I'll take some notice of you when you come back here and tell me how to bring up my thirteen." '

The shouting of the men broke into our laughter and hurriedly taking my leave I ran down to the shore where Lachy and Ruari were waiting to stow me into an impatient *Seagull*. The engine was already throbbing and as soon as I was aboard we started off, the poor old boat struggling valiantly to tow the rowing-boat with its quivering, snorting cargo of cattle. Even to my unpractised eye it looked decidedly overloaded, for not only was it crammed full of beasts but the bottom had been partly filled with shingle so as to provide a level base upon which the animals could stand. I said as much to Murdoch who was perched on the bow of the towed boat, his coat-tails almost touching the water.

'Ach, cattle's got sense; they're not like humans,' he retorted with so much acerbity that I concluded he himself was a little apprehensive.

For perhaps a mile we plodded on without mishap and then *Seagull* started to roll; so also did the cattle-boat.

'It's the tide rip!' roared Ruari. 'I told you we'd meet it. By God! you'd best watch out now.'

Murdoch answered with a cool nod and taking out his beloved pipe he began to fill and light it methodically. His position on the bow looked precarious but, refusing to show the least sign of perturbation, he settled the pipe more comfortably in his mouth and puffed at it with satisfaction. I turned to watch the weaving line of the tide rip coming nearer and nearer. How the catastrophe happened I never really knew, but it was probably due to a sudden movement of some of the beasts coinciding with a particularly severe roll of the boat. I heard first a concerted yell from the *Seagull*'s crew and wheeling round saw that the heavily laden rowing-boat lay over on her side with the sea pouring in over her gunwale; that the cattle were struggling in the water and bellowing with terror, and then, after a moment of anguish, that the boat had vanished beneath the waves. Fortunately someone had the presence of mind to slash the tow-rope or *Seagull* might have suffered the same fate. It was not until some moments later that I realised there was no sign of Murdoch.

'Murdoch!' I screamed and scanned the water for a trace of him among the panic-stricken beasts who were already swimming strongly and most sensibly back towards Rhuna. It seemed an age but must have been only a matter of seconds before Murdoch's white head appeared some twenty yards away from the side of the boat and, despite the dreadful anxiety of the moment, I remember noticing how large and red and bulbous was his nose. Angus, Ruari and Lachy stood staring stupidly at the scene, their attitudes expressive of something very like indifference.

'Can he swim?' I shouted distractedly.

'No,' answered Lachy, and pinioned my two arms behind my back as I tried to slip off my coat. 'No you don't,' he said firmly, 'one corpse is enough.'

'He won't be a corpse if you'll let me go,' I argued, but Ruari turned angrily upon me.

'Stay where you are!' he commanded. 'We can throw him a rope.'

'For God's sake throw it then!' I sobbed, feeling sick with panic and frustration. 'Don't let him drown. Do something!'

146

In the space of the last few seconds, or perhaps at some equally perilous moment in his career, Murdoch had apparently learned to tread water, since he remained visible for a considerable time. Angus grabbed a coil of rope and threw it towards the unfortunate man. The aim was excellent; it fell within a few inches of Murdoch, but as Angus had forgotten to keep a hold of the other end it was wasted effort. Murdoch's voice came plaintively over the water: 'I canna' keep this up much longer. Save me! I'll drown!'

'It'll take more than a bit of watter to drown you,' comforted Ruari, and picking up an oar he hurled it with such accuracy that it looked as though he intended to put Murdoch out of his misery quickly rather than assist in his rescue.

There was no shadow of doubt that Murdoch was in imminent danger of drowning before our very eyes and yet, in spite of the seriousness of the situation, one half of my mind was conscious that the whole episode smacked of farce. Fortunately, however, Murdoch managed to grasp a second oar that was thrown; another coil of rope went out to him, this time with all four of us hanging on to the end, and he was safely hauled aboard, where he gasped and shivered for some minutes. He seemed comparatively undaunted by his experience and taking a flask of whisky from his pocket he tipped it to his lips and drank deeply.

'Did any of you see my pipe?' he asked when he was sufficiently stimulated. 'It was in my mouth when I went down.'

Murdoch contrived to be ludicrous even in the most unsuitable circumstances. The four of us shook our heads.

'There was somethin' in your mouth when you went down,' said Lachy, 'but whether it was your heart or your pipe I couldna' tell.'

'Indeed it was my pipe,' responded Murdoch.

'Ach, then I expect you swallowed it,' said Lachy.

'I did not then,' replied Murdoch. 'My insides would be warmer than they are now if I'd swallowed my pipe —it was lit, I tell you.'

Everyone laughed rather more than the remark or the occasion warranted, and though Murdoch that day came within an ace of losing his life, or so it seemed to me, I never heard him refer to the incident except to bemoan the loss of the best pipe he'd ever had.

The mishap caused some delay in our programme and there was talk of taking Murdoch and Angus along with us to pick up the geologists. I, maintaining that the old man should get into dry clothes as soon as possible, prevailed upon Ruari to deliver him to his family before he should involve us in any more hair-raising experiences. As soon as this had been accomplished, *Seagull's* bow was turned once more towards the hills. We were already an hour later than the time we had promised to return and when we again chugged into the little sheltered harbour there was neither sight nor sound of the geologists. Ruari stopped the engine and the sudden quiet pressed on our ear-drums. Lachy stepped ashore.

'Give a shout,' he urged Ruari, and straightway Ruari let forth a bellow which split the intense quiet like a bomb and resounded among the hills for some moments afterwards. There was an echoing sound, scratchily feeble, in return, and after tying the boat the three of us went along the steep track towards it. It was not long before we met two of the geologists tottering down towards us, carrying between them a heavy sack.

'What the devil!' began one of the men truculently, but was soon subdued by Ruari's suave but picturesque excuses for our late arrival. 'Well, we'll go and round up the others,' the geologist replied sulkily. 'We've all been down to the jetty once, but when we found you hadn't turned up we thought we might as well keep working until you did.' He gestured towards the heavy bag which had been dropped on first seeing us. 'Here,' he instructed Ruari imperiously, 'you can carry that down to the boat and put it aboard.'

The two left us to go in search of the rest of their party while Ruari, with Lachy's assistance, lifted the sack on to his back. Ruari, as I have said before, was a strong man but his load was a heavy one, and he was quite distressed by the time we eventually reached the jetty. He deposited the sack with a bump on the rocks and rubbed his back tenderly.

'My God! That sack's so hard and heavy you'd think it was stones they had in it,' he grumbled.

'It is stones,' answered Lachy, who was more familiar with the ways of geologists.

'Stones?' Ruari almost spat. 'I'll give them stones if they try to play tricks like that on me,' he threatened. He looked at me for confirmation.

'Of course they're stones,' I told him, my face breaking into a smile at his outraged expression. He eyed me suspiciously from beneath knitted brows and his fingers plucked at the string which tied the neck of the bag. Out of the corner of my eye I perceived the party of geologists coming out of the dusk down the track towards the boat. Lachy saw them too.

'Look,' I told Ruari. 'If you don't believe me you can ask them for yourself, for here they come now.'

But Ruari had the sack open and was fingering the samples of gneiss and gabbro which would no doubt afford material for research for many months to come. He turned menacingly towards the approaching group. 'You buggers!' he yelled angrily. 'I'll teach you to play a joke like that on an old man. You ought to be ashamed of yourselves!' And before anyone, least of all myself, realised his intention he had turned the bag upside down and tipped the whole of its contents into the water.

There was a heartrending groan from the weary geologists and some of them raced forward impetuously in a vain attempt to save the treasure they had so industriously gathered. Their groans tailed off into sighs and their sighs melted into a stricken silence as they sank down hopelessly on the nearby rocks and stared dispiritedly at the ever-widening circle of ripples on the water where their treasure had disappeared. Ruari continued to glower at them with implacable wrath. I glanced uneasily at Lachy who was bending over the engine of *Seagull*, an unlit cigarette between his teeth and a superfluously intent expression on his face.

'Ruari,' I began timorously, feeling it incumbent on me to say something, 'they were not just ordinary stones. These men were not playing a joke on you. They're samples,' I floundered as Ruari bent his chilly gaze on me, 'specimens for studying,' I faltered.

'Is that so?' asked Ruari in somewhat mollified tones. I nodded.

'Yes, these men are students,' I persevered. 'They get a degree for this sort of thing.'

The words 'students' and 'degree' Ruari understood at once. He turned with a conciliatory smile to the group of scowling men.

'Well, if that's it now you must excuse me, but I thought it was a nasty bit of a game you were playin' on an old man, makin' him carry a big bag of stones down the mountain side,' he apologised magnanimously. 'But ach,' he went on, 'it's lucky indeed I havena' thrown away the sack itself and I'll have it full for you in a couple of minutes just.'

The geologists, still in a state of mental and physical overthrow and utterly bereft of speech, stared glumly while Ruari bent and began to fill the sack with shingle from the beach.

'That's no good!' the leader found his voice. 'For heaven's sake let's get home!' he snapped sullenly.

'Ach, but it's no trouble at all,' Ruari declared, with an extravagant flourish of his hand, 'and what harm I've done I must try to undo as best I can.'

'You're a damn fool!' returned the irate one ungraciously, and snatching the sack from Ruari clambered gloomily aboard *Seagull*.

'Well if I mustn't, I mustn't. I dare say you know best yourselves,' murmured Ruari with a puzzled nod.

As soon as the rest of the party were aboard we cast off and *Seagull* gambolled ponderously towards the Bruach shore. Talk was desultory, for Ruari was surprisingly abashed after his experience, while Lachy and I hovered between profound sympathy and irrepressible mirth.

It was an exceedingly melancholy party of 'jolly gees' who were landed at Bruach and who climbed stiffly and slowly up the brae towards the special bus which awaited them. Ruari watched them go, a sly expression on his face. 'Yon men are fools,' he observed as he baled out *Seagull* while I secured the tiller.

'It's you who were the fool,' I told him. 'You should have known that the stones wouldn't be ordinary stones.'

'Me? A fool?' exclaimed Ruari indignantly. 'Is it me that's the fool, when they've had to hire my boat to take them again tomorrow?'

'You wretch!' I chuckled.

'I'm thinkin',' said Ruari, cocking a speculative eye at the cloudless horizon, 'that we're in for another fine day tomorrow. You'll be comin' with us again, Miss Peckwitt?'

'No,' I said with a shudder. 'I can't face that crowd again.'

Ruari turned to Lachy who had just come alongside in the dinghy to take us ashore.

'What was you talkin' about to yon man?' he asked.

I had noticed that Lachy seemed to be having quite a voluble conversation with one of the geologists while he was taking them ashore.

'Ach, he wasn't a geologist at all,' replied Lachy. 'He called himself a cartyographer or somethin' like that.'

'A what?' demanded Ruari.

'A cartyographer,' repeated Lachy. 'I had some fun with him I can tell you.'

'How was that?' asked Ruari.

'Well, he was wantin' to know all the place names in Gaelic and in English,' said Lachy.

'But I distinctly saw you pointing to Rhu Corran, and calling it Allt Rhunan,' I accused.

'So I did,' agreed Lachy cheerfully. 'And I told him Corry Dhy was Cnoc Dhanaid, and plenty others wrong besides. The old nosey parker he was.'

Ruari chuckled appreciatively.

'But Lachy,' I expostulated feebly. 'If he said he was a cartographer you should have told him correctly. It's very important.'

'Ach,' said Lachy scornfully, 'what does he want to know the right names for? He doesn't live about here at all. He's only after makin' a map.'

8

A Ceilidh

The acquisition of the Gaelic is, I believe, a necessity for those who wish to lead a full life in the Hebrides, and accordingly I purchased a Gaelic grammar and set myself the task of mastering the idiosyncrasies of that much-exalted tongue. Languages have never been my strong point but having the advantage of actually residing and conversing with natural Gaelic speakers, I estimated that by the end of three months I should have achieved a reasonable degree of fluency.

'It's quite easy to learn,' encouraged one of the accepted scholars of the village when he heard of my intention. 'The Gaelic is pronounced exactly as it is spelled so you will not find it half so difficult as other languages.'

I was enormously cheered by his words and was tempted to cut my estimate to six weeks, but the discovery that 'Cnoc' was pronounced 'Crock', 'Dubh' as 'Doo' and 'Ceilidh' as 'cayley' convinced me that his statement had been somewhat misleading. When I found that a simple phrase like 'I have a cat' is in the Gaelic distorted to 'A cat is at me' I felt that I must double my original estimate and, even so, doubted whether I should ever realise that to say 'The dog is at me' indicated possession and not attack.

Previous to commencing the study of Gaelic I had noticed that the inhabitants always seemed to be slightly nonplussed by my formal English greeting of 'Good morning!' or 'Good evening!' Naturally I used 'Good

morning' as a salutation, not as an observation on
weather conditions, and I was not to know then that in
such matters the Gael believes in being specific. In
my anxiety to say the right thing I asked Morag to tell
me the Gaelic way of wishing people 'Good day'. She,
taking me literally, taught me to say 'He Breeah', a
phrase which, I later learned to my dismay, meant 'It is
a good day', in the sense that 'the weather is fine', and it
was singularly unfortunate that for practically the whole
of that season there were no days when 'He Breeah'
could have been called a suitable greeting. Through rain
and cold, through wind, hail and snow, 'He Breeah!'
I called gaily, and received in reply politely bewildered
'He Breeahs' from dejected figures whose boots
squelched wetly and from whose sou'westers the rain
streamed steadily. 'He Breeah!' I greeted the embittered
roadman as he sheltered in his inadequate little hut from
the merciless flurries of sleet which swept incessantly up
the valley. 'He Breeah!' I hailed startled milkmaids as,
blue-fingered and red-nosed, they huddled miserably
under the cows' bellies, seeking refuge from the torrential
rain.

The villagers accepted my misuse of the phrase with
amused tolerance and were unfailingly complaisant, as
is their way, but my suspicions were at last aroused when
one old soul, battling homeward against a fierce north-
westerly gale, her sodden cape billowing wildly in spite
of her effort to restrain it, returned my 'He Breeah'
promptly and then added conscientiously, 'But there's
a fearful lot of wet along with it now, isn't there?' That
night I learned to say 'He Fluke' (it is wet) and 'He
Fooar' (it is cold) and by so doing ensured the finest spell
of warm dry weather that the Island had experienced for
some years.

Though my Gaelic studies were not conspicuously
successful they did at least help me to understand the
propensity of my new friends for investing anything and
everything with the masculine or feminine gender, for,

like French, the language has no neuter. A shoe for instance is a 'she', while a coat is a 'he'. The professions are all masculine, though the noun 'work' is feminine. (It is easy to understand the significance of this when one has lived in the Hebrides for a short time.) The circumstance that an object might be feminine in the English language yet masculine in the Gaelic added to the confusion, as did the complications of soft and hard consonants and shortened vowels; and when I heard of cows with calves at foot being referred to as 'he' I began to doubt very much whether anyone among the Bruachites was capable of classifying sex with any certainty.

This use of either the masculine or the feminine gender persisted among the crofters even when speaking English, and I was frequently considerably agitated on hearing remarks which seemed to suggest all manner of nefarious or ludicrous practices.

'When he's done barking, Ruari's going to hang him on the clothes line for an hour or so,' I overheard Bella telling Morag one day, and was greatly relieved to discover that 'he' was nothing more animate than a fishing-net. For one like myself, possessing only a limited capacity for controlling my countenance, there were agonising moments such as the occasion when I met an old crofter and his wife stumping morosely along the road. The weather, which earlier had looked promising, had turned treacherously to rain and as we paused to commiserate with one another on this fact the woman bent down to tie her bootlace. Her husband studied her bent back, a lugubrious expression on his lined face. 'Yes,' he grumbled disconsolately, 'and I did think we'd have got to the peats today, but it's no use now she's gone and turned wet on me.' I need hardly point out that in this case the weather was the 'she'.

Apart from the curious idiom I was often disconcerted by the precise old ladies who, having little knowledge of English except for the English of the Bible, attempted to converse with me in distressingly scriptural

155

language, utterly oblivious of the fact that many Biblical words are not used in polite conversation these days.

To familiarise myself with the language and thus help along my Gaelic studies, I should have acquired the ceilidh habit. These ceilidhs, which were really nothing more than the impromptu dropping in of neighbours, were going on almost every night of the autumn, winter and spring, but whereas most writers on Highland subjects deem it their duty to depict the ceilidhs with a romantic pen—lamplight; peat fire flames playing on a cluster of honest friendly faces; rich Highland voices, joking, singing and story-telling; cups of tea and home-baked scones—I was never able to forget that the room was likely to be ill-ventilated; that the tight-packed bodies would be hot and unbathed; that the pipe-smoking old men would be spitting indiscriminately; that the boots of the company would be caked with dung and mud; that more than one of my neighbours might be belching with threatening violence, and the clothes of others reeking of stale peat smoke and sour milk. As a consequence I was inclined to view the ceilidhs with disfavour; so that I was not at all pleased when Morag relayed to me a most pressing invitation to attend such a gathering at the home of the village's pet widow. I was tempted to refuse point-blank but, recalling that the house in question was comparatively large and airy and that the widow herself was an exceptionally genial lady, I decided that I might do worse than accept.

Morag was delighted, and about nine o'clock on a bright, starlit November evening we sallied forth. All day there had been a sharp frost and now our footsteps rang with a clear, staccato echo instead of the customary sloshing plod. A silvery glow behind the hills heralded the rising of the maturing moon and suddenly and impressively it emerged above the dark peaks, spilling light and shadow with superb artistry into the tranquil valley. My companion and I walked briskly; not because we expected to be late for the ceilidh—that would have been well nigh impossible as the Bruachites kept astonishingly late hours—but because of the invigorating effect of the chill air. Morag, never at a loss for some topic of conversation, pointed out various dwellings and amused both herself and me by recounting stories of their occupants past and present. Just as we came abreast of a low, thatched house on the high road the door was flung open and a woman of demi-john proportions stood silhouetted in the lamplit space. Morag immediately called out a greeting which was shrilly returned by the fat woman, along with the additional information that she would be catching us up presently.

'Yon's Anna Vic,' said my companion. 'You'll know her likely?'

I certainly knew Anna Vic both by sight and reputation. Ruari had described her to me as being 'so fat that if you saw her on the skyline you didna' know if it was herself or two cows standin' side by side', while Lachy asserted that 'if you can see daylight between the ankles then it canna' be Anna Vic'.

'She is indeed a very big woman,' I said.

'Aye, and her heart's the biggest part of her,' replied Morag warmly. 'My,' she continued with barely a pause for breath, 'but she holds a lot of water that one.'

'Who does?' I gasped.

'Why, that fine rainwater tank beside the house there,' answered my landlady, inclining her head towards the house we had just passed. 'I must be seein' about gettin' one of them for myself.'

Our ears were assailed by a piercing shout and, turning, we beheld the panting Anna Vic waddling after us like an excited duck.

'How fast you walk,' she grumbled pleasantly as she toiled along beside us, but neither her corpulence nor our speed proved the slightest impediment to her conversational powers.

'Why,' she panted after a little while, 'it's warm enough walkin' but in the house I was feelin' the cold

157

terrible. Indeed I was sittin' that close over the fire that when I came to put on my stockings my legs was tartan with the toasting I'd given them.'

We laughed, and so entertained did she keep us that it seemed no time at all before we were pushing open the door of the ceilidh house where we found several people already comfortable ranged in front of an enormous peat fire. On the inevitable wooden bench sat Alistair the shepherd, Angus, Murdoch, Adam the gamekeeper and one-armed Donald. Roddy and Callum, the hostess's bachelor brothers, sat determinedly in their favourite armchairs. A wooden chair was shared awkwardly by twin sisters whom I had already christened 'Giggle' and 'Sniggle'; Johnny the bus-driver was perched precariously on one end of the roughly hewn kerb, while Elspeth, the young schoolteacher, sat, with arms akimbo and knees locked virtuously together, on a corner of the table, her feet resting on a low stool. Greetings were exchanged and the men, after catching the intimidating eye of our hostess, executed a sort of 'general post' as they outdid one another in their anxiety to make room for us. We settled ourselves on a horsehair sofa drawn close to the fire; the conversation was resumed and in no time at all Anna Vic and Morag were involved in an argument with Donald as to the price of whelks for the previous season. I listened impartially, being far more interested in the setting than in the dispute.

The room was cosily warm; the mellow lamplight, reflected by the varnished wood walls, whitened the hair and smoothed the wrinkles of the aged, while it burnished the hair and enhanced the already ravishing complexions of the young. On the gleaming hob two sooty kettles spouted steam and beside them a magnificent brown teapot squatted complacently. Against one wall stood a homely dresser bedecked with gay china, and flanked on either side by 'Vesuvius in Eruption (daytime)' and 'Vesuvius in Eruption (at night)'. On the opposite wall, nearly surrounded by its festoon of weights and chains,

158

hung an old-fashioned clock, its pendulum lazily swinging the night away; its ticking rivalled only by the repetitive sniffs of the company, for sniffing is as sure an accompaniment to a ceilidh as is the popping of corks to a champagne party.

Tea and biscuits began to circulate and the conversation ranged from such topics as the prospect of winter herring to the existence of witches; from the price of whisky to the efficacy of willow bark for cold sores; from the condition of the cattle to the miraculous traffic lights of Glasgow. It was Murdoch who regarded the latter thus, explaining carefully to his unsophisticated audience that: 'When the lights is blue the cars can go; when they're yellow they can still go; but when they're red!' the old man's fist dropped expressively on to his knee and his voice became emphatic. 'Why 'tis just like a tether on their wheels,' he told them, 'and they canna' move, no not an inch!' After one glance at his spellbound audience he added knowledgeably 'It's the electric d'you see?'

It was plain that Murdoch believed the secret of the traffic lights to be a powerful electric ray which effectively immobilised all engines in the vicinity, and it says much for Glasgow motorists that Murdoch, who had studied them intensively during the fortnight he had spent in the city, had apparently never seen a car 'jump' the lights.

'Have you ever seen them?' he asked me.

'Yes,' I told him. 'We have them in England too.'

Murdoch regarded me with a sceptical stare. 'Is that so?' he murmured with polite disbelief.

Tea drinking was well in progress when the rampant Lachy burst into the room, followed by Euan the half-wit. Without ceremony Lachy snatched the stool from beneath Elspeth's feet, ignoring her sudden collapse as blandly as he ignored her profane remonstrance. He seated himself on the major portion of the stool and generously allowed Euan to make himself comfortable on the remaining two inches. The latter opened his mouth

159

to begin a vituperative protest but a quelling glance from his hostess not only silenced his protestations but also appeared to paralyse the muscles of his jaws, so that he sat for the remainder of the evening staring stupidly before him, his mouth with its one front tooth gaping as rigidly and seductively as a baited mousetrap.

So far as I was concerned Lachy's arrival was inopportune, for the discussion had turned to old country cures —a subject in which I was intensely interested—and I had made mental notes of numerous, half-remembered remedies. As I have mentioned previously, Morag's mother was reputed to have possessed great skill in concocting medicines from plants, but Morag always appeared embarrassed when I tried to pump her for information. It was as though she was ashamed to confess her knowledge. Tonight, however, she was not averse to discussing the subject and I heard her prescribe sea urchins for the cure of asthma; scabious roots for jaundice; plantain leaves for poultices and plasters; clover heads for cancer, and a fantastic-sounding remedy for a soaring temperature as in the case of fevers, etc., which was to split and fry a red herring, then to tie the halves to the soles of the patient's feet. This treatment, though claimed to be efficacious, was considered to be rather drastic and was accompanied by the warning that in the case of an adult the fish should not be left on the feet for more than twenty minutes by the clock; while in the case of a child ten minutes was the maximum for safety, otherwise it might do more harm than good. I hope I may never have occasion to try out this cure; nor, for that matter, would I care to try out the recommended cure for piles, which was to 'sit in a bucket of pneumonia every night for half an hour before going to bed'.

The manner of Lachy's entrance had thrown everyone into a state of expectancy and though I attempted several times to bring the conversation back to cures my efforts were unavailing.

'D'you know who I've just seen?' the newcomer demanded.

Everyone professed ignorance.

'I saw Hamish MacAlistair Oulliam,' announced Lachy dramatically.

His statement was greeted with cries of 'Oh, my, my!' and 'Surely not after all this time?' and 'Whoever was expectin' to see him again indeed?'

'Well, he's home again this night, true as I'm here,' affirmed Lachy. There were even more exclamations and in the middle of them he turned to me.

'You never knew Hamish MacAlistair Oulliam, did you, Miss Peckwitt?' he asked, and then continued: 'No, you couldn't have.'

I had to admit that I had never heard of Hamish Mac-Alistair Oulliam.

'Well, I'm tellin' you, Miss Peckwitt,' he explained solemnly, ' 'tis three years now since that fellow—and he was only eighteen or thereabouts at the time—he jumped on a sheep and away he went and not a soul has seen breath, nor line, nor trace, nor shape of him from then until he walked into his own house tonight.'

As I have said, the talk during the evening had touched upon various aspects of the supernatural; I had listened to the most impressive tales of present-day fairies, tales which would be vouched for by witnesses still alive and of impeccable character. As a result I was in a particularly receptive mood, but even so the existence of an enchanted sheep which could carry away a man was too much for my prosaic mind. Covertly I studied the circle of intent faces, watching for the slightest quirk of the lips or glint in the eye to confirm my suspicion that the story was a deliberate attempt at pulling my often too-susceptible leg. I could, however, discern nothing in their expressions save profound interest.

'I don't believe a word of it,' I said decisively.

My words brought a chorus of indignant and sorrowful rebukes from the company.

'Why, there's plenty knows the truth of it,' they told me.

'Indeed,' someone insisted, 'he'll like as not be tellin' you the truth of it for himself soon enough.'

Their earnest asseverations were obviously made in the sincere belief that the sheep had indeed run away with the man, but try as I would my faltering imagination boggled, first at the idea of any sheep being able to carry on its back even the smallest of men, and then at the possibility that, even in such a wild part of the country, the steed and its rider could disappear completely for three years. It was a tale for the superstitious Gael or an infants' school; not for a town-bred Englishwoman.

'Sheep don't do that,' I insisted. 'It's not possible.'

'They don't?' Murdoch enquired haughtily. 'I'm tellin' you, Miss Peckwitt, if the sheep is carryin' a mixed cargo she might be away for even five years. It all depends on the cargo and the Company.'

The ensuing silence was broken by a snatch of song. So long as the Gaels stick to their own melodies I like to hear their singing, there being a primitive and unrestrained passion in their music which perfectly expresses the spirit of the wild hills and lonely glens of their land, and completely suits the curious vibrancy of their untrained voices. Listening sometimes I had the vague feeling that the beat of the tom-toms was missing, so strangely reminiscent are some of their songs of those of native tribes.

Adam the gamekeeper was considered to be Bruach's best male singer and it was he who started now, nodding the beat of the music to himself as he sang, and interspersing each verse with a colossal guttural sniff which twisted his nose like the thong of a whip, and jerked his head up from his chest like a marionette on a string. Everyone joined in the choruses and I could not help noticing that the mannerisms and facial expressions of all the singers were almost identical.

162

It was the custom for every person present at the ceilidh to be asked to sing, and it was equally the custom for everyone to deny that he or she could sing. Giggle and Sniggle were addressed when Adam had finished.

'Come on, girls, what about a song from you?'

Giggle and Sniggle hung their heads shyly and of course giggled and sniggled in unison. They undoubtedly would have provided a long-drawn-out duet of giggling and sniggling had there been room enough on the chair for them both to breathe out at the same time. Persuasion having proved fruitless in their case, Elspeth was next entreated.

'Come now, you Elspeth, you're a good singer.'

Elspeth too hung her head and giggled. 'I can no sing,' she disclaimed unenthusiastically.

'You can so.'

'Ach, I can no.'

'Indeed you can so.'

Thus the cajolery and contradiction continued and between each unconvincing denial Elspeth surreptitiously but very determinedly cleared her throat in preparation for the song she had every intention of singing throughout every one of its fifteen verses.

As the night wore on the singing and the gossiping became more sporadic until there was only the voice of Anna Vic, who for the greater part of the evening had been regaling our patient hostess with shrilly despairing confidences regarding the shortcomings of the fat woman's youngest son. Her affronted voice pierced a temporary silence.

'Supposin' I stand on my head he won't do it for me,' she complained. There was the echo of a sardonic laugh from Lachy.

'Supposin' you stand on your head, nobody would notice the difference. You're the same shape either way up.'

His quip was received with a roar of laughter from the assembled company and the fat woman looked momentarily uncomfortable. The shepherd, still grinning widely, got up to go. He was tired, he told us, after having had such a heavy day, 'there'd been that many docks chasin' ships all over the hills'. He directed a meaning glance at Murdoch who was reputed to own the worst sheep-worrying dog in the district, but, affecting to be deaf, the old man continued to stare steadily at the fire.

'The merry dancers are puttin' on a good show tonight,' called Alistair as he went out; 'it means a change in the weather one way or another.'

Morag and I decided that it was time we also should be making a move, and Johnny, Lachy, Angus, Anna Vic and Murdoch, though loth to break up the ceilidh, made up their minds to come with us. The night was still clear and the slightly toothachy moon sailed serenely along through a froth of white cloud. From behind the hills rose the flickering green-gold cone of the Northern Lights, its apex directly above our heads.

'Aye, aye, a change in the weather right enough,' confirmed Murdoch as he minced along in front of us, holding his pipe to his mouth in the manner of a small child blowing bubbles. We three women followed, arms linked together, and behind us came Johnny, Lachy and Angus. The talk eddied from one to another and the background to our conversation was the sucking rasp of the breakers on the shingle and the infrequent cry of some night-flying bird. And then we became aware of another sound: a weird, rhythmic, burring wail which none of us could identify.

'Good God! Whatever's that?' burst out Anna Vic apprehensively.

After pausing to listen we decided that the noise was coming from somewhere along a stretch of road now under repair. The men turned their steps inquisitively in that direction and we followed, keeping close to their heels, dropping our voices to whispers. The noise grew gradually more distinct and was now punctuated by an eerie, choking moan. Anna Vic clutched at my arm, but whether it was for her own comfort or mine I could not tell. If it was the former she was likely to be disillusioned, for after the evening's ghost stories my nerves were not exactly steady. After walking for some distance the men halted and we were at once relieved and surprised to hear Murdoch's asthmatic chuckle. Following the direction of his pointing finger, we saw, a short way in front of us, a dark mass which we soon identified as the small hut where the 'gaffer' of the roadmen lived. It was from the hut that the strange noise was coming.

'My, but that man can snore,' declared Johnny with grudging admiration.

Anna Vic's tightly held breath escaped in a thankful sigh and she slackened her hold on my arm.

'He must be ill,' I said.

'Not him,' replied Murdoch sagely. 'It's whisky that makes him snore like that, not sickness.'

'How that man can drink!' Angus observed in accents of awed humility.

'You should have seen him on Friday,' said Lachy. 'He was that drunk it took four of us to get him over from the bus to his hut. And when we got him inside, Johnny here lights the Primus to make him some tea to try would it sober him up. There was no watter, so we had to take a pail and go to the burn and by God! when we got back we found the old bodach sittin' on top of the lighted Primus itself.'

'Indeed it was lucky for him he'd sat in a few bogs on the way home,' said Johnny, taking up the story, 'or he'd have been in a worse mess than he was.'

'Was he burned bad?' demanded Murdoch.

'Burned? Him?' asked Lachy incredulously. 'Why, when we pulled him off the stove he said he must have been sittin' in a patch of thistles some time. Thistles!' went on Lachy. 'Can you believe it? And the bottom burned out of his pants and his backside as red as a

165

cock's comb in spring. I'm tellin' you that fellow has a skin like the sole of a tackety hill-boot.'

Lachy's enthusiastic description of the gaffer's misadventure lasted while we retraced our steps to the road.

'My, but he's a character that one,' remarked Murdoch. 'And I've never in my life seen a man that's wilder in his drink,' he added respectfully.

'He doesn't have to get drunk to get wild,' interpolated Johnny. 'He wanted to smash my face in the other day because I told him the Government would lose the next election.'

'Aye, aye, he's a staunch Tory,' averred Murdoch.

'And so you are yourself for that matter,' muttered Johnny sulkily.

'And why shouldn't I be?' demanded Murdoch with some heat. 'People that's lived as long as I have is always Tory. You grow in sense as you grow in years you know.'

Johnny retaliated with some incoherent remark reflecting upon the senility of the Tory party in general and the comparative youthfulness of Socialism.

'Socialism! Why, I'd sooner have rheumatism than Socialism. It's easier to c-cure,' stuttered Murdoch, who had never felt the slightest twinge of either malady. 'You young people,' he went on, 'shouldn't be allowed to have a vote at all, and then Socialism would never have come to fret us in our old age. You have no sense at all,' he finished disparagingly.

'I'm no so young,' objected Johnny. 'I'm gettin' on for forty.'

Murdoch spat with elaborate contempt. 'Forty!' he exclaimed scathingly. 'Forty!' he repeated. 'Chicken's age is forty. You shouldn't get your vote till you get your old age pension. You should qualify for the two of them together.' Haughtily he resumed his place at the head of the procession and ventured no further remark until he wished us good night at his own bedstead gate.

'So Johnny's a red-hot Socialist,' I observed when Murdoch had gone.

'Aye,' put in Lachy, 'he's been a good Socialist all his life except on polling days.'

Johnny laughed self-consciously.

'That was one of those social nosey parkers we had on the trip today,' resumed Lachy.

'You got a trip today?' asked Morag with surprise.

'Aye, we did, and the social woman was pretty sea-sick I can tell you.'

'What did you do with her?' asked Johnny.

'There was nothin' I could do with her,' replied the other indifferently. 'She was done for. All I could do was drag her up the beach and leave her above the tide.'

'Oh, but you should have done more than that for the creature,' scolded Morag. 'Could you no have done somethin' to try would you bring her round?'

'Me? Bring her round?' echoed Lachy. 'Why should I try bringin' her round?' And then apparently divining a reason for Morag's admonition he added with materialistic reassurance: 'It was all right, I didn't need to bother, she'd already paid her fare.'

The talk of sickness in humans veered to the far more important topic of sickness in animals. We reached the dyke and as I was about to 'leap' over it, Morag began asking minutely about a cow of Lachy's which had been ailing for some time.

'It's no right for her to go on like that,' he told her. 'She's old and she's sick and I've made up my mind I'm goin' to shoot her in the mornin'.'

Morag agreed that it was high time the beast was disposed of and later, when I was filling my hot-water bottle, she emphasised, in reply to my question, that Lachy could be trusted to make a far easier and better job of putting the beast out of its misery than would the 'Cruelty'.

During the night, as Murdoch and the Aurora Borealis had foretold, the wind changed its direction and brought with it a couple of hours of torrential rain from the west. By morning the ground was again sodden and the black-currant bushes stood sadly in the middle of a sheet of water.

'And did you shoot your poor old cow?' I asked Lachy when I met him.

'No, I did not then,' he replied morosely. 'I believe I'll have to be gettin' the Cruelty to do it yet.'

I felt that I understood. 'It cannot be very nice to have to shoot an animal you've had all these years and grown fond of,' I suggested sympathetically.

'Ach, it's no that at all.' Hastily Lachy repudiated the suggestion that his failure to accomplish the deed had been in any way due to sentiment. 'I was goin' to shoot her right enough,' he went on stoutly, 'but when I came to do it I found she'd gone and got damp in the night and swollen so big I couldna' push her into the gun.'

He resolved this statement of patent impossibility by producing for my inspection an undeniably swollen, but far from effeminate-looking, shot-gun cartridge!

9

The Dance

FIRST WARNING

A Grand Concert with Artists from Glasgow
followed by a dance and a Competition to find
the Prettiest Girl is to be held on Friday 30th
next

Men 4s.   Ladies 3s. 6d. & pkt soap
      flakes as usual (no splitting)

Come on, lassies—Now's your chance to shine

In aid of charity

(D.V.)

I studied the carelessly scrawled notice in the window
f the grocer's shop; the black crayon lettering on a
ughly torn sheet of white wrapping-paper looked like
child's first attempt at printing. The poster was some-
hat overshadowed by another one which advertised a
3rand Sale of Females' on the following Saturday. This
as of no interest to me personally as it referred only to
sale of heifers, but the dance 'warning' was definitely
orth attention. I translated the 'no splitting' into a very
rudent desire on the part of the organisers to avoid
ther the concert or the dance being a financial failure,
s might be the case if a separate charge were made for
ach.

The demand for soap flakes was a little puzzling, but
had lived long enough in Bruach to appreciate that

many of their customs had survived from Biblical times and though I had not yet observed the practice it was not wildly improbable that solicitous hand-maiden would, with true Biblical courtesy, bathe the feet of all patrons on arrival. The 'D.V.' struck me as being anomalous, but from reports I had heard of the dance secretary's flagrant misappropriation of funds, I knew that its position on the notice was significant.

The organised social activities of Bruach were practically non-existent; a circumstance which was partly due to there being no public hall of any kind, and partly to the fact that both the head schoolteacher and the council representative were so Calvinistically opposed to entertainment that they would perjure themselves pink to prevent the schoolroom being used for anything but its everyday purpose. It was fortunate, therefore, that a neighbouring village which boasted a nebulous and often lethargic 'Community', and also a disused barn which was styled grandiloquently as the 'Public Hall', would occasionally exert itself sufficiently to sponsor a concert or a dance—generally in aid of some obscure charity —and would invite the patronage of any Bruachites who might feel so inclined. The prospect of such entertainment invariably aroused a good deal of interest throughout the district and almost every inhabitant, except those prevented by religious scruples or rheumatic twinges, could be relied upon to attend. In the present case the 'Committy' was evidently determined to excel itself and a beauty competition would undoubtedly prove an irresistible attraction for young and old.

Pushing open the creaking door, I ventured into the poorly lighted shop where a boy in a threadbare brown kilt and dung-caked tennis shoes stood resting his face on the counter, while from behind the counter the grocer himself dexterously manipulated a pair of scissors over the boy's dark head.

'Well, well, well! Good afternoon, Miss Peckwitt,' the grocer greeted me, in tones which tried to deny that

I had, for the past five minutes, been undergoing his close scrutiny from between a pair of hand-knit socks and a showcard advertising warble-fly dressing. As he spoke the head on the counter jerked upwards, but it was instantly rammed down again by the grocer's impatient fist.

'Be still you, Johnny!' threatened the amateur barber, vindictively grasping a handful of the boy's hair. 'You be tryin' to turn round and stare and it's this big bunch I'll be after cuttin' off.'

The head, which I now recognised as belonging to my erstwhile fishing instructor, remained obediently rigid. The grocer treated me to a prodigious wink.

'This is what comes of leavin' your hair to a Saturday to get it cut,' he muttered banteringly. 'And then it's such a rush you're in to get it done for the Sabbath, eh, Johnny?'

The head on the counter grunted and as the grocer diligently resumed his task I watched with fascination while an irregular-shaped patch of Johnny's scalp was laid almost bare and the sheaves of crisp, black hair fell stiffly on to the counter. The grocer, stimulated by my interest and sublimely confident of my admiration, continued to snip and chat pleasantly until one half of Johnny's head resembled fine sandpaper and the other half a gale-battered hay-cock; then I was treated to a second wink.

'There now, what d'you think of that, Miss Peckwitt?' he asked, laying down the scissors with an air of finality. 'Does that not look handsome?' And to the boy: 'Run you away now, Johnny, I've finished.'

Johnny, without raising his head, ran an explorative hand over his hair and let out a muffled groan.

'Away with you,' repeated the grocer, pushing the boy's shoulder, 'I'll finish the rest on Monday.'

The boy's head did not move, but a snigger squeezed its way out from between it and the counter.

'Very well.' The tormentor relented with a smile. 'But

you'll have to wait until I've given Miss Peckwitt what she's wantin'.'

The head nodded uncomfortable acquiescence but I insisted that the hairdressing should be completed before I was attended to. I was, I declared, in no hurry whatever. But, I pointed out, this could not be said of a diminutive fellow of about seven years of age who had darted breathlessly into the shop on my heels and who had since stood, studiously ignored by the grocer, tapping a half-crown discreetly on the edge of the counter. My reminder made the grocer fix the boy with a repressive frown.

'What are you wantin' all in your haste, Ally Beag?' he asked sharply.

'I'm wantin' half a pound of bakin' sody,' whispered Ally Beag with a terrified glance in my direction.

'It's near seven o'clock,' said the grocer severely. As the shop made no pretence of closing until around eight or even nine o'clock, I was puzzled by this seemingly irrelevant remark. 'What's your mother wantin' with bakin' sody at this time on a Saturday night?' he continued, still frowning fiercely.

Ally Beag wilted visibly. 'She's wantin' it for bakin' scones,' he faltered.

The grocer's eyebrows shot up. 'She is indeed?' he asked superciliously. 'Tonight you say?'

Ally Beag nodded in awed confirmation.

'No she is not then,' gloated the grocer. 'She's goin' out to ceilidh with Anna Vic this night, and it's fine I'm knowin' she'll no have time for bakin' scones as well.' He paused, and stressing his words by tapping the scissors on Johnny's head, continued: 'It's bakin' scones on the Sabbath she'll be if I give her sody tonight. Go you home and tell her I've no bakin' sody till Monday,' he commanded, and then added cryptically, 'she'll understand.'

Ally Beag's freckled face reddened, but as he made no attempt to argue it is possible that he too suspected

172

his mother's intention to desecrate the Sabbath. With eyes fixed despairingly on the grocer's unyielding countenance he sidled slowly out of the shop.

'If it had been her stomach she would have got it,' the grocer excused himself virtuously as he resumed clipping. 'I'm no a man to deny a thing when there's real need.'

After a few minutes had elapsed a crestfallen Ally Beag returned and silently helped himself to three damp-looking loaves from the cardboard box beside the counter. With eyes downcast he again proffered the half-crown and the grocer, with a righteous pursing of his lips, accepted the money and clapped the change on to the counter. The vanquished Ally clasped his burden of loaves to his chest and slunk out of the shop watched by the grocer who squinted at him from between the shelves of the window and nodded his head knowingly. I should mention that the grocer was an Elder of the church and the duty of an Elder (in addition to preventing the minister from becoming too secular) is to discourage the deviation of the flock from the path of righteousness. How he could reconcile his Calvinistic piety with the poster displayed in his window was one of the inconsistencies of Bruach which I never managed to fathom.

When Johnny's scalp was shining beneath what was no more than the merest suggestion of stubble, he was released and, while the barber surveyed his handiwork, the victim, with a sheepish grin at me, vigorously rubbed shape and colour back to his crushed apology for a nose. With his arm the grocer swept the dark mass of hair from the counter and, as Johnny skipped away, he turned to me with a smile of unctuous enquiry.

'Half a pound of baking soda,' I said audaciously, though baking soda was not one of the items on my list. Perhaps I imagined the flash of chagrin which touched his heavy-lidded eyes. I think I must have done, for there was no trace of hesitation or reluctance as he reached up to the shelf and handed me a packet already made up. Apparently my soul was beyond hope of redemption.

'You'll get some apples and pears if you're wantin' them,' he offered magnanimously. 'They came yesterday on the bus.'

'Good!' I exclaimed. 'I love them both.'

'Aye,' he agreed quietly, 'I know that fine.'

I must explain that fruit of any kind could rarely be obtained in Bruach, and when it was available it was rationed like golden sovereigns.

'It's queer about the pears though,' the grocer remarked conversationally as he lifted the basket on to the counter for my inspection. 'D'you see there's somebody been and taken a bite out of each one of them.'

He held up the pears one by one. Every pear, though otherwise perfect, bore the indisputable imprint of teeth —and very good teeth too.

'What a disgusting thing to do!' I commented, mentally reviewing the dentitions, both false and true, of the neighbourhood. The grocer, who had two front teeth missing, was obviously not the culprit.

'Yes, indeed, it's a shame right enough,' he agreed as he carefully replaced them in the basket. 'But you see, Miss Peckwitt, the bus-driver swears they was perfectly all right when he took them on, so it can only have been someone from round about here who's been at them.' And as I was wondering why he offered that as consolation he added ingenuously: 'Of course, if it had been anybody from the mainland I daresay I might not have been able to sell the half of them.'

I said I would take a pound of apples.

'You have good teeth yourself,' he complimented me tactlessly as he weighed out the fruit.

Huffily I refuted the implication, whereat he protested with suspicious vehemence that such a thought had never entered his head. This assertion he immediately contradicted by letting slip the information that his enquiries had shown I had not been among the bus passengers.

174

My innocence must, however, have been proved to his satisfaction for I would undoubtedly have been classed as a tainted mainlander and consequently the pears would have been totally unsaleable.

There is no point in brooding over insults in Bruach. 'So there's going to be a concert and dance,' I managed to say pleasantly.

'Oh yes indeed,' admitted the grocer, and with an obvious shock of recollection he reached into the window and discreetly turned the notice front to back so that the advertisement should not profane the Sabbath.

'I'm glad they've given us due warning,' I said.

'They'd need to do that,' he answered with complete seriousness. 'Folks has to make their plans.'

'Why the soap flakes?' I asked.

'To make the floor slippery,' he explained; 'though I'm thinkin' it's whole bars of soap they'll need for fillin' up the holes where the rats have eaten through.'

I wondered why they did not use french chalk.

'French chalk?' he echoed. 'I don't sell that. What like of stuff would that be?'

I enlightened him regarding the properties of french chalk but he was not impressed. Soap flakes, he maintained, were the best thing in the world for sticking to the men's tackety boots. 'Makes them lighter about the feet,' he added. It was my turn to be supercilious.

The prospect of a dance where one's partners were likely to be wearing tackety boots was not inviting to me, but it acted as no deterrent to the rest of the village. Very soon after the appearance of the notice and the announcement that voting for the Beauty Contest was to be left entirely to the men, the lassies, with smiles and coquetry, were beginning to woo the male population as assiduously as a prospective M.P. woos his constituency. If the grocer could be believed, there was a noticeable increase in the cosmetic trade, which hitherto had been a despised and slow-moving sideline, relegated along with the picture postcards, toilet rolls and souvenirs, to the umplumbed (except in the tourist season) depths of the shop. If Lachy could be believed, five damsels had already offered to pay for his ticket if he would promise them his vote and with placid impudence he expressed his intention of accepting all five offers. Even the Gaffer, who was a case-hardened bachelor if ever there was one, complained of being disturbed by the nightly serenading of female voices, while even the village half-wits claimed to have discerned a strange tendency to amiability in girls who had previously greeted them with sarcastic reflections upon their shortcomings.

The lassies taunted one another mercilessly with the sole design of calling attention to one another's imperfections. They posed; they hung on every word their menfolk uttered, contriving to be gay, alluring or brazen as occasion demanded; they frizzed their hair; they rolled their eyes and batted their eyelids; they studied dress catalogues intently; they experimented liberally with lipstick and face powder and, not forgetting the time-honoured way of ensnaring men's hearts, they concentrated a little of their attention on the baking of scones and oatcakes. And the men, well aware of what was going on, and the reason for it, watched the artifice and subterfuges of the aspirants with cool, enigmatic smiles.

As the day of the dance drew nearer I was constantly coming upon people of all ages and sizes, and of both sexes, furtively rehearsing dance steps. At the peats one day I watched from behind a convenient hillock while a hefty maiden in gumboots and tattered skirt tripped awkwardly round the stack, gathering up the peats and throwing them into the creel as she went. As the creel on her back filled the steps became less recognisable but even when it was quite full she refused to give in and my last glimpse showed her striving to strathspey her homeward way across the sucking bog.

Some days later, when rounding a bend in the road, I came upon a gang of lusty roadmenders who, despite

176

enormous iron-shod boots, were jigging and posturing their way through a 'Dashing White Sergeant', their shovels and picks deputising for female partners. The music was being supplied by the Gaffer, who performed with less skill than enthusiasm on a miniature mouth-organ, while a short distance away a forsaken steam-roller panted its indignant chorus of protestation. When the musician tired he announced that it was past five o'clock, whereupon the men, ignoring his energetic de-nunciation of their desertion, abruptly abandoned their 'partners' in a clattering heap beside the road and melted away. Sourly the Gaffer pocketed his instrument and walked over to the steam-roller. There was a final puff from its tiny chimney, a long-drawn-out sigh, and then silence.

'Are you going to the dance?' I called out.

'Not me,' replied the Gaffer scornfully. 'There's too many women and too much beer drinkin' at them dances.'

The latter part of this remark coming from a man who so recently had been too drunk to know whether he was sitting on a lighted Primus stove or a thistle was con-founding.

'Don't you believe in drinking?' I asked him.

'Not beer,' he replied. 'Beer drinkin' will kill a man quicker than anythin' else.'

'Is that so?'

'Surely it will,' he said authoritatively. 'Just the other day for instance I had word from two of my friends tellin' me they was dead. Two of them mind you and beer drinkers both of them.' He shook his head sadly. 'Yet look at me,' he continued as we paused for a moment beside his little hut: 'I bin a whisky drinker since I was twelve. Gallons of it I must have drunk in my time and never a minute's pain or illness as a result.'

As he bent to open the door of the hut my attention was caught by the vivid circle of tartan which provided the seat of his otherwise drab trousers.

The day of the concert was cold but dry; the night was even colder. Dusk was only beginning to creep over the mainland hills and only one star twinkled faintly as Morag and I, having decided not to risk being crowded into the ramshackle bus, set out to walk to the 'Public Hall'. We took a short-cut across the crofts; past low thatched byres where cattle chains clinked companionably; past crude little sod huts where hens questioned and ducks quacked apprehensively; past a potent-smelling dung heap—at least I should have gone past it had I not been lost in contemplation of the night sky and had not my companion been engrossed in the contents of a neighbour's clothes-line. Morag skirted the dung heap by inches. I ploughed into the middle of the beastly thing.

'Oh darn!' I ejaculated crossly, peering down at my filthy shoes and stockings.

'Ach, dinna' be frettin',' comforted Morag. 'Likely it'll keep your legs warm.' She giggled. 'Keep your chin up. Isn't that what the English say when they're in trouble?'

I admitted it was and kept my chin up, but it was not fortitude but the stench of the manure which forced me to take her advice so literally.

Reaching the high road we met the postman's sister who was also on her way to the concert. The meeting reminded me that I had been expecting a letter to which I particularly wished to send a speedy reply, but the excitement of the evening had ousted it from my mind until this moment.

'Goodness!' I said in dismay. 'I should have waited for the postman. I was expecting a letter.'

'I don't suppose there'll be any mails tonight,' the postman's sister explained kindly, 'or only very few, anyway, for my brother's intending to go to the concert.'

'Oh,' I said with some surprise, 'doesn't he deliver the mails when there's a concert then?'

'Why, no indeed, how could he get the mails done and

178

the concert beginnin' at eight o'clock?' she asked reasonably.

I admitted that it would of course be impossible. 'But,' I persisted foolishly, 'what happens if someone is depending on a letter? I mean, what if there should be something really important? How would he know?'

The contempt of her glance withered me from the top of my permanently waved head to the toes of my manured feet.

'Well then,' she reproached me icily, 'do you think, Miss Peckwitt, that my brother has never been to school? D'you think he is not able to read?'

I grovelled abjectly, denying that I had intended any such implication, and Morag, rushing to my aid, reproved the woman for believing that Miss Peckwitt would suggest such a thing. Why, didn't Miss Peckwitt know fine the post could read, and write too? Didn't she know he always signed the receipts for her registered parcels himself instead of troubling Miss Peckwitt to do it? Slightly mollified by Morag's words, the sister condescended to change the subject. Her manner, however, remained frigid and I believe that she never really forgave me for what she considered to be an outrageous reflection upon her brother's education. Morag explained later that the present postman's predecessor had in actual fact been unable to read and this perhaps had led the sister to be slightly touchy on this point.

'How did he manage to deliver letters if he couldn't read?' I asked.

'Surely he just used to give us the bundle and we'd choose our own,' replied Morag.

Despite the mishap at the dung heap we were in good time for the concert, the hall being only about half full when we arrived.

'Come and we'll get a good seat,' said Morag and hurrying forward she laid claim to two portions of a long wooden bench with drunken-looking legs, on to which we lowered ourselves experimentally. I thought I had seen the benches somewhere before.

'They're the seats from the church,' explained my companion.

'I'm surprised the missionary allows them to use the church seats for a concert,' I said. 'Does he approve of this sort of thing?'

'No, no, indeed,' responded Morag, 'and they wouldn't have got them if he knew anythin' of it.' She went on to explain that the 'Committy' had just helped themselves to the seats without so much as a word to the missionary; an undertaking which, considering that the Mission House lay on the road between the church and the Hall, must have been accomplished with a good deal of stealth. I said as much to Morag. Her expression as she turned to me was a remarkable blend of pity and mischievousness.

'Sure you can trust the missionary to keep his eyes shut if there's a thing he doesna' want to see,' she said, and added guilelessly: 'He's no bad really like that. I'll say that much for him.'

We continued to sit on our unsteady 'pew' for a long time; Morag rising every now and then to wave a greeting to some friend on the other side of the hall; but it was not until about a quarter of an hour after the concert was due to start that the place began to fill with any rapidity. People began to gather in groups and, indifferent to the compelling pianoforte chords which issued from time to time from behind the stage curtains, became absorbed in conversation. Without warning the curtains suddenly swept apart and the audience prepared to give the stage a proportion of its attention. After a moment, however, the curtains swung purposefully together again, a performance that was greeted with piercing whistles and derogatory Gaelic phrases from the back of the hall where the gossiping groups showed little sign of subsiding.

'Ach, they're only practisin' to see will the curtains

work.' A cloud of hot peppermint and whisky assailed us as a large, fiery-faced youth leaned forward to give us this titbit of highly confidential information. His statement was borne out by the fact that for the ensuing ten minutes the curtains continued their career of advance and retreat, achieving with practice and a little lubrication a performance which ranged from the weightily majestic to ecstatic abandon, and disclosing to the interested spectators nothing more inviting than a deserted stage. Everyone was the more startled therefore when, after a particularly impressive meeting, the curtains were parted by a bowing figure, resplendent in full Highland garb, who announced that the concert was about to begin and that the first item on the programme was to be a song entitled 'Blast you, Euan, can't you leave that alone!' This title was later corrected to 'The Bonnie Bonnie Hoose o' Airlie', the mis-statement apparently having been caused by the sudden decision of the curtains to recommence their cavortings—presumably at the instance of one Euan—coupled with the misfortune that the announcer happened to be standing on the hem of one of them and had narrowly escaped being precipitated on to the bald head of the illustrious chairman, who sat, rigid with importance or terror, in the centre of the front row. It was also explained that their own pianist having been taken ill, we should accord a warm reception to the local cobbler who had volunteered to act as accompanist. At this juncture the stocky figure of the cobbler who, according to Morag, had 'picked up the piano' during the war, burst with flaming cheeks on to the stage and, ignoring the grateful plaudits of the audience, commenced to manœuvre the piano into a suitable position much in the manner of a guncrew manœuvring a bogged gun. Satisfied at last, he struck a few chords in a very professional fashion—his own profession—and thereafter pounded away with such violence that he had perforce to pause every now and then to suck his bruised fingers. There was no doubt about the warmth of the

181

cobbler's reception. The audience cheered themselves hoarse (judging from the voices of some of the singers, I rather think they did too), and did not desist until the first artiste appeared on the stage, when they settled themselves into their seats with a thoroughness which was, under the circumstances, definitely risky.

It surprised nobody I think when, after the first couple of songs, the rest of the artistes decided to perform unaccompanied, and the cobbler thus released shambled to his seat, explaining to his admiring supporters that he'd have been better if he hadn't been loadin' the sheep these last few days and gettin' his hands soft with the fleece grease.

The singers, most of whom were attired in Highland dress, delivered their repertoires with serious concentration, and the audience except for the unquenchable groups at the back of the hall, listened with rapt attention until in the middle of a spirited rendering of a 'waulking song' a strident scream from Anna Vic shattered our ears. The interruption revealed that Murdoch, who was trying to accustom himself to a new pipe, had been so carried away by the performance that he had thoughtlessly knocked out his pipe on the low collar of Anna Vic's dress, thus sending a stream of hot ash down the unfortunate woman's neck. Still exploding volubly the fat woman was escorted from the hall by her two daughters, one of whom, encouraged by titters and advice from all sides, tried unavailingly to hold the dress away from her mother's ample back. The singer, undeterred by the wandering attention of his audience, continued valiantly, and it was not many minutes before the maltreated Anna Vic was back again, casting indignant glances on a highly amused Murdoch but seeming little the worse for her experience. She stubbornly refused to resume her seat and remained standing for the rest of the concert, but whether her determination was due to apprehension or blisters I could only conjecture.

There were many songs sung that night, some of them with more vigour than skill, the choruses being taken up by everyone present with fervid uproariousness and each being acclaimed with a verve and enthusiasm that was as damaging to the seating accommodation as it was to the ear. There was, too, a comedian, who pleased the audience immensely, though they smothered their mirth in their handkerchiefs and received every joke in a desolate silence. For a time the comedian struggled along manfully but, despairing at last of evoking even a single audible titter from his listeners, his patter soon faded into insignificance and he retired defeated from the stage.

When the curtains had closed for the last time we shuffled out slowly in twos and threes, to gather in the usual chattering clusters. From inside the hall came thuds, bangs, giggles and melody, the inseparable accompaniments of the busy Gael, which told us that the floor was in process of being cleared for dancing. I was introduced to a dry, aloof-looking woman who had acquired, at some period of her life, a spurious Oxford accent with which she now proceeded to afflict me. We were invited to take tea at her house during the interval and as our throats were parched after the heat and the choking smells of the hall we were both extremely glad to accept.

'Wasn't the singing good?' asked our hostess as she handed out the steaming cups of tea.

'Indeed but my hands is sore with the clappin',' answered Morag fulsomely.

'Mine too,' replied the woman. 'What did you think of the concert, Miss Peckwitt?'

'I'm afraid I didn't think much of it at all,' I replied bluntly.

'Well now, neither did I,' rejoined Morag easily.

'No to be sure.' Our hostess accomplished the *volte face* without so much as the flicker of an eyelid. 'I've heard better singing than that in my own house.'

'Yet you've just been saying your hands were sore with clapping,' I taxed them.

'Of course we clapped,' agreed Morag plausibly, 'but d'you see they've come a long way to sing for us, and they think they're awful good, anyway. It wouldn't be right to disappoint them.'

'No indeed,' responded our hostess feelingly, 'one couldn't do that. But myself, I'm not so keen on these Mod medallists, they sing too much like the wireless.' (A Gaelic 'Mod' is the equivalent of the Welsh Eisteddfod and is held for the competitive singing of Gaelic.)

'No more am I,' affirmed Morag, her mouth crammed full of buttered oatcake. 'They sound more like seagulls with larningitis.'

'What a pity people didn't give the comedian any encouragement,' I said, when the two women had ceased to laugh. 'I felt rather sorry for him and some of his jokes were quite good.'

'He was a good laugh, right enough,' they agreed.

'But nobody laughed aloud at his jokes,' I said.

'Ach, but you canna' be laughin' at a man to his face just as though he was a sort of animal,' replied Morag.

I pointed out that comedians thrive on laughter, but our hostess cut me short.

'No, but that's just the English way of it,' she corrected. 'It's not our way.'

'We leave the laughter to the English,' tittered Morag, 'the same way as we leave them the love. Why, the way English folks goes on about fallin' in love you'd think love was a thing you could put into a parcel and take home with you.'

'Haven't you ever loved anyone?' I asked.

'There's not such a thing as love,' she said.

'You've been married,' I told her. 'Weren't you in love with your husband?'

'In love! In love! Listen to it I tell you. Indeed it's true I've been marrit. I marrit a good enough man and he had a good enough wife in myself and between us we

184

had five children. What for would we be wantin' love for as well? Surely I know as much about love as I know about 'lectricity and I want nothin' to do with either of them if I can help it.'

So spake the practical Morag, and it was difficult to believe that hardly less than an hour ago I had seen her dabbing furtively at her eyes during the singing of a particularly sentimental song.

Some time later, having taken leave of the Oxford accent, who was not coming to the dance until she had seen her old father safely to bed, we returned to the hall. It was soon evident that the majority of the revellers were still drinking strupaks with their friends or, in the case of the menfolk, drinking illegal whisky at the near-by hotel, for except for a listless group of females who had draped themselves round the doorway like wilted flags, the place was strangely deserted. The girls aroused themselves briefly from their torpor to greet Morag and me and then sank back into attitudes that seemed to add to the general lifelessness of the place rather than detract from it. Inside the hall lights were burning, but there was no sound from within. I looked at my watch. The dance had been advertised to begin at eleven o'clock and it was now half past that hour.

'What's happenin'?' Morag addressed the bevy of girls who stared dully in reply.

'It's the band,' one of them at last managed to answer.

'The band? What's wrong with the band?' asked Morag.

'They're out at the back there fightin' like bulls,' the girl said morosely.

'They're fightin'? Why is that?'

The girl who had volunteered the information shrugged her shoulders apathetically. The rest remained comatose. The band was having a fight, and the fact was accepted philosophically as though to be 'fightin' like bulls' was a characteristic habit of all dance bands.

'It's swearin' to strangle one another they was a few

185

minutes ago.' Another girl jerked herself to life momentarily and threw out this piece of intelligence with gloating satisfaction.

'How many players are there in the band?' I asked, visualising something in the nature of a musical rugger scrummage.

'Three,' answered the first girl; 'the pipes, the fiddle and the melodeon.'

'And who's swearin' to strangle who?' asked Morag.

'Ach, the fiddle says he's for stranglin' the melodeon and the melodeon says he's for stranglin' the fiddler.'

'And the piper?'

'He's too drunk to strangle anybody but himself.' The girls sniggered smugly.

My landlady and I had, while extracting this information, become aware of varying sounds of battle which emanated from somewhere at the back of the hall.

'I'm goin' to take a look,' said Morag bravely, and hurried towards the scene of conflict.

'I wonder what has happened to the M.C.?' I asked the girls after ten minutes had ticked by, and there was still no sign of the dance beginning.

'He's out at the back too,' the girls told me. 'He was tryin' to stop them from quarrellin', but they take no heed of him at all.'

Being confident of Morag's ability to quell the musical strife and noticing that the girls still hugged their packets of soap flakes, I suggested that we should do whatever we were expected to do with them. 'Just empty them on the floor as you go in,' they told me. I led the way in and they proceeded to tear open the packets and strew the contents on the floor. Conscientiously I followed suit.

The grocer's statement that the floor needed whole bars of soap to fill up the rat-holes was certainly not far wrong. There were some treacherous holes and even those parts of the floor which the rats had left alone were splintered and rough. Boards creaked and groaned and in places black mud oozed up between the joints as they gave under our weight. It could not by any stretch of imagination be called a dance floor, but I daresay it was good enough for tackety boots.

More people began to arrive and just as we had finished our nose-tickling task Morag appeared on the threshold solicitously shepherding two tragic and muddy figures: one with a black eye and bleeding nose; the other with a swollen chin and a gory ear. They were closely followed by the M.C. supporting or being supported by a rotund and beaming piper, who was assuring everyone happily that he had succeeded in persuading the two musicians to postpone strangling each other until after the feshtertivities, for it was a shame if folks wash to be dishappointed. (His last words, I assumed, referred to the dance and not to the strangling duet.)

Thus inauspiciously the dancing started and there were some of us who wished before the evening was very far advanced that the piper's powers of persuasion had not been so successful, for the erstwhile combatants seemed to have imbued their instruments with their own disharmony and our ears were assaulted by an incessant riot of discordancy which Morag aptly described as being 'worse than a bullin' cow'. Regardless of strife the dancers leaped and stamped their way through innumerable schottisches and reels, their shrill 'yeeps' and screams outrivalling the frantic efforts of the belligerent instrumentalists who, with carefully averted eyes, played with the single-mindedness of two greyhounds chasing a hare and with much the same result; the fiddle invariably reaching the winning post two or three bars ahead of his antagonist.

The piper who 'spelled' the fiddle and melodeon was determinedly hilarious and did not degenerate until shortly after the refreshment interval, when his piping developed an alarming bubbling undertone, an intrusion which the M.C. dismissed as due to there being 'so much beer got into the pipes they won't play right', and while first aid was rendered to the instrument the piper himself

187

was permitted to sleep off his excesses at the rear of the stage, from whence his nasal organs continued to accompany the dancing with only slightly less sonorousness and decidedly more rhythm than had been discernible in his previous efforts.

A bashful young blood was quick in offering to make up for the piper's lapse and produced for this purpose an ordinary mouth-organ. A dance was duly announced and entered upon by the dancers but except for a chord at the beginning and another at the end the only indications that there might be a musical accompaniment were the bulging eyes and the distended cheeks of the musician and the position of his eyebrows which were a good two inches above normal.

The announcement that voting in the Beauty Contest was due to begin released all the musicians temporarily and the fiddle and melodeon were escorted from the stage in opposite directions by anxious friends. The girls meanwhile were requested to form a circle in the centre of the room and the men were handed pencils and paper and asked to record their votes. I had been asked to present the prizes, so I now made my way to a small table at the front of the stage, upon which a box of lace-edged handkerchiefs and a pair of silk stockings—the first and second prizes—were displayed, together with several half-bottles of whisky and one or two boxes of cigarettes which were to be spot prizes. The efforts of the M.C. to persuade the circle of girls to perambulate and display their charms were unavailing; they either huddled together in exaggerated modesty, as false as it was infuriating, or stood with heads bowed in attitudes of knock-kneed shyness, yet resolutely ogling the men from beneath lowered eyelids. Various ribald remarks percolated through the buzz of talk, and then the M.C. gave instructions for the papers to be collected. 'And the pencils,' he added meaningly, as some of the men endeavoured to secrete the latter in breast pockets. Capfuls

188

of paper were soon being emptied on the table and between us the M.C. and I went through them.

'Number sixteen!' announced the M.C. and, amidst a roar of applause, number sixteen, a hefty buck-toothed young woman, sturdy as an oak and just about as supple, came lurching ferociously towards the stage. Clumsily she negotiated the steps, or rather failed to negotiate them, and tripping over the top one clutched my proffered hand desperately as a support rather than as the salute I had intended it to be. I congratulated her solemnly and handed over the prize but, overcome by an excess of shyness, she was unable to articulate even the most perfunctory acknowledgment. The M.C. also shook her hand and the dancers, seizing the opportunity for fun, clamoured that he should kiss the winner. The two looked at each other and then away again. The M.C. smiled fatuously. The girl shook her abundant hair over her flaming cheeks.

'Kiss!' The clamour became insistent, and dutifully the M.C. obeyed, but as he too was preceded by very pronounced buck teeth it was a difficult feat to accomplish. The noise of the impact put my own teeth on edge.

'Number twenty-eight,' called the M.C. next, and with another burst of applause the second prize-winner came lumbering forward like a frenzied calf into a sale ring. Buxom, scarlet-faced and perspiring, she was afflicted with a wall-eye, thick ankles and a depraved taste in scent. Her thick red hair was adorned with a posy of white flowers which, as I reached hastily for a handkerchief, I identified as the ramsons, or wild garlic. She shook my hand limply, grinned gummily and, evading the proffered hand of the M.C., plunged down the steps to her friends.

It may be suspected that the men were perpetrating a colossal joke, or that the girls had won their votes more as objects of compassion than of admiration. But this was not so. The Islanders viewed beauty purely from the utilitarian standpoint. For a woman to possess allure she had first to possess bulk, for in windy climates a thin or normally developed woman has distinct disadvantages. Anna Vic's husband was a much envied man, particularly during hay harvest, because not only could his wife carry immense loads on her broad back but on breezy days he could build quite substantial hay-cocks in the shelter provided by her girth; less fortunate men with skinny wives had either to leave their hay at the mercy of the weather or build it in low cocks through which any rain would soak in no time. There could be no doubting that the men had chosen according to their desires.

The next prize was a bottle of whisky for which tickets had already been sold. The winner was a tall, pasty-faced, Bruach youth who I had hitherto glimpsed retiring clandestinely around the backs of houses, or disappearing into convenient cattle byres. Tonight he was in no mood for self-effacement and swaggering up to the stage he took his prize, pulled out the cork, and then walking to the centre of the floor he held up the bottle, threw back his head dramatically and drained the contents at one single draught. I fully expected him to drop down senseless but instead he stalked majestically to the open door and in a reedy but penetrating voice demanded naïvely: 'Where's that bloody policeman? Isn't it his job to be lookin' after drunks like me?' As though in answer the uniformed policeman appeared in the doorway, his face split from ear to ear by a grin. The prize-winner lurched forward and took him most companionably by the buttons of his tunic. 'I'm Duncan MacAllister,' he asserted in accents that were rapidly becoming more blurred. 'And I'm that drunk I'm not fit to be at large. I ought to be locked up where I'm safe.'

In spite of the policeman's obvious reluctance, Duncan grasped his arm compellingly and amid jeers and encouragements the two disappeared. Dancing was resumed, and when, about half an hour later, the policeman returned alone, he was heard confiding to enquirers

190

that he'd got so fed up with Duncan hangin' round his neck and insistin' on bein' jailed that he'd pushed him in through a little narrow window at the back of the hall, told him it was a prison cell and cleared off as quickly as he could. It transpired that the 'little narrow window' belonged to the ladies' lavatory!

At three o'clock in the morning the dancers were still in fine fettle and old men and young men, dowagers and damsels, were capering about the soapy room with the exuberance of two-year-olds, the fervour of their dancing banishing the missionary and his prophecies of Hell-fire to the regions of their inspiration. The men had discarded their jackets, collars and ties and were dancing in shirt sleeves, their expressions a mixture of ecstasy and bliss. At the commencement of each dance they approached the girls with condescending masculinity, using the same phrase, the same peremptory voice and intonation when requesting them to dance as they used when they wished to move an obstinate cow. It sounded suspiciously like the English farmer's 'Get up there, Daisy!' The roadmen were much in evidence, inches of their sunburnt bull-necks emerging above constricting neck-bands, their shirts soaked with perspiration. Boisterously they skipped and vaulted about the uneven floor, wielding their partners as they had wielded their picks and shovels, though I should say that the latter had received the more consideration. Their dancing was an ungainly combination of capers, lunges and caprioles and was attended by an incessant chorus of male and female shrieks; the former rapturous, the latter agonised. It struck me that none of the roadmen had changed his boots. Lachy, hot and dishevelled, pranced vengefully across the floor brandishing his two partners as though he was practising for 'tossing the caber' rather than leading them through the intricacies of a 'Dashing White Sergeant'. Johnny was being propelled hither and thither by Elspeth the schoolteacher; his legs looked as though they were moving mechanically; his eyes were tight shut.

191

It was quite possible that he was fast asleep! Watching the dancers I recalled a phrase of the 'warning' notice —'lassies now's your chance to shine'. The lassies were certainly shining and if they had not mopped their pretty faces profusely (borrowing one another's handkerchiefs for the purpose) they would have shone a good deal more; the perspiration showed as dark patches which reached from the armpits almost to the waistlines of their flimsy blouses. The wooden walls of the room were running with condensation; the air was blue with tobacco smoke, and cigarette butts and empty packets were being trodden and kicked around the floor by the feet of the dancers. At the end of each dance the men dropped their partners as though they were hot—perhaps the simile is not inappropriate—and hurried outside.

At one time during the evening I ventured outside myself for a breath of fresh air and was surprised to hear the sound of a spade being plunged into earth.

'There's Miss Peckwitt.' The remark came out of the darkness and a moment later Lachy's voice was asking me if he'd 'get a shine of a torch'. Obediently I went towards the voice and found a group of men gazing with puzzled intensity at a newly turned patch of earth. Lachy bent down, unearthed a bottle, and held it in the beam of the torch.

'That's no ours, Lachy,' said Johnny who was also one of the group.

'What brand was ours then?' asked Lachy.

'It was no that one anyway,' insisted someone; 'haste and put that back.'

'Then were the hell is ours?' asked Lachy irritably as he replaced the bottle and covered it over. 'I'm damty sure it was somewhere here we put it.'

He set to work again in a slightly different spot and this time his digging brought to light a bottle which they were all satisfied was their own.

'I have another one I buried earlier over by the dyke there,' said Johnny. He turned to me: 'Miss Peckwitt will be thinkin' it's awful strange to be buryin' the drinks,' he said ruefully, 'but you canna' dance with bottles in your pockets and you canna' trust folks here when it comes to whisky.' He addressed Lachy again. 'Come and we'll get my bottle while we have the light,' he said eagerly.

'Not on your life,' replied Lachy. 'Leave that one where it is for now. We'll drink this one first—it won't take long.'

It certainly did not take them long and within a short time they were again borrowing my torch. How many bottles of whisky had been buried in the grounds of the hall that night I had no idea, but whenever I went in search of fresh air there was always one group or another busy digging.

'How is it that there happens to be a spade at the hall?' I asked Johnny. 'Surely the committee don't provide that, do they?'

'Of course they don't,' he rejoined. 'We picked it up from the burial ground on our way here.' And misunderstanding my look of surprise he went on: 'It's all right, we're goin' to put it back on our way home.'

'The trouble with these girls is that they canna' dance,' grumbled Lachy as we sat watching the progress of an aptly named reel. His wandering eye fixed briefly on a full-blooded young siren who had draped herself sinuously over a couple of chairs and was raking the 'stag lines' with hungry eyes. 'That's the only one here who knows how to dance properly,' he finished. I recognised the girl as the missionary's daughter.

I pointed to an extremely pretty girl with a glorious mop of blonde curls. 'Who is she?' I asked.

'Ach, she doesn't rightly belong here at all,' said Lachy, and after a few minutes cogitation whispered: 'Not properly she doesn't—one half of her comes from Glasgow.'

The next dance was one which was utterly unfamiliar to me and though I studied the steps of the revellers

I could see no two couples who followed the same pattern. 'Tripping the light fantastic' might have been a fair description of some of the steps executed by the more lissom of the damsels, but 'fantastic' was the only adjective applicable to those of the rest of the dancers.

'Come and dance,' invited Lachy.

'I'm sorry, I'm quite unable to do this one,' I apologised.

'Neither can anybody else,' said Lachy; 'but who's worryin' so long as we enjoy ourselves.'

It was difficult to refuse Lachy because he was always much too ready to feel that he was being snubbed, so I suffered myself to be bobbed and bounced through something that might have been a jig but was more akin to a judo lesson.

'I like the way you townsfolk seem to be able to dance on your toes,' panted my partner admiringly.

'You're dancing on them too,' I replied with a ghostly chuckle that was half irony and half agony.

'Me? Dancin' on my toes?'

'No,' I retorted brutally, 'on mine.'

'I thought I must be,' said Lachy simply, and with no trace of remorse; 'I could tell by the way your face keeps changin'.'

'What did you think of the evening's beauty?' I enquired as we sank exhausted into our seats.

'She'd make a damty fine heifer,' he said dispassionately.

'She wasn't your choice, then?'

'No indeed. It was the one with pink hair I voted for.'

I had long since discovered that colour shades in Bruach bore no resemblance whatever to those recognised by the rest of the world. A red and white cow, for instance, is known as a 'grey beast'; a black one will be described as 'blue'; but pink hair was worth investigation. I asked Lachy to point out the freak. For a few minutes he scanned the weaving dancers and then he pointed to a young girl with pale, sandy-coloured hair who was at that moment engaged in executing a frolicsome schottische. She caught our glance, waved cheerily and continued dancing with zest. I was surprised to see her there for it was only recently that I had heard she had secured a good post as a lady's maid in Edinburgh. I mentioned this to Lachy.

'Oh, but she had to give it up and come home,' he replied. 'Did you not hear? She's been on the club for a few weeks now.'

'Is there something wrong with her?' I asked dubiously, my eyes following the girl's fast-moving, nimble figure.

'Indeed there is!' said Lachy. 'Did you not know she has terrible rheumatics in her feets? My, I hear it's that bad sometimes she can hardly put her legs under her.'

The lassie had 'her legs under her' tonight all right, and it looked to me from the way she was skipping about the floor that she might have the legs of a few other people under her before very much longer. My own shins were already bruised after encountering her as a neighbour in a 'Strip the Willow'.

'How did you like the second prize-winner?' I demanded of Lachy.

'Oh, she wasn't bad,' he said. 'Her hair was all right. That's real Highland hair.'

'That's real hennaed,' contradicted Morag who had just seated herself on the empty form beside us. 'I'm tellin' you, Miss Peckwitt, that second prize-winner is the girl Lachy has a fancy for marryin'.'

'It is not,' repudiated Lachy. 'I'm after marryin' nobody but an Englishwoman like Miss Peckwitt here. They're good workers the English.'

At five o'clock, the floor was noticeably clearer and even the younger dancers were beginning to show signs of fatigue. There being no more prizes to present, Morag and I decided we could unobtrusively withdraw from the festivities. We were tired, I more so than my landlady for she had done little but sit and ceilidh during the whole evening. Rescuing my coat from the packed cloak-room, I flung it over my shoulders, and was following Morag to the door when suddenly a wild-eyed figure burst into the room.

'The hotel's on fire!' he bellowed. 'Help! Help!'

The response from even the most jaded dancers among us was immediate, and in less than a minute the hall was emptied of dancers, onlookers, officials and musicians and we were all racing as fast as we could in the direction of the hotel. The smell of burning soon met our nostrils, and, callous as it may seem, it was a welcome change from the pungent odour of soap flakes and sweat I had been breathing all evening. As we rounded the corner we came upon the hotel, where one of the garret windows sprouted fierce tufts of flame and billowing clouds of smoke.

The policeman, hatless and jacketless, was already attempting to form the revellers into a bucket chain, assuring everyone meantime that he had despatched someone to ' 'phone for the Brigade'. His task was well nigh hopeless, for the Bruachites and their neighbours were nothing if not fierce individualists and they retained their individualism even in the face of fire. He might just as easily have tried to organise a chain of live eels as organise a chain of Gaels. His exhortations, entreaties and threats were in vain; the crowd obeyed their own inclinations entirely, clinging tenaciously to the belief that personal effort would always be superior to communal effort. The few who were not bewitched by the conflagration seized pails and ran to the loch, but the blazing lights of the hotel were so dazzling after the darkness that people and pails were constantly colliding and at least as much water was spilled on the ground as eventually reached the flames.

'Them lights near takes the eyes out of you,' coughed Morag as she came over to join the knot of women whom I had more or less coerced into forming a straggled and inefficient chain. But even with the eyes near out of her she was worth at least three of the other women. Her presence shamed them into action; her tongue stirred action to alacrity, and soon buckets and jugs were passing to and from the loch. Several men stood by, their admiration divided between the burning building and the bucket chain.

'What can I do? What can I do?' The distracted hotel housekeeper ran out from the kitchen and stood wailing, and wringing her hands, in the midst of the confusion.

'Get me half a dozen darning needles to stick into some of these louts!' shrilled a voice which I was faintly surprised to recognise as my own. From the way the spellbound watchers were electrified into activity it might have been supposed that the darning needles had been produced forthwith.

'Get into the chain will you!' the sorely tried policeman shouted as he descried an old man, the occupant of a thatched cottage dangerously near to the burning building, returning from the direction of the loch.

'I will not then,' retorted the old man defiantly. ' 'Tis my own chamber I got and 'tis my own watter that's in it, and 'tis my own bit of flame I'll be after quenchin'.'

The reply typified the attitude of the crowd and, with a despondent shrug of his shoulders, the policeman watched the lone fire-fighter trotting purposefully in the direction of the cottage, his utensil held in front of him as though he was a competitor in an egg-and-spoon race.

Tired as everyone must have been, we worked like Trojans that night but, though every utensil a hotel could provide was commandeered for fire-fighting, our efforts had only a negligible effect on the flames. If the helpers had directed their energies as efficiently as they wagged their tongues we might have accomplished more, but the Gael's inability to co-operate is congenital and his loquacity is, if anything, increased by peril or panic.

Over an hour later there was a cry of relief as a small, grey van slid elegantly towards the hotel and braked to a decorous halt. Then began a scene which could only have been described as high comedy.

'He Breeah!' The driver, who was in fireman's uniform, greeted us all with true Hebridean politeness, unfailing though sometimes exasperating. He and his two mates alighted from the van, and, bestowing confident smiles on the bunch of sodden fire-fighters, seemed undecided whether to come and shake hands with each of us in turn.

'My, but what a time you've taken,' complained one of the onlookers peevishly.

'Indeed, and you're lucky we're here at all,' the driver responded with some heat. 'Didn't the fool who gave the message forget to tell us where was the fire?' He turned to his mates. 'What a job we've had knockin' up folks all the way to find where we should go.' (At that time in the morning I am quite sure that many of the crofters would have told them where they should go— and in no uncertain terms.) The driver's mates nodded agreement and I wondered if, having now arrived at the scene of the fire, they had yet noticed it.

At this moment the policeman, harassed and sooty, raced impetuously towards the fire engine.

'Put everythin' you can up there!' he commanded. 'It's ragin' like a furnace.'

The fireman-driver, who was obviously also in command, looked through the policeman's broad chest.

'In my job,' he retorted coolly, 'it's me that says what's to be done.'

The policeman received the rebuff in silence and turning to the bystanders, who, upon the arrival of the fire engine, had forsaken their utensils, he beseeched them to bring their pails and follow him. About a dozen men obeyed and tore after the policeman into the hotel, where, a short time later, we could see them charging in and out of the upstairs rooms, silhouetted like figures on a frieze.

With a deliberateness that was probably thorough,

but was nevertheless irritating to the onlooker, the firemen coupled up their hoses and started the engine of the pump. The youngest of them, a lean youth with a mop of cherubic curls peeping from beneath his stiff cap, lumbered heavily towards the hotel with a length of hose. By this time the policeman and his retinue were throwing linen and blankets through the open windows, to be salvaged by willing hands below.

'Right?' called the chief fireman to the cherub.

'Right!' replied the cherub. He positioned himself to direct a jet of water at one of the windows when, without warning, he went down beneath a large double bed mattress which hurtled from somewhere above.

'Hi!' yelled the crowd, while gesticulating rescuers ran to extricate the fireman.

'Hi!' they yelled again as the rescuers themselves were buried beneath a veritable shower of mattresses, all aimed with a precision that would under other circumstances have looked suspicious.

'What's happened?' asked the chief fireman curiously.

'They've flattened him,' supplied an onlooker equably.

'Flattened him?' echoed the chief with a bellicose glance at the window where the policeman had last appeared. 'What for? He's done no wrong.'

Meanwhile the second fireman ran forward with his own hose, but as he crossed the lawn he too was knocked for six, not by a mattress but by a large wardrobe which someone, in an excess of zeal and panic, had thrown recklessly from a second-floor window. Two anxious faces appeared at the window from which the wardrobe had descended but their concern was for the fate of the furniture, not for the unfortunate fireman who lay prostrate in the middle of the lawn; a lawn which his still-gushing hose was quickly transforming into a miniature lake.

The chief fireman, furious at the treatment his men had received, was still standing beside the engine excitedly flinging orders at all and sundry. What the orders may have been nobody knew, for of course nobody took the slightest notice. The policeman reappeared on the scene.

'Look here, man,' he addressed the chief witheringly; 'what's the use of pouring water into the cellars when it's up in the roof the fire is. A hose on the roof will have it out in no time.'

'You've near killed my mates,' retaliated the chief angrily. 'Now what d'you expect me to do about your fire?'

'Me? Killed your mates?' demanded the policeman, who was quite unaware of the mishap to the firemen. 'Well, it's likely they'll have more life in them dead than alive. But if you don't get up there quick I'll report you,' he went on savagely.

The chief fixed his adversary with a pair of horror-stricken eyes. 'Me?' he expostulated. 'Me? Go up on that bloody roof?'

'Why not?' returned the policeman with admirable restraint. 'That's where the fire is, isn't it?'

It looked for a moment as though the chief was about to dissolve into tears, but instead he hitched up his trouser leg and turned abjectly on the policeman.

'Have you seen that?' he asked piteously, displaying his wooden leg for inspection. 'Can you rightly expect a man like me to go clamberin' and climbin' stairs, let alone roofs?'

'Oh no, that's different.' At once the policeman was contrite. 'You'd best give me the hose and I'll go up myself,' he offered.

'Are you sure you'll manage?' asked the chief considerately.

'I'll manage,' returned the policeman through clenched teeth, and ran forward to take up his duties as chief fireman.

As he had claimed, a hose on the roof had the fire out in a comparatively short time. Within an hour the threatening flames were subdued and the charred and dripping ruin of the roof emerged from the pall of smoke. A fine drizzle of rain began to help along the good work.

'Come round to the kitchen,' said Morag. 'There's tea for everybody there.'

Thankfully we adjourned to the kitchen where we found the two injured firemen who, having been rescued from their predicament and given first aid, were now reclining comfortably in easy chairs beside the stove and regaling themselves liberally with whisky supplied by a grateful proprietor. They were, someone explained, 'waitin' on the ambulance takin' them to hospital'. They were obviously hoping the ambulance would be a long time coming.

The policeman, with torn shirt, was hardly recognisable under his grime as he tottered into the kitchen and dropped into a chair.

'I think I've sprained my wrist,' he muttered. Someone pressed a roll of bandage into my hand and I bound up his wrist as well as I could. 'God! What a night!' he said as his chin sank wearily on his chest.

The experience being safely over, cups began to clatter merrily and the night's adventures were gone through over and over again in detail, as people sipped tea and poked whole biscuits into their gabbling mouths.

'The sooner the ambulance comes and these men get skilled attention the better it will be for them.' A high authoritative voice briefly silenced the hurly-burly of the kitchen. The two firemen directed baleful glances at the speaker and hastily replenished their glasses; the crowd resumed their chatter.

'Oughtn't we to get hold of the nurse?' I asked the policeman.

'Impossible,' he replied. 'The nurse is on holiday in Glasgow.'

'Well, what about the doctor?' I persisted. 'Is he on holiday too?'

The policeman permitted himself a grim smile. 'In a

way he is,' he said. His smile broadened into an expansive grin. 'I had to lock him up on Thursday—drunk in charge again.'

It was long past breakfast-time when Morag and I set out to walk home, there being no sign of the bus anywhere.

'I wouldn't have minded bein' a bitty crowded to save havin' this walk on top of the night we've had,' mourned my landlady, and as I dragged beside her along the stony path with the brittle heather stems rasping against the remains of my silk stockings I sincerely echoed her sentiments.

The drizzle was by this time showing signs of developing into a real downpour and the newly turned potato and corn patches were speedily changing their pale dun colour for a moist blackness. The rain sizzled through the sparsely leafed bushes and in the grey murk above a skylark soared, pouring out melody as though compelled to rid itself of its jubilation before it could bear to seek shelter. The burn rippled sportively under the old lichen-patterned bridge.

'Them's voices,' said Morag suddenly, and leaning over the parapet we beheld the 'fiddle' and the 'melodeon', one arm embracing their instruments and their free arms embracing each other. They were making repeated claims that ' 'twas my fault sure as I'm here', and so engrossed were they in their new friendship that neither of them was aware of our presence. We thought it wiser not to disturb them.

'They look very comfortable in spite of the weather,' I said.

'They should be comfortable,' replied Morag. 'Did you no see it was the piper himself they was sittin' on? He's one that won't get wet anyway.'

We did not go to bed when we reached home but busied ourselves with the sedentary tasks of the house. The letter I had been expecting was duly delivered by a red-eyed and befuddled postman, somewhere about lunch-time. I managed to summon up enough energy to take my answer up to the pillar-box. On my way home I perceived a group of tired men sheltering just inside the doorway of Lachy's cow byre. They included Duncan the whisky drinker and, remembering his performance of the previous night and also the policeman's remedy, I called out to ask him how he had liked his spell in prison.

Duncan grinned pallidly. 'Prison's all right,' he said. 'But them damty wardresses won't give a man a minute's peace and quiet.'

10

Mary's Visit

It had been, if I remember rightly, during breakfast one
morning in our flat, soon after the proposal of my migra-
tion to the Hebrides, that Mary, with her customary
bluntness, had raised the subject of sanitation. It was a
subject which I had at the time been reluctant to discuss,
largely I suppose because I knew instinctively that one
could not expect such refinements as flush lavatories in
isolated country villages, and just at that particular hour
I recoiled from envisaging the only alternative.

On my arrival in Bruach Morag had soon introduced
me to the niceties of rural sanitation, pointing proudly to
a horridly conspicuous little hut, painted a torturous
pink and almost surrounded by an abundant growth of
nettles, which stood in splendid isolation at the far end of
the 'park'.

'I empty her in the sea every day,' Morag had said,
and I had immediately enlightened Mary as to the nature
of the 'refusals'. 'When I knew you was comin',' continued my landlady, 'I painted her all over inside and
out, and I got Ruari to shift her from where she was
beside the hen house over to here.' She chuckled briefly.
'And bless me, but the fool didna' realise the paint was
wet, and he comes up behind her, puts his two long arms
around her, lifts her up and carries her to where she is
now,' she finished triumphantly.

I was a little confused by her recital and it must have
seemed to her that I was not sufficiently impressed by
her brother's feat.

'If you dinna' believe me, just take a look at her behind and you'll see the shape of Ruari on her yet,' she assured me earnestly.

I at once feigned a convincing interest in Ruari's prowess, for the menacing appearance of the nettles completely overruled the impulse to 'take a look at her behind'.

The 'wee hoosie', as Morag called the lavatory in my presence—though when I happened to overhear her mentioning it to Ruari one day she referred to it by a far more robust name—looked exceedingly fragile and, I imagine, depended a good deal for support on the large heaps of stones which were piled anyhow against its sides; it was possible that the nettles also made some slight contribution to its stability. Ventilation was lavish, and at night one was thankful for the ubiquitous cycle lamp—a candle would not have remained alight for an instant in the fierce draughts. The door, I found to my dismay, could not be secured except by means of a piece of string looped round a rusty nail: a flimsy and far from reassuring arrangement, but when in occupation the numerous ventilation holes gave advance glimpses of any intending visitor, and a throaty cough at an opportune moment was all that was necessary to divert the would-be intruder to the pursuit of an imaginary bird's nest or an industrious weeding of the garden. So far as Morag and I were concerned the arrangement worked admirably, but during a visit from one of my landlady's male relatives—a fellow utterly lacking in sensitivity—I so nearly coughed myself into an attack of laryngitis that I insisted on purchasing a handsome and effective brass bolt, and prevailed upon Ruari to fix it on the door. Ruari undertook the task with thinly disguised scorn but his subsequent remark that the door would be 'the better for that bit of strengthenin'' convinced me, in spite of Morag's silent criticism, that my one and ninepence had been well spent.

The supply of toilet paper was erratic, the grocer re-

ceiving a consignment only once a year, at the beginning
of the tourist season, and when that was exhausted
Morag attempted to remedy the situation with an accu-
mulation of well-thumbed periodicals covering an extensive range of subjects. I ensured an adequate supply
of toilet rolls by post but I must admit that my education,
during the summer months at any rate, was enormously
improved by the regular perusal of the magazines. Before I had been in Bruach a year I was well versed in
such subjects as: 'How to prepare the ideal growing
mash for newly weaned pigs'—this was wasted study as
there were no pigs in Bruach, at least not the four-legged
ones; 'How to distinguish a pipit from a skylark'; 'How
M.S., Glasgow, could cure his headaches' and 'Housewife in Perth' could avoid getting chilblains, and 'How
to make a scruggin cake'—though I never discovered
what scruggins might be. I could even recite parrot-
fashion the correct shades of make-up for blonde, brunette and red-head, and also reel off a list of the historic
monuments of Scotland with hardly a pause for breath.
I like to think that some day the information may prove
valuable.

It was not until my second summer in Bruach that
Mary decided to risk visiting me in my new home, and
directly she announced her intention Morag and I began
a belated but furious onslaught on the spring cleaning
and the enhancing of improvements which had originally
been undertaken in my honour. I had of course become
inured to many of the crudities of Island life, but I could
still recall my own repugnance on first coming into contact with many of the accepted arrangements, and I had
no wish to give Mary the impression that I had become
completely degenerate. Though Morag's house was one
of the cleanest in Bruach, that which passes for cleanli-
ness in the Hebrides would be looked upon as slovenli-
ness by the average urban housewife, so my landlady
and I scrubbed, polished and mended and at intervals

wielded moulting paint-brushes with more vigour than skill.

'My, but you do come in handy,' Morag exclaimed admiringly after one of my artistic orgies had transformed the drab brown staircase into a glistening and unsullied white.

After the house, the next objective was the 'park', which besides half a dozen tall rowans and what Morag described generously as a 'seeds mixture grass'—though 'weeds mixture' would have been my more fitting description—boasted only a few ancient blackcurrant bushes which to my knowledge had never produced anything more attractive than curled leaves and earwigs. Ruari, having been persuaded to lend a hand, mowed grass steadily, and just as steadily emitted a comprehensive stream of expletives as his scythe came up against an appalling number of stones which, if he could be believed, had been hidden there with deliberate and spiteful intent. It was a thrill for me to watch the superb effortlessness of Ruari's rhythmic, graceful swing; it was an education for me to listen to the effortlessness of his abuse. In desperation Morag went out to him.

'Ruari, shut your noise,' she implored. 'Miss Peckwitt's after hearin' every word you say.'

'If she don't like it she can come out here and cut the grass herself,' replied the undaunted Ruari, and carried on swinging and swearing without noticeable pause.

Gradually, our labours showed their effect. The garden no longer resembled a garbage dump, and after I had enjoyed the privilege of seeing Ruari 'wash down with lime' the house itself looked as spick and span as it was possible to make it.

'Everythin' in the garden's lovely,' trilled Morag inspiringly, the evening before Mary's expected arrival, but I was glaring at the 'wee hoosie' whose garish pinkness had, by my efforts, now been modified to a sober green.

'I wish,' I remarked testily, 'that you had left the "wee hoosie" where it was beside the hen house instead of having it moved to its present position.'

'In that case, I'll tell Ruari to shift her back as soon as he has a moment,' promised my landlady confidently.

'Oh no!' I entreated hurriedly, mentally coupling Ruari's deafness with his genius for doing the wrong thing at precisely the wrong moment. 'I beg of you, please leave it where it is.'

'Ach, but he'll do the same as he did before, I expect,' rejoined Morag. 'He'll just up with her in his arms and away.'

That was exactly what I was afraid of.

'No,' I replied firmly. 'Please don't mention it to him at all.'

'Just as you like,' agreed Morag with resignation, and so the 'wee hoosie' with its dado of nettles remained where it was.

The following day I made the trip to the mainland to meet Mary, whose determinedly optimistic mood was reassuring. Her arrival coincided fortunately with a spell of fine though blustery weather, but unfortunately with the breakdown of the only available hire car. The driver, though promising to do his very best to provide a substitute, had not been particularly hopeful, so it was an immense relief on our arrival at the pier to see his smiling face blooming above a flamboyant suit of dissonant checks. I introduced him to Mary and this being accomplished he condescended to busy himself with our luggage, only pausing to suggest cheerfully that he would not mind waiting while we took a cup of tea at the nearby tearoom. I could see that Mary was already favourably impressed, and was quick to point out that this willingness to oblige was a common trait among the Islanders. Our tea was excellent, the waitress who served was smiling and efficient, and I congratulated myself that Mary would soon come to understand the fascination the Island held for me. Feeling refreshed and full of pleasant satisfaction we were emerging from the tea-room when a funeral hearse, sombre and stately, drew up at the door. Mary gave it a startled glance and I managed to recollect that in England one does not expect to see a hearse parked outside a café while the driver goes for a cup of tea. I felt a little explanation was necessary.

'I told you they're very unsentimental about funerals, didn't I?' I began, 'and this hearse has probably come all the way from Glasgow. You never know how far they may have travelled and I expect the driver ...' The rest of my words died away for it was at that moment that I beheld the driver. Eager and effusive, he climbed down from the driving-seat and greeted us for the second time that day.

'Enjoy your tea?' he asked hospitably, and without waiting for an answer turned to Mary. 'I've put your luggage aboard, miss,' he told her happily. 'There's nothing I might have forgotten now, is there?'

I turned to my companion. Never, 'while the Lord spares me', shall I forget the expression on Mary's face as she stared, not at the coffin she expected to see, but at her own suitcases and parcels piled neatly among the silver appointments. I experienced a moment of dismay as I realised suddenly the full force of the shock she was about to receive when the driver should fling open the glass doors and wait courteously to give us a 'leg up' inside. Of course it was all my own fault for I had taken great pains to impress upon the driver the necessity of providing some alternative form of transport to the broken-down taxi. I was prepared for a journey by lorry, by the cattle float, or even a borrowed horse and cart, but never in my wildest moments had I dreamed that anyone would think of substituting a hearse for a taxi. No doubt at first my own expression was equally tense, but, having grown accustomed to the unorthodoxy of Island transport and the general indifference to death,

I was very quickly able to accept the situation with something approaching equanimity, even to see the humour in it.

'There's nothing else for it except Shanks' pony,' I whispered urgently to Mary.

'Does he expect us to go in that thing too?' she demanded in outraged tones. I nodded.

The driver discerned our hesitation. 'You two ladies can just sit in front with me,' he said, accompanying his invitation with a grin of ineffable superiority. 'It's only the wife's old mother I have there and she'll go in the back with the luggage easy enough.' He motioned blithely towards the cab of the hearse and, after a circumspect peep, I was able to confide to Mary that the 'wife's old mother' was neither coffined nor embalmed, but, on the contrary, appeared to be exceedingly agile. As if the words were a signal the old woman bustled obligingly out of her seat and, though I felt rather doubtful as to the propriety of allowing one obviously so much nearer the grave than myself to go joy-riding in the back of a hearse, I was relieved when she refused to accept my half-hearted suggestion that I should take her place.

'It's quite comfortable, my dear,' she told me, her old face wreathed in smiles. 'You see, with it bein' for the corpuses it has to be nice and bouncy.'

'Come on,' I muttered inflexibly to Mary. 'It's our flat feet if you don't.'

Yielding reluctantly, she allowed herself to be handed with decorous solicitude into the front seat where she stayed, stiff and straight, for the whole of the journey. The hearse, after an *arpeggio* on the horn for the benefit of the crews of several fishing-boats, started off at an irreverent speed, and as he accelerated the impenitent driver discoursed upon the superiorities of the hearse above all other forms of transport, remaining callously indifferent to the rigid anxiety of Mary's face and a silence between the two of us which could only be described as deathly.

Morag, her face expressionless, was waiting for us as we drew to a majestic stop beside the wall. She eyed Mary uneasily, but I hastened to explain in an aside that my companion's aloofness was due not to hauteur but to the shock of having to travel in a funeral hearse. The uneasiness was instantly replaced by a smile of warm welcome. While Mary was being introduced to Ruari, I paid the driver (the exact fare) and, while Morag and Ruari were wrestling with the luggage, I turned to the 'wife's old mother', who by now had been hauled out of the glass doors and was ready to resume her place beside her son-in-law. I hoped she had been comfortable.

'Och aye, nobody could mind dyin' for a ride like that,' she replied.

'That one,' commented Morag sourly as the hearse disappeared, 'she'd say anythin' just to get folks to hire the hearse for their funerals. And as for that driver fellow, he's after swankin' round the place in it ever since he bought it. Indeed you'd think it was for takin' folks to Heaven itself instead of to the burial ground.'

She examined our clothes closely. 'It's to be hoped he cleaned it out after takin' yon calf to the sale in it this mornin',' she said.

'Oh surely not!' protested Mary.

'Surely indeed,' asseverated Morag. 'And isn't he after takin' the scholars to school in it these three days past?'

The experience being safely over Mary was able to smile wanly. We negotiated the wall with an adroitness that was on my part due to long practice and on Mary's part to long legs, and soon the two of us were eating bacon and eggs and oatcakes and chattering away as though it was only yesterday we had said goodbye. Eagerly we fired question after question at each other, and outside in the whispering rowans a thrush echoed us interrogatively. Sleep overwhelmed us before even a tenth of our confidences had been exchanged, and as

211

soon as we woke the next morning our tongues were at it again. Mary was still tired after her long journey and the two of us sat lazily beside the open window after a late breakfast, our conversation outrivalling the scandal-mongering of the starlings on the chimney pot.

Suddenly Ruari's bellow assaulted the walls of the house like a battering ram.

'My, but that man shouts loud enough to wound a body,' we heard Morag complain, as she opened the door. The two voices continued in high altercation for some minutes and then a momentary quiet was followed by a perfunctory tap on the door. Morag burst into the room, but as she never allowed distress of any kind to interfere with good manners, she began by hoping we had enjoyed our breakfast. We assured her that we had.

'Is anything the matter?' I asked.

Morag looked apologetically at Mary. 'It's yon man,' she said plaintively, 'they're after tellin' me he's runnin' all over the place stabbin' all they cattle.'

'Good gracious!' Mary and I ejaculated together.

'I'm wonderin' if you'd help me take my own beasts to the hill?' Morag went on. I nodded assent.

As I have said earlier, Bruach possessed more than its fair share of mental defectives but I had not so far heard of one who was afflicted with bovicidal tendencies. That the position was serious we judged from Morag's manner, so I jumped up from my chair and pulled on gum-boots (necessary because of the inevitable bogs which, unreasonable as it may sound, are always more numer-ous the higher one climbs). Mary watched me with wide-eyed astonishment.

'Shall I come with you?' she asked in a voice that in-vited refusal.

'No,' I told her. 'You lock the door after us and you'll be all right. He won't come here.'

I was not in the least apprehensive about her safety but was in fact secretly rather pleased that she should so soon learn how 'handy' I had become with the cattle.

Morag had already reached the cow byre and there I sped after her. A slam of the house door indicated that Mary was following my instructions.

'If you'll take the stirk, I can take the cow,' said Morag as she deftly untied the two beasts, and in a jiffy we and the animals were out of the dark byre. I assumed that as the stabber was beyond control we should be taking the beasts to some appointed place in the hills where the men of the village could combine and act as a bodyguard until the maniac was got under control.

'Which direction?' I called, as the stirk, his tail stiff as a poker, galumphed impetuously across the 'park'.

'To the glen,' she answered.

With an ominous bellow the beast bounded forward and as I grasped his head-rope firmly our memorable trek began. To say that I took the stirk to the glen that day would be an utterly erroneous description of our journey. It would be more correct to say that the stirk took me, for, winding the cattle on the hill, he raced off like a thing demented, and, like something equally demented, I careered after him, resolutely hanging on to his rope. Behind me I thought I heard Morag shout, but it was quite impossible for me to check the beast in his mad flight. Out of the corner of my eye I saw old Murdoch wheeling a barrow-load of manure from his byre and as we flashed past him he nearly overturned the barrow in his astonishment.

'Where are you away to?' he shouted.

'I'm taking the beast to the glen,' I yelled back, as I panted in the rear of the stirk's exuberant rushes. The echo of a cynical laugh fell upon my throbbing ears.

Over the hill my charge and I tore with heedless abandon, plunging through intimidating bogs, vaulting lightly over ruined dykes and sailing airily over peat hags until I began to feel that one at least of my progenitors must have been a deer. Never before had I been conscious of possessing legs that moved like wheels, but like wheels they worked that day. Round and round they went as though they were jointless and muscleless, until I was doubtful if I could ever stop them from going round and round. It would perhaps have been an exhilarating experience had I been in the mood and training for it, but I was in far too much of a panic about the stabber for there to be the faintest possibility of enjoying myself. To me the trek was a nightmare, though to Bruach it subsequently became an epic: one eye-witness relating that 'Indeed I didn't know it was a woman at all he had with him. It looked like some cow flyin' one of they big kites.'

At length we reached the glen where a motley collection of cavorting cattle were mooing and lowing in every key from double bass to falsetto, and a number of conspicuously idle men squatted in the heather. The stirk, his flanks heaving, stopped dead in his tracks, lumbering only a couple of paces forward when I, having half his number of legs and consequently less efficient braking power, cannoned forcibly into his stern. Gasping, I collapsed on the ground, my throat feeling like emery paper. Ruari's thundering voice penetrated my exhaustion.

'You shouldn't have set the beast a pace like that,' he reproved me; 'it's bad for him.'

I glanced reproachfully in his direction, too breathless to disclaim responsibility in the matter.

'Will they be all right here?' I asked Lachy when I had regained sufficient breath to speak intelligently.

'Aye,' replied Lachy, who was always prominent among any loungers, 'I daresay he'll attend to it soon.'

I possibly looked as enlightened as I felt.

'Who will?' I asked.

'Why, the vet of course,' responded Lachy. 'Isn't that what you've brought the beast for?'

Comprehension dawned slowly and, dragging myself

wearily to my feet, I went over to where a knot of spectators were clustered about a belligerent but securely held cow. I had already made the acquaintance of the veterinary surgeon; an Edinburgh man with a keenly developed sense of humour.

'Is it you who's the maniac running about "stabbin' all they cattle"?' I taxed him with mock severity.

The vet glanced significantly at the hypodermic in his hand. 'I believe it must be,' he said with a wry grin. 'Watch how I do it.' Clipping a tiny patch of hair from the cow's neck, he inserted the needle.

'Testing for tuberculosis,' he muttered, 'and dashed high time too.'

Silently I cursed the literalness of Morag's descriptions. It was by no means the first time they had caused me stress and embarrassment; probably it would not be the last. My landlady herself arrived at this moment, rather breathless and more than a little anxious for my welfare. She too chided me on my unseemly haste.

To save us the tedium of waiting, the vet obligingly 'stabbed' our two beasts and, that done to everyone's satisfaction, he turned to a mangy black cow which was being led forward by a decrepit old man whom I knew as Shamus Beag.

'He has a nasty cut on his udder,' I heard Shamus telling the vet, and saw the latter bend down to examine the cow.

'I don't like that at all,' he said as he straightened up again. 'There's an awful queer smell about it.' Again he bent down and sniffed. 'It doesn't smell right at all.' He frowned deeply. 'Have you been putting anything on it, Shamus?' he asked.

'I have so,' admitted Shamus. 'Indeed I have the stuff here with me now.' Fumbling in his capacious pocket he produced a tube and held it out for the vet's inspection. I did not need to glance twice to recognise the alluring label of a much advertised and highly scented

215

vanishing cream. The vet took a cigarette and clamped it between his twitching lips.

'Why on earth d'you go putting stuff like that on a cow's udder?' he asked Shamus.

Shamus, ignoring the ribald comments of the interested spectators, scratched vigorously at the sparse hair beneath his cap.

' 'Tis all what I could get from the tinks when they was round,' he explained with grave simplicity. 'And I do believe it's been doin' him good.'

'Maybe, maybe,' agreed the vet quickly as he snapped shut his cigarette-case. 'But look here, Shamus, I'll send you some better stuff than that for the cow. You can give that scented stuff to your wife.'

Shamus directed a puzzled glance at the speaker. 'My wife has no cut on her——' he began.

'No!' interpolated the vet loudly. 'For her face of course.'

'My wife has no cut on her face,' replied the old man with a slow shake of his head, and then added innocently. 'That would be her mouth.'

Laughter gurgled among the onlookers and the vet cupped his hand around the match flame to try and hide his own furtive smile.

Shamus bade everyone an indifferent farewell and plodded away with his cow.

The calm of the morning had by this time given way to a bullying breeze that frisked our hair and tore at our jackets. Leaving the cattle to find their own way home Morag and I retraced our steps across the moors. Mary unlocked the door with a scared face.

'Everything all right?' she enquired.

I nodded briefly.

'Your friend must be awful nervous,' said Morag in my ear, for naturally she had not heard my parting instructions to Mary.

'Yes,' I whispered treacherously, 'I'm afraid she is.'

216

Poor Mary! Already she was beginning to think that 'Bedlam' was a more apt name than Bruach for the village, but my explanation of the lunatic stabber and a description of my own hectic cross-country flight sent her into peals of laughter.

'Becky,' she prophesied joyfully, 'I do believe you'll make an Olympic runner yet.'

For the remainder of the afternoon and until late in the evening I lay on the sofa in a lethargy born of exhaustion. Mary was quite content to rest also and as she sat by the window in the growing dusk, sipping her hot milk supper, she said: 'You know, Becky, I believe your Island does have a certain charm in spite of its uncouthness.'

I grunted sleepily.

All day the wind had been steadily rising and now it had whipped itself into a full summer gale. Mary stared fascinatedly at the rowan trees bowing themselves to its onslaught.

'I say, Becky,' she began suddenly, 'I saw some funny white birds fly past the window then. What could they be?'

'I don't know,' I said, and reluctantly heaving my aching limbs from the comfortless sofa I went to the door. There was still some daylight left in the sky, for the summer twilight on the islands lingers long—too long. I peered outside and could see no sign of any birds, but even as I watched some white shapes hurtled by me. Calling to Mary I propelled her round the end of the house and down the 'primrose path'.

'There's one sure thing,' I gloated. 'I may some day make an Olympic runner, but you'll never make an ornithologist. There! Look at your "birds".'

Mary's eyes followed mine, and we both burst out laughing as we stood watching the 'wee hoosie' where the boisterous wind, having sought and found the brand-new toilet roll, was now mischievously whipping it through one of the larger ventilation holes and tearing it into garlands which caught in the branches of the dark trees, making them look like gaunt presbyterian spinsters attired for some stygian ball. Streamers of migratory toilet paper whisked away up the village to festoon themselves around clothes-line posts, chimneys, byres and even on the horns of a perplexed cow. I called to Morag and she, seeing what had happened, skipped nimbly across the grass, intent on retrieving stray wisps of the precious paper. She came to me offering a crumpled armful, which I accepted only to sacrifice it to the appetite of the storm.

'My, but that's a shame,' Morag reproached me as the last length of the roll, now unwound to its extremity, sailed swiftly towards the hills. But I only smiled at her concern and made a mental note to keep to that particular brand of toilet paper, for the manufacturer obviously gave good value for money—there seemed to have been miles of it.

'Well, I think it's spiteful of her then,' said Morag.

'Who?' asked Mary, but a dig in the ribs from me warned her not to pursue the question.

In the privacy of our own room I explained that it was the wind that was 'spiteful' for having taken away the toilet roll.

'The wind is a "she" then?' asked Mary.

'It depends who you happen to be talking to,' I told her. 'It's a "she" with Morag; it might easily be a "he" with the next person you meet. They don't waste time on trivialities like sex.'

'What a language,' said Mary.

'What a people,' I murmured.

We finished our supper and were going upstairs to bed, pausing to say good night to Morag who was standing just inside the outer doors watching a car with unnecessarily bright headlights tearing up the road.

'That's the taxi-driver and his wife and a crowd of

218

other folk goin' off to the dance,' she informed us conversationally.

'Oh,' I said innocently, 'then he must have managed to repair the taxi at last?'

'Not him,' said Morag serenely, 'that's the hearse itself they was in.'

11

Getting Ready for the Wedding

'In the spring', sings the poet, 'a young man's fancy lightly turns to thoughts of love.' But in the Hebrides that is indeed no truism. In the spring the crofter's materialistic fancy turns to planting, for though he can contemplate a future without love, a future without potatoes would be unendurable. It is for this reason that weddings, for the most part, are confined to the autumn and winter and, because he is invariably in no hurry for marriage, the terms 'autumn' and 'winter' are frequently symbolic of the time of life at which he chooses to take the fatal step (except in those cases when, in polite language, the bride finds it necessary to prepare the layette before the trousseau).

One autumn a whisper began to percolate through Bruach that it was to witness a wedding and before the rumour had circled the village three times it had become an established fact. Bruach was indeed to have a wedding; a real white wedding with bridesmaids, hotel reception, and even printed invitation cards. Morag sniffed contemptuously at the last piece of information.

'Them things is just a waste,' she said. 'When my own daughter was married in Glasgow she sent out them cards and she had R.I.P. printed on the bottom of them so she'd know how many was comin'.' She shook her head sadly. 'But nobody did—they're so ignorant about here.'

There had already been two or three weddings during

my stay in Bruach but being of the sort just referred to in parentheses they had involved little more than a clandestine visit to the mainland, a few hurried minutes at a register office and, on the return home, had meant nothing more romantic than the addition of an extra pair of hands to the *ménage* of the in-laws more in need of labour or less cramped for room. In this case however the bridegroom was a doughty young fisherman of not more than thirty years of age and the bride, who was only a few years his senior, an attractive waitress from the hotel in the neighbouring village; a village moreover which boasted not just a church, but a church with a belfry and an organ. The hotel had undertaken the catering for the wedding breakfast and never before had the Bruachites enjoyed such an exciting prospect. From the first spectral whisper until at least a year after the solemnisation of the event weddings, past, present and future were the sole topic of conversation wherever one went.

'Ach, but weddings isn't like they used to be,' lamented the old folk. But Anna Vic, whose wedding had taken place as recently as thirty years previously, spiritedly refuted the criticism.

'Indeed after my own weddin' my Uncle Roddy and my Uncle Hamish was missin' for three whole days,' she argued firmly. 'And where did we find them at last but in yon Allta cave. Barricaded themselves in they had, with crates of beer and whisky and them vowin' they wouldn't come home till they'd drunk their way out.'

The uncles Roddy and Hamish, their patriarchal appearance betraying no indication of their riotous youth, were present to hear and corroborate the fat woman's assertion.

'And we near managed it too,' said Roddy proudly, turning his flushed face away from the fire for a moment. 'There was but one full bottle left when you found us.'

'So there was,' agreed Hamish, nodding reflectively.

'And if the beer and whisky was as good today as then, I'm no doubtin' but what we could do the same again.'

'Whist, whist!' counselled some of the women, with doubtful glances at me.

'And for the three nights it was freezing solid and everyone thought they'd be very near dead with the cold,' went on Anna Vic indomitably.

'I never remembered bein' warmer in my life,' objected Hamish, directing a satisfied stream of spittle into the glowing peats.

'I should think not,' put in the roadman sarcastically. 'Why, man, it's thirty years since and amn't I still findin' empty bottles in that cave?'

His remark was greeted by a chorus of delighted chuckles which lingered until Lachy was heard asking if anyone remembered the Skean wedding. It appeared that everyone did.

'Tell Miss Peckwitt about that one, Lachy,' said Johnny, and Lachy, needing no further persuasion, embarked on his story.

'This weddin' at Skean,' he began. 'We was all there most of us, and the bride and bridegroom was standin' nice as you like in front of the minister. Well that bridegroom was as drunk as blazes. He was that drunk it was the best man havin' to hold him up from behind all the time—and he had a job to do that. Of course the minister he'd been born and reared in the place as you might say, so he didn't mind at all that the fellow was drunk. "Will you take this woman?" says he.

' "I'll take her for a whiley," says the man. "Just till I get tired of her."

' "You're that drunk you don't know what you're sayin'," the minister tells him. "I know your own mind better than you do yourself." So he carries on with the service without botherin' to ask the fellow again. Ach well, everythin' was all right till after about six months the fellow goes back to the minister.

' "I'm tired of this woman," says he. "I'm wantin' to get rid of her."

' "Man, you can't do that," the minister tells him.

' "I can so," says the fellow. "It's the conditions I took her on and there's all my friends and relations at the church will swear that I made it plain to you I was only takin' her on those terms."

' "Man, man," groans the minister, "I would be thrown out of the Church entirely if it was known I'd married a man as drunk as you were yourself that day."

' "I'm no carin' what happens to you," says the fellow. "But I want to be rid of this woman so that I can get a good milk cow. I canna' afford both."

' "Listen here," says the minister, "I have the best milk cow on the Island, and if you'll keep your mouth shut and keep the woman I'll make you a present of the beast."

'Of course the fellow knows that fine, that's just what he was after. He wasn't tired of his wife at all and it was just a put-up job between the two of them. At the end of another six months he goes again to the manse and says he's wantin' a horse; a bit later on he's needin' a good ram, and so on. The Lord himself knows what he might have got with time, but the poor old minister went and died on him. I wouldn't be surprised if it was worry that killed him,' finished Lachy complacently.

Naturally I doubted the truth of the story but strangely enough everyone was well acquainted with the couple concerned and their admiration for the husband's astuteness was patent.

'How long ago did all this happen?' I asked.

'Ach, not more than twenty or twenty-five years back,' replied Lachy, 'and that man's a rich man now, Miss Peckwitt.' I was not surprised.

The Bruach wedding, though not scheduled to take place until some weeks after I had first heard of it, managed to interfere with my own plans, for I had decided o pay a prolonged visit to Mary and I was expecting to stay in England until after the New Year. But this wedding promised to be too interesting to miss and consequently I announced my intention of cutting short my holiday so as to be present. Straightway I was deluged with commissions to purchase innumerable articles from the English shops, for, notwithstanding their contempt for the English as a race, the Bruachites were firmly convinced of the superiority of English merchandise. The requests were made diffidently but with a pathetic optimism that made refusal impossible, and my shopping list grew longer with each day that passed. The bride-to-be wanted a pair of white silk stockings, a lacy handkerchief and, blushingly, a pair of pink frilly garters. She had, she told me, already procured her dress, veil and shoes from one of the mail order firms which, to the best of my belief, specialise in supplying outlying places with outmoded fashions at outrageous prices. Giggle and Sniggle, who were to be bridesmaids, wanted head-dresses—blue ones.

'Very nice,' I complimented them, for they both had pretty blue eyes. 'And are your dresses blue too?' But they didn't yet know. The dresses were being purchased second-hand from a shop in Glasgow, 'seein' as they'll only be needed the once', and the colour would depend on what the store could provide. My suggestion that they wait until the dresses arrived before deciding on the colour for the accessories was received with an indulgent smile. 'Any colour suits blue,' they told me loftily, and, with a resigned sigh, I entered the blue head-dresses on my list.

Morag wanted gloves—black ones.

'For the wedding?' I murmured.

'They'll do me for church and funerals too,' she replied.

Lachy, still hankering after an English wife, pressed me to bring one back for him.

'Blonde or brunette,' I asked jocularly with my pencil poised ready.

'Ach, I'm no carin' one bit,' he said. 'I'm willing' to take whatever you bring for I think by now you know my tastes pretty well. Just be sure she's no wearin' one of them weeks.' It took me a moment of puzzled thought before I could translate 'weeks' into 'wigs'.

Kirsty, the gaunt and wrinkled spinster, peeped shyly in through the door one evening shortly before my departure. She clutched a paper in one hand.

'I can never get a hat that will suit me,' she mourned as we settled down to a strupak, and anyone who had ever seen Kirsty's homely features could well believe her complaint. 'See, will you get me a hat like this one,' she continued nervously unfolding the paper and pointing to an advertisement which depicted several hats of alluring designs. Her dry, knobbly finger came to rest on one of them. 'A peek-a-bo style', ran the caption, 'a debutante's dream'. I studied it carefully, trying hard to visualise it surmounting Kirsty's tired face from which all trace of the debutante had vanished a quarter of a century ago.

'I think I will suit it, don't you?' she enquired timidly.

'What colour were you wanting?' I asked evasively.

'My coat is brown and I was thinkin' blue would go awful nice with it.' Her tones became apologetically firm and as any attempt at argument would have been construed as unwillingness to make the purchase for entirely different reasons, I merely nodded and ventured only an apathetic suggestion that green might look better.

'But my eyes are blue, and they say blue-eyed people always suit blue,' she replied with childlike candour. Her pale eyes met mine briefly and slid away again and, not for the first time, I cursed the authors of the 'twopenny loves' with their inevitable blue-eyed heroines, wearing the equally inevitable 'little blue dress' which 'deepened the colour of her forget-me-not blue eyes'. Fatalistically I folded the paper and tucked it inside my shopping list which by this time had grown to considerable length.

The very evening before my departure I was doing some last-minute ironing when there came a timid knock on my door and in response to my invitation there entered Euan the half-wit. I was very surprised to see him, for though he sat sometimes in Morag's kitchen he had not so far invaded the precincts of my own room. His presence was by no means welcome, but having by this time resided long enough in the Hebrides to have acquired a little of the Gaelic courtesy, I suggested half-heartedly that he should take a seat. In reply Euan swallowed twice, grinned widely, but remained standing awkwardly beside the door. Deeming it wiser to ignore him until he chose to speak, I carried on with my ironing.

'You go England?' His voice jerked into my thoughts as I slid the iron carefully between the intricate frills of a blouse.

'Yes, I am,' I agreed.

Euan blinked rapidly in acknowledgement, but said nothing more.

'Are you wanting me to get you something?' I asked banteringly, being well aware that he had no money of his own.

'Yes!' The word burst from him with startling vehemence and was followed by a number of convulsive swallows.

'Well, tell me what it is and I'll do my best for you,' I encouraged, and overwhelmed with pity for his feeble-mindedness resolved that if it was at all practicable I would get what he wanted.

'Bring me . . .' he stuttered pleadingly, his eyes starting so far out of his head that I expected them to drop on to the floor at any moment.

'Yes, bring you what?' I coaxed.

'Donkey!'

I stared at Euan so long that the iron scorched an ineradicable angle on my blouse.

'A donkey!' I exploded. 'What sort of a donkey?'

'With legs,' he replied timorously.

'Do you mean a real donkey?'

He nodded and blinked vigorously, but words failed him. They nearly failed me.

'Goodness gracious! I couldn't possibly bring you a real donkey,' I told him. 'How on earth do you think I could manage with a donkey on the train?'

His expression changed abruptly from eager anticipation to utter dejection. Slowly, and without another word, he turned and, closing the door quietly behind him, crossed the passage to Morag's room. It was not until some minutes later that I heard her sending him home. When the outer door had closed after him Morag herself entered my room. The first thing I asked was whether Euan had told her of his request that I should bring him a donkey.

'So he did,' she replied, 'and I was askin' him if he'd ever seen a donkey to be pesterin' you to bring him one.'

'And has he?' I enquired.

'He was sayin' no he hadna' rightly but he thinks a donkey looks like a squashed horse. He doesna' think you've seen one either.'

'Me?' I echoed. 'Why not?'

'Well, he was sayin' if you'd ever seen a donkey it's fine you'd be after knowin' it wouldna' need to go on the train. He says you'd know that it has its own legs and can walk.'

'I wonder what he expects me to do with it?' I asked drily. 'Ride on it, walk beside it, or hitch it on to the back of the train?'

Morag laughed. 'Ach, but Euan doesna' know but what England's any further away than Shuna,' she excused him. Her eyes came to rest on my open, neatly packed bags on the sofa. 'So it's all ready for off you are,' she observed.

'Yes,' I told her. 'But I shall leave my cases open and pack the crushables at the last moment.'

She nodded, briefly confirmed the rest of the arrangements for the morning, and said good night.

After a broken night during which my sleep was continually interrupted by dreams that the clock had stopped or had failed to ring; that my luggage had mysteriously disappeared; or that I had mislaid my purse and was unable to pay for my ticket, the strident burr of the alarm startled me into wakefulness. I lit a candle, slid reluctantly out of bed and threw a dressing-gown around my shoulders. As I poked my feet into bedroom slippers I became hazily aware of the sounds of most unusual activity downstairs. There was the noise of windows being thrown open, doors flung back on their hinges and a muffled roaring, coupled with the acrid smell of smoke.

'Come quick, Miss Peckwitt! My house is on fire!' I doubt if there is another sentence in the English language which can galvanise a person into activity as quickly as that which my landlady had just uttered. Frantically I tore downstairs and bursting into my room was confronted with the sight of a tremendous fire which raged in and around the grate, while a deluge of glowing soot cascaded from the chimney on to the floor and smouldered fiercely on the linoleum.

'Shut the door and the window!' I commanded, recollecting the instructions I had once seen on a cigarette-card. Obediently Morag leaped to the window and shut it down with such a bang that the two lower panes of glass shattered. The next few minutes were utter confusion. Morag sensibly grabbed a brush and swept the red-hot soot towards the hearth and immediately the odour of singeing bristles mingled with the choking smoke. I grabbed pails and raced down to the sea but, as luck would have it, the tide was out and it was quite impossible to fill the pails unless one waded until one was almost knee-deep—no enviable task on a dark, cold and frosty morning. With two full pails and a torch it is difficult to race and I should have known better than to try to leap up three steps at a time. I fell heavily and the chill water flowed round and under me before I could arise. Back to the sea again to refill my pails, one of which now leaked shockingly, and with as much speed as could be combined with caution I hurried back to the house. Morag was still sweeping for all she was worth, that is if pushing soot about with a bald and smouldering broomhead can be called sweeping. The room was so full of smoke that it was well nigh impossible to see. I sluiced the water over the floor, but during my absence the tablecloth had caught fire and the wallpaper above the fireplace was rapidly browning with the heat.

'Run for Ruari!' sobbed Morag. 'Run for him quick.'

Seizing the tablecloth I flung it outside to burn away harmlessly on the grass, and then ran for Ruari. There is no doubt that there are times when deafness seems to be the worst affliction anyone can suffer. Certainly I thought so as I pounded at the door of Ruari's house and flung handfuls of pebbles at the window, but though I had the assistance of the dog, who from his kennel contributed to the uproar to the full extent of his capacious lungs, there was no acknowledgement from within. Discovering that the door was only latched I went inside, continuing to yell unceasingly for Ruari. The only reply was a duet of serene, undisturbed snores from above. I climbed half-way up the stairs, still calling; I gained the landing; I went into the bedroom from which the snores were coming and grasping Ruari's flannel-clad shoulder shook it vigorously. With my mouth close to his ear I entreated him to wake up and come and help. At last aroused, he shot upright with such suddenness that his head bumped my teeth.

'Wuff, wuff, wuff!' he spluttered as might a bulldog that has been compelled to take a cold plunge.

Quickly I explained what had happened, insisting that

the house was in imminent danger. With surprising speed one of Ruari's legs appeared from under the bedclothes but, recollecting himself, he hastily tucked it in again.

'I canna' get dressed with a woman watchin' me,' he said reprovingly.

'Sorry,' I said, and retreating from the room started downstairs.

'Hi! where are you goin' with that torch?' came a shout. 'I canna' see what shape I am and where is my clothes without a light, can I?'

Returning to the bedroom I found Ruari, still a little dazed, sitting on the edge of the bed in his nightshirt. At the sight of me with the torch he immediately scrambled back beneath the clothes, pulling them right up to his chin.

'Woman, woman!' he chided me. 'Let me get into my breekis in private will you!'

'But I can't see my way down again without a light,' I retorted. 'I don't know my way about your house in daylight, never mind in the dark.'

We effected a compromise by my holding the torch round the edge of the door into the bedroom while the rest of my body stayed outside.

'Is your eyes shut?' demanded Ruari.

'Of course!' I snapped back.

Muttering and breathing heavily, he attired himself in clothes which were, I suspected, both in quantity and quality, more suitable for an expedition to the North Pole than for wrestling with a fire in a neighbouring house. Having accomplished this much he decided to wake Bella who had slept profoundly throughout the disturbance.

'Come and get watter to quench Morag's fire,' he bade her shortly. As we hurried downstairs Bella's querulous voice pursued us, demanding to know how she was going to see to dress herself without a light. I affected not to hear: it was no concern of mine that Ruari and Bella made a habit of staying in bed until daylight.

'Wait now while I get my boots on,' said Ruari as I made for the door and, while I seethed with impatience, he retrieved his boots from under a chair and sat down leisurely to put them on. As soon as he had tied the second bootlace I bounded outside and bolted back to Morag's, leaving him to be guided by the glow of the fire, which could now plainly be seen through the windowless window. Once again I recalled the instructions on the cigarette-card.

'Salt!' I shouted, rushing into the room, 'plenty of salt to dout the fire.'

'My God!' whimpered Morag, 'I used the last pailful of it only yesterday for the herrin' and I havena' as much left as will salt the potatoes.'

Ruari appeared, and with a determination born of panic Morag seized his ear.

'Salt!' she yelled in her turn. 'Get me salt, plenty salt!'

Ruari shook his head. 'We have none,' he replied flatly, 'we hadna' enough for all the herrin' we got and the grocer has none either.' His hand went to his ear as though to protect it from further savagery.

Morag's expression was tense. 'We'll need to sacrifice the salt herrin',' she decided heroically.

I shook my head doubtfully, for though I am at all times only too willing to sacrifice salt herring I wondered if salt in this form would serve the same purpose. Before I could voice my doubts Ruari had charged off into the shed, had heaved the heavy barrel from its corner and, spurning my inefficient help with an untranslatable growl, was stumbling with it back into the house.

'Clear oot the way!' he warned Morag and she, dodging nimbly into a corner, only just managed to avoid the cataract of herring, salt and liquor as Ruari hurled the contents of the barrel on to the fire. There was a fierce sputtering, and choking smoke billowed out once more into the room; the house began to smell worse than a kipper factory, but the fire was considerably quelled and by the time a strangely attired Bella arrived with more water and wet sacks, the steady roar had become fretful and was gradually, but unmistakably, subsiding. Daylight was breaking as we carried more water to douse the hot walls and the charred linoleum and Ruari climbed up on the roof to ram wet sacks down the chimney from above.

'Why did you start that?' he demanded truculently as soon as we were able to breathe again.

'Indeed wasn't I in such a fret to get Miss Peckwitt's breakfast, and then this spiteful old fire goes sleepy on me,' exclaimed Morag with a malevolent glare at the red-hot grate. 'I was wantin' her to have a nice bitty warm before she went out, so I dosed her with plenty paraffin and bless me but puff! the old bitch went and flies away up the chimbley.'

Summoning a wan smile, I glanced at the clock, and Morag, seeing the direction of my glance, climbed on a chair and rubbed the coating of soot from the glass with a corner of her apron. It was exactly the time my train should have been leaving the mainland station. 'Why, you've gone and missed your train,' she remarked superfluously.

'So I have,' I agreed as I wearily surveyed the sooty contents of my suitcases, and collected my freshly ironed crushables for relaundering.

'Oh well,' said Morag comfortably; 'that's the very first time I've felt sure that old chimbley was really clean.'

No further calamity occurred to prevent me from setting off for England the following day and after an uneventful journey the train drew into the station of my home town where Mary was awaiting me. The return to town life was exciting and I revelled once more in 'all modern conveniences'; in the wearing of light shoes; in nice peaceful church services, and in eating thin bread and butter. My shopping expeditions were amazingly successful, though the pink frilly garters necessitated some diligent seeking. We unearthed a sumptuous pair at last in a decaying little shop in an insignificant side street; they were speckled with rose buds, bordered with lace, and tufted with swansdown, and I could be very certain that the bride-to-be would be enchanted with them. Kirsty's 'debutante's dream' was purchased and despatched to her in a debonair hat box. The bridesmaids' head-dresses, very blue and very beguiling, were packed safely in the bottom of one of my cases. Eventually all the items on my list were scored through—Lachy's wife and Euan's donkey excepted—and I could safely concentrate on my own plans.

For some time I had been toying with the idea of purchasing a small car for use in Bruach, and now I set about putting my plan into action. As I explained to Mary, I was tired of being allotted a space in the cattle float or distorting my body to fit into the backs of inadequate vans on the very frequent occasions when the Bruach bus was unfit for service. The hearse too was still a disturbingly regular feature of Island transport and, though up to the present I had always been fortunate enough to have the seat beside the driver, I could not help feeling a little apprehensive that the time might come when this would prove impracticable. I was lucky enough to purchase an old Morris two-seater car which we promptly christened 'Joanna', and at once I embarked on a course of driving lessons from a reputable instructor. At the end of a few weeks I was confident of my prowess and, saying goodbye to England, 'Joanna' and I set off, a little uncertainly to begin with perhaps, on the four-hundred-mile journey to Bruach, intending to reach our destination rather less than a week before the wedding.

The sensation of homecoming which I experienced when I drove 'Joanna' off the ferry boat and introduced her to the Island—the crossing was mercifully calm—

was strange indeed for a town-bred Englishwoman. The charm of the Island struck me afresh and, although it was December and what slight breeze there was stroked my cheeks with icy fingers, I drove with both windows of the car lowered, and drew deep, eager breaths of the fresh, invigorating air. To the left of me the loch stretched out, placid and still, reflecting the dark, rain-washed hills, the anchored fishing-boats, and the slow flight of the homeward-bound gulls. The setting sun was no more than a sliver of vermilion above the horizon, while to the north the rapidly purpling sky was laced with brilliant green. I was glad to come upon the first thatched houses of Bruach looking for all the world like sturdy brown mushrooms that a snail has eaten its way through; from the snail hole curled the now familiar blue of peat smoke mingling its fragrance with that of scorching flour, reminding me that it was Saturday evening and the Sabbath baking would be in progress. Bringing 'Joanna' to a stop beside the wall, I jumped out, and a beaming Morag came hurrying to greet me. It would have been churlish to try to avoid the embrace she had so obviously determined upon and, before it was over, Bella had appeared, to bestow upon me similar evidence of affection, while a flushed and smiling Ruari waited impatiently to shake my hand with ferocious warmth. The fervour of the welcome from all three of them was impressive and made that which I had received in England seem frigid by comparison. It was difficult to repress a feeling of elation, for the geniality of the Gael, despite its lack of sincerity, is an endearing trait. While the women prodded my limbs to see if I had lost weight, and enthused over 'Joanna' and over my new clothes, Ruari busied himself with my cases. Back again in my own room I was fussed over and petted and repeatedly assured that my company had been very much missed, and by the time I was ready for bed that night I was feeling so flattered by their attentions that I experienced no regrets at all that town life was once more behind me.

My return was the signal for a chain of visitors who came to welcome me, to inspect me, and to hear the latest news from England. Among the first were the bride and bridesmaids. All three professed themselves delighted with the purchases I had made for them and were eager to tell me that the bridesmaid's dresses had arrived from the second-hand shop. Though neither the shade nor the style of the dresses was identical, as they had been hoping, the girls were plainly thrilled. 'One is a sort of pink,' they told me, 'and the other is a sort of orange'—a colour combination which filled them with rapture and me with regret. Not far behind the bridal retinue came Kirsty, no less enamoured with the hat I had sent her from England, which I was to be permitted to see her wearing on the following Sunday. Hard on Kirsty's heels came Padruig and Euan. Once again I had to endure the former's description of his visit to 'Buckram Palace', and during the recital Euan, apparently bearing me no ill-will after my failure to bring him a donkey, sat watching me with eyes full of dog-like devotion.

'Euan doesn't seem to be fretting that I haven't brought his donkey,' I observed to Morag after they had left.

'But he thinks you have brought him one,' she replied.

'What!' I exclaimed feelingly. 'How can that be?'

'Indeed havena' the boys been after tellin' him you brought one back for him and that he's to come to Ruari's croft here tomorrow to practise will he ride it?'

'That really is the limit,' I said angrily. 'Goodness only knows what they've let me in for now. I shall be having the fellow trailing me all over the place.'

'Ach, they've let you in for nothin',' she soothed. 'The boys has borrowed a park deer from over the other side of the Island and they're after tellin' Euan it's an English donkey. That was the idea when they put him up to askin' you for a donkey in the first place.'

I discerned a touch of the combined genius of Lachy,

Angus and possibly Johnny in the ludicrous plan and vowed vengeance on all three of them.

'It'll be all right,' continued my landlady, 'Euan's never seen a donkey.'

Having emphatically refused to stay and witness the meeting of Euan and the deer, I have only my landlady's narrative as to the eventual outcome of the escapade. She, almost delirious with laughter, described the spectacle vividly and, as may be expected, in language peculiarly her own. It appeared that while a few of the men—Angus, Lachy and Johnny prominent among them—held on to the deer, Euan was persuaded to throw his leg over the saddle. As soon as he complied the men let go their hold and the deer, with prodigious leaps and bounds, made for the hills. Miraculously, no one attempted to explain how, the jockey had managed to cling on and, accompanied by the vociferous encouragement of the onlookers, was carried fully a third the length of the croft before he slid over the beast's stern and landed flat on his back in the mud. The deer fled precipitately and was soon out of sight and Euan, after slapping the mud from his trousers and retrieving his cap, flew in pursuit. He too was soon lost to sight and it was two hours later that the gamekeeper reported having seen him—still running.

It was a relief to me to hear that Euan had eventually returned and to know that the poor fellow was in no way hurt.

'He'll never forgive me,' I complained.

'Forgive you? Why should he forgive you?' argued Morag. 'He thinks it's a wonderful donkey. He's done nothin' but boast and swank of his English donkey ever since.'

I groaned. 'What is going to happen now that it's gone then?' I asked.

'Ach, stop frettin'. He thinks it's run all the way back to England and he's quite certain you'll get it for him when next you go,' she returned placidly.

236

Though it was difficult to believe such a hoax could have been carried through as successfully as the perpetrators claimed, I must admit that Euan seemed to be in no way disappointed with the performance of his counterfeit donkey. On the contrary, he continued to regard me with an embarrassing devotion which showed not the least sign of diminishing.

12

The Wedding

As the great wedding day drew near, the Bruachites bent themselves to the task of writing congratulatory telegrams.

'What are you goin' to put in your own message?' asked my landlady one evening, and when I replied that, as I had every intention of being present at the ceremony, it seemed unnecessary to send a telegram, she was genuinely surprised, and insisted that it was the custom for telegrams to be sent whether or not one would be there in person. It was also the custom, she told me, for some of the self-styled bards of the village to compose congratulatory messages in verse, and suggested that one Peter would 'make a verse' for me if I so wished. I shook my head; my acquaintance so far with local compositions had forced me to the conclusion that, provided rhyming, metre and grammar could be discounted entirely, their work might be tolerably good—certainly not otherwise. My landlady's cousin, a master in a Glasgow secondary school, had, she confided, supplied 'a grand verse' for her own telegram. 'My, but he's right good at them. Just wait till you hear it,' she exalted with a girlish gleam in her eyes, and added coyly: 'I shan't tell you now though for fear of spoilin' it.'

I murmured something about contenting myself with the prosaic 'congratulations and best wishes', whereupon Morag stared at me with the stricken expression of a child who has been punished for a sin it is not aware

238

of having committed; and abruptly changed the subject. She did not mention the telegrams again.

A belated dawn heralded the wedding morning itself and after rubbing a clear patch on my window I saw that it promised to be a dull, depressing, typical December day. Downstairs my landlady was humming Gaelic airs to herself as she scuttled about her morning chores, for she was intending to leave early, having promised to lend her assistance in the kitchen for the major part of the day. The cows were to be left in the byre instead of being turned out on the hill as usual, and I had promised to give them their evening feed before setting out for the church after lunch. When Morag had gone, I spent the morning in polishing 'Joanna' who, in spite of her age, was in remarkably good condition. At lunch-time I cooked and ate a rather frugal meal—the frugality being in anticipation of the menu for the wedding feast proving somewhat onerous. I was on my way, in gum-boots and mackintosh, to give the cows their feed before changing into my wedding finery, when the vehement blasting of a horn made me look round, and I beheld the taxi-driver in an opulent new taxi signalling furiously in my direction. I crossed the park to the road.

'Isn't that fellow the biggest fool in the Island!' he burst out passionately, without making even the expected allusion to the weather. I sensed instantly that something was seriously wrong.

'Which man? And what has he done?' I asked, puzzling as to why I had been chosen as confidante.

'Why, Sandy, the bridegroom, of course,' the taxi-driver explained. 'He's gone off in his boat round to Lochnamor this mornin' before they were up, they're tellin' me, and there's no sign of him comin' back yet. I've been waitin' over half an hour on him.'

I looked at my watch. It said ten minutes past two and the wedding was timed to take place at three. Lochnamor was an hour away by boat, but there was a rough track across the glen which, if it proved to be negotiable

239

all the way, should take 'Joanna' there in about twenty minutes. The taxi-driver's expression was eloquent.

'I suppose you want me to take my car through the glen and get him?' I said.

'Well, Miss Peckwitt,' he answered humbly, 'I'm thinkin' it's the only way to get hold of the man, and this thing'—he paused and glared with perfidious disdain at the front wheels of his luxury model—'she's too low in her body for me to think of tryin' it.'

'There's precious little time,' I pointed out, 'and I have yet to feed the cows.'

The taxi-driver alighted quickly from the car. 'I'll feed the cows myself,' he offered obligingly.

I thanked him and started off towards 'Joanna'. 'And you'll have to water them too,' I called as I ran. 'The well is over there.'

'Ach, I'll put them outside for a while and they'll drink their own water,' returned the taxi-driver.

'Oh,' I said unhappily, but shrugging my shoulders I left him to do what he pleased, for there was no time to argue. I was glad that 'Joanna's' engine had already been running that morning so that she responded to the first pull on the starter and I was quickly able to back and turn her into the road. Putting my foot down as hard as I dared, I headed her towards the glen. The track was sinuous and rutty; loose stones flew on all sides of us and rattled with distressing frequency on the car's underparts. The bends were nerve-racking, but she skidded round them contemptuously with the air of a thoroughbred on familiar ground, and we eventually reached the spot where the track widened into the shore of a tiny, sheltered bay. The tide was well out, and high and dry above the line of surf was a fishing-boat on 'legs', beneath which two dungaree-clad figures crouched industriously scraping barnacles off the keel. They were far too engrossed in their task to notice my arrival and doubtless the noise of the sea had muffled the sound of 'Joanna's' engine. I turned the car back towards the way

240

we had come and then raced down to the beach.

'Hey, Sandy!' I addressed the bridegroom, gasping as I inhaled the strong smell of fish, seaweed and tar which hung around the boat. 'You're going to be terribly late for your wedding.'

'Good God!' burst out one of the figures as it squirmed from beneath the boat. 'It's surely not today, is it?'

Sandy, a slim, brown-haired fellow, sporting a moustache that made him look as though he had just taken a bite out of a hedgehog, stared incredulously first at me and then at the other dungareed figure who had emerged from under the boat's stern. It was obvious from their expressions that both had completely forgotten the wedding.

'I did want to bottom her today,' mourned Sandy, staring sadly at the half-scraped hull of his boat.

'You'll be bottomed yourself if you don't turn up for your wedding,' I threatened him with a smile.

'I'll have to go.' Despairingly he turned to his confederate. 'You'll have to stay and bottom her by yourself,' he told him.

'But I'll need to come. I'm your best man,' expostulated the other.

'Wedding or no wedding, we canna' leave the boat like this for the tide to come up,' objected Sandy.

'We could rush back in time for the tide maybe?' suggested his partner hopefully.

Sandy appeared to reflect for some moments on the propriety of rushing away from his own wedding in order to attend to a boat.

'No, I might not be able to manage it,' he said, his tones betraying the degree of temptation he had been subjected to. 'You'd best stay and see to it yourself.'

Reluctantly the best man resigned himself to his martyrdom and I set about coercing the vacillating tar-spattered bridegroom into 'Joanna'. Once again I drove at reckless speed through the glen and at ten minutes to three Sandy, impatient enough by now, tumbled out of the car and into the arms of his family who were waiting on the doorstep. His mother was holding his wedding trousers; his aunt was holding his shirt and his grandmother his jacket; his father, an old man almost crippled with rheumatism, hovered in the background meekly offering a collar and tie and a pair of shoes. Outside on the road the taxi-driver, his hair and shirt front decorated with stray wisps of hay, fretted uneasily beside the luxury model. How the family accomplished the feat of inserting Sandy into his wedding attire I have no idea, being intent on manœuvring 'Joanna' round and past the taxi; but as I drove away home I caught a glimpse of the bridegroom rushing down to the burn, both hands clutching at his trousers, followed by the taxi-driver-cum-cowman brandishing a pair of braces and a towel. I had pulled up outside Morag's house and was scrambling out of my seat when the taxi, with engine revving and horn blasting merrily, surged past. A man's white handkerchief fluttering from one lowered window of the car acknowledged my small part in the proceedings.

There remained still the task of making myself presentable and it was plain that, even if the wedding were delayed by the late arrival of the bridegroom, I should still be lucky not to miss the ceremony. With fumbling fingers I changed into my suit and, after a quick glance around the kitchen to ensure that everything was in order, hastened once more to 'Joanna'. Just as I was settling into my seat a voice hailed from a distance and, fuming with impatience, I craned my neck round the door to see the rheumaticky figure of the bridegroom's father toiling gallantly up the hill towards me. Breathlessly and with the sweat pouring from his furrowed brow, he attained the car and collapsed against it with a plaintive bleat.

'Are you coming to the wedding?' I asked.

'No,' he panted sorrowfully. 'Somebody has to stay and see to the cows.'

'Don't tell me then that Sandy has forgotten the ring,' I prompted, pulling at the starter.

'No indeed. It's worse than that.'

'Worse?'

'Aye, he's forgotten this,' announced the old man gravely, and produced from his pocket a small bundle wrapped in a white handkerchief.

'What is that?' I asked suspiciously.

'It's his teeths,' he replied, 'and he canna' get marrit without them.'

'Oh, they won't really make any difference,' I consoled, but the old man drew himself erect and spat with unexpected vigour.

'It will to her,' he said. 'She's always at him, at him, like a mouse at a taty, for not wearin' his teeths, and if he turns up for the weddin' without them, sure the bitch will turn on him even in the church itself.' He spat again. 'You'll take them for him will you?' he cajoled, and there was both distress and urgency in his voice. 'You'll haste, won't you?'

I took the handkerchief-wrapped bundle and laid it on the seat beside me and then, bidding the old man goodbye, I let in the clutch. 'Joanna' screamed her way up the hill. By the time I had covered a few miles the humour of the situation had begun to strike me, but, even before I could raise a smile, a wildly gesticulating figure appeared in the middle of the road. 'Someone's been left behind,' I grumbled to myself as I braked to a stop. An old man, whose attire was in no way suitable for a wedding, rammed at the window with fingers that must have been about as sensitive as skittles.

'Ach, but it's cold, cold, cold,' he began conversationally as I lowered the window.

'It is,' I agreed shortly. 'But I'm in a tearing hurry. What is it you want?'

He looked mildly hurt at my brusqueness. 'Are you goin' through the village?' he enquired, leaning his elbows on the door of the car.

'I am. Please tell me what you want,' I repeated testily.

Shocked by my reply, his manner developed a certain hauteur.

'She's wantin' to know will you take a chicken to the post for her?' He nodded condescendingly towards the house where presumably 'she' was.

'I can't wait one second more,' I told him, one foot already on the accelerator and the other on the clutch. 'If it's quite ready I'll take it.'

'She's just after finishin' pluckin' it now,' he said languidly. 'Will you no be comin' in for a wee moment?'

'Look here,' I replied exasperatedly, 'I'm on my way to the wedding and I've simply got to get there in time because there'—I pointed—'in that bundle are the bridegroom's false teeth and he cannot get married without them.'

'Can he no?' queried the old man.

'No he can't,' I replied tersely.

His countenance assumed an expression of mingled pity and curiosity. 'Why can he no get marrit without his teeths?' he enquired, and then giving me an immoral wink went on: 'Sure, he'll no be marryin' her just to bite her, will he?'

Fiercely I let in the clutch and 'Joanna', leaping forward like an outraged debutante, left him gurgling contentedly at his own witticism. The halt, though it had entailed only a few seconds' delay, made me despair of ever reaching the church on time and I drove as I had seldom driven before. The minute hand of the clock on the dashboard seemed to race almost as madly as the car and it was pointing to nearly half past three when I at last arrived outside the church. Debating as to how I was to get the precious bundle to Sandy, I hurried into the porch where, pausing to take stock of the situation, I heard the minister intoning the marriage service in a voice that was suggestive of the spell-casting demons of pantomime. Hope sank, but rose again as I realised that the service had only just begun and that there were still some few minutes before the fatal moment arrived. Stealthily I tiptoed up a side aisle to the front pew, before which were grouped the young couple, the two bridesmaids, the sponsor and the taxi-driver who, having already acted as valet, driver and cowman, had now been pressed into service as groomsman. Taking a deep breath which served as an aromatic reminder that Sandy's toilet had indeed been a sketchy one—the church reeked with the mingled odours of fish, seaweed and tar—and ignoring the faintly hostile glances of the occupants of the pew, I urged them to make room for me. The slight disturbance made the minister look up from his prayer book and direct upon me a frankly enquiring stare. I gazed with the utmost reverence at the hassock by my feet. Cautiously I nudged my neighbour. 'Here are Sandy's teeth,' I hissed. 'Pass them on; don't drop them whatever you do.' With bated breath I watched over the progress of the white bundle along the pew until a plainly audible 'Hi!' told me that it had nearly reached its objective. The taxi-driver stepped back a pace, reached behind him surreptitiously, stepped forward again and a moment later, after a barely perceptible movement of his arm, the teeth were safely deposited in Sandy's pocket. It was just in time.

'Wilt thou take this woman . . .' the minister began. Sandy's hand went into his pocket and then to his mouth. He appeared to be stifling a prolonged yawn. '. . . so long as you both shall live?' concluded the minister. The bridegroom's 'Adam's apple' rose and fell twice.

'I will,' he responded thickly.

The minister turned to the bride and repeated the question. Sandy took the opportunity to bestow upon her a devastating smile.

'. . . so long as you both shall live?' The minister's voice ceased and the congregation waited in hushed expectancy. The bride flicked her husband-to-be with a brief, speculative glance.

'I will,' she replied firmly.

The tension over, I relaxed as well as I could into the small portion of pew allotted to me by the well-cushioned relatives. The minister closed his book and the organist, a diminutive woman with a round, rosy face and tight coils of hair, which supported a blue straw hat heavily overladen with cherries, suddenly began to writhe like a hooked mackerel as her short legs laboured at the pedals. Almost before the hymn was announced the organ whinnied forth into the opening bars of 'The Voice that breathed o'er Eden', in which the congregation joined half-heartedly. At the end of the service the principals disappeared into the vestry and as soon as the door closed upon them the organist snatched off her high-heeled shoes and began to massage her feet tenderly. The congregation broke into a buzz of conversation which included a good deal of awed comment on my late arrival and the reason for it. My explanation attracted so much interest that in no time at all quite a number of people had gathered round me asking for more details. Even the little organist tiptoed from her stool to stand, in stockinged feet, listening to my story. I had just reached the point where the old man had wanted me to wait for the hen, when, without warning, the vestry door swung open and the happy couple emerged, both grinning toothily. The guests melted back to their places and the organist, after one horrified glance at the vestry, flew back to the organ and strove vainly to reach the pedals. The bride, who was expecting to hear the triumphal strains of the Wedding March— having paid for it—looked questioningly towards the mute organ beneath which a dishevelled little figure was now searching desperately for her shoes. The blushing bridegroom, with arms stiff and fists clenched, studied his feet intently, while in the background the minister could be seen furtively wiping his mouth with the back of his sleeve.

I slipped outside to get my camera from 'Joanna' and

found that the threat of rain had now resolved itself into a fitful shower. I had no sooner taken up my position than the bridal couple and their retinue appeared at the door of the church, belatedly accompanied by a crashing discord on the organ which matched in harmony the cerise and orange of the well-washed, but quite un-ironed, bridesmaids' dresses. The music came to an abrupt conclusion, and almost simultaneously the determined but rather rumpled little organist came charging through the church door, still in stockinged feet, and clutching in one hand an outsize bag of what I took to be confetti; in the other, the cherry-laden hat. I checked my camera, besought the guests to stand out of the way of the group, clicked a few times and nodded that I had finished. I was wishing that rice or confetti had been obtainable, but the grocer had run out of the first and had never stocked the second. I found old Murdoch beside me.

'I've been savin' up all my eggshells for weeks. There's no better confetti than crushed eggshells,' he told me as he hurled a fistful at the newlyweds. The organist began pouring generous quantities from her bag into the eager palms of those not so fortunately equipped. I saw that it was not confetti but semolina, the fact that semolina could be used as a substitute for rice in puddings evidently being sufficient recommendation for its use as a substitute for rice at weddings. The bridal party ploughed their way to the waiting taxi through a mixture of pudding ingredients and good wishes, their footsteps crunching as though they were walking on fresh cinders. As the door of the taxi slammed upon them a shrill yell rent the clamour of greetings and we turned to see Lachy, already in a state of mild inebriation, lurch towards it. With a merry toot of the horn the taxi drew away from the kerb, the bride and bridegroom waving gaily from inside. On the edge of the kerb teetered Lachy, pointing jubilantly to the rear bumper of the taxi, from which dangled a pair of easily identifiable high-heeled shoes.

The crowd roared in approval and like frolicking children the main body of it surged after the taxi and turned the corner to vanish in the direction of the hotel. From the scattering of people left behind the organist detached herself, and advancing vengefully upon Lachy she proceeded to bespatter him with a stream of formidable Gaelic which the uncontrite recipient acknowledged with fatuous grins. Somehow or other Lachy must have managed to placate her, for as I bent to crank 'Joanna' I heard a series of whoops and yelps and beheld the lady herself undergoing a 'piggy-back' from the shoe thief. With one hand pressing her hat securely on to her disarranged coiffure and with the other clutching resolutely at the 'piggy's' goitre, she looked far from happy about the performance of her steed. She was touchingly grateful for the lift I offered and, during the short journey to the hotel, was loud in her condemnation of Lachy's trickery.

At the hotel, Morag, flushed with pleasure and the heat of the kitchen, but very much in her best attire, greeted me volubly.

'Why, there's ninety people catered for and over a hundred and thirty turned up, so the housekeeper was sayin',' she told me. Fortunately it had been taken for granted that there would be gate-crashers and the easy-going hotel staff were more pleased than perturbed at having a couple of score extra mouths to feed. It is on occasions like this that one thanks God for the Gael.

'It's them men that was loadin' sheeps,' continued Morag by way of explanation. 'They said they wouldna' be able to get, but I doubt they meant to come all the time. Here they are anyway, and here they'll be stayin' till they think better of it.'

Here they were indeed, and certainly here they appeared to have every intention of staying; men who had been lifting sheep on to lorries all day; men whose clothes were covered with grease and sheep dung; men whose hands looked as though they had been playing with greasy coal. Here they were, their hobnailed boots planted firmly on the carpeted floor of the hotel lounge, their tired bodies leaning on rough crooks while their dogs, bewildered by the strangeness of the surroundings —they would have been quite at home in the bar— threaded their way warily among the legs of the assembled guests and paused every now and then to look at their masters with mute enquiry.

'Of course,' Morag's voice began again in my ear, 'with there bein' so many of us we'll need to take our meals in layers.'

'Relays,' I corrected automatically, but her attention had already wandered elsewhere.

The guests had now begun to file past the newlyweds and, after a handshake, each man pressed a slim envelope into the groom's hand. (I heard later that Sandy made forty pounds profit on his reception—ten pounds more than he had reckoned on making.) Next, the wedding cake, under the careful supervision of the minister, was cut by the simpering bride and handed round along with glasses of port wine and sherry. The guests congregated into hilarious little groups, sipping their wine self-consciously and endeavouring to swallow their cake without chewing it—they are taught at school that this is the essence of refinement. The sheeploaders, mingling freely with those more suitably attired, clutched their glasses in strong calloused hands and tautened chapped dry lips to sip daintily at the wine. They shuffled constantly from one foot to the other, a habit which I have noticed to be prevalent among hill-reared people.

Almost everyone I had ever met in Bruach was present at the reception even to the most decrepit of the old folk. The Gaffer, looking strangely unfamiliar without the string which usually adorned the knees of his trousers, leaned an arm on the shoulder of old Farquhar who was clad in a greeny-black suit, the pockets of which bulged so suspiciously that I wondered if he had brought his rats with him. ('No,' said Morag, 'that'll

249

just be a couple of bags so's he can take home what he canna' eat.') The uncles Hamish and Roderick were peering with thinly veiled contempt into the bottom of their empty glasses. Ruari and old Mac sat in a corner bellowing pleasantries at each other until the vacant chairs about them seemed to shudder with the impact. Adam the gamekeeper slumped in his chair, sniffing contentedly, while the old crones from Rhuna gabbled confidences across his broad, tweed-clad chest. The policeman, hardly recognisable in plain clothes, talked animatedly with Dugan and tried not to notice the intoxicated Lachy, who was crawling around the floor on his hands and knees searching for his lost spectacles. As Lachy had never in his life owned a pair of spectacles to lose, his search looked like being a prolonged one.

A maid appeared and, pointedly ignoring the bride and bridegroom, mumbled a few words in the minister's ear. He nodded understandingly.

'Come and take your dinner!' he commanded forcefully, and as he took upon himself the task of escorting the bridal couple into the dining-room the guests obediently fell in behind.

The repast itself was by Island standards luxurious, and was partaken of with a vigour and relish which could undoubtedly have been heard a mile or two away. Plates clattered; knives and forks pinged against plates, glasses and false teeth; tongues wagged, chairs scraped, stomachs rumbled and feet shuffled, while throughout the several courses the dishes were passed and re-passed across and around the table in a manner more reminiscent of a rugby football field than a dining-room. At the end of the meal the minister proposed the health of the couple in a long speech which, if one could judge from the laughter it evoked, was also a vastly amusing one, but as it was in Gaelic there was little of it I could understand. The bridegroom refused point-blank to reply to the toast and so did the bride. The best man also begged to be excused and, as everyone was impatient for the reading of the telegrams, the minister, sensibly refusing to argue with his stubborn protégés, gathered up the sheaf of congratulatory messages and began to read them out in English.

Those telegrams! Never in my life had I heard such pointed ribaldry as I heard then. Never before could I have imagined that a minister of the Church would condone, still less participate in, such vulgarity. Yet there he stood in his clerical collar and black suit, trying vainly to conceal his own enjoyment as he read each message slowly and meaningly. At one time I was conscious of hearing my landlady's name being called as the sender of one of the telegrams, and chancing to catch her eye at that moment I saw her gleeful smile. The bride could hardly tear her shining eyes from the minister's face, except when she wished to prod her abashed husband into a better appreciation of the 'humour'. In her white garb of chastity she displayed about as much inhibition as a tom-cat.

When the telegrams came to an end we returned to the lounge, where a white-haired fiddler, nearly as advanced in liquor as he was in years, played a 'Strip the Willow' with exaggerated caution.

'Quicken it up a bit, Peter,' urged the bride, who was partnered by the taxi-driver-cum-cowman-cum-best man, her husband having adjourned to the bar with a few friends. Offended at the criticism of his playing, the fiddler accelerated hard, and the bride, in order to keep the pace, had to leap and bound with a calfish recklessness that traced her movements with a clearly marked pattern of semolina. Her exertions were, however, not wholly successful in dislodging the stray pieces of eggshell which still adhered to the tendrils of her well-frizzed hair.

The dancing continued, with several breaks for refreshments, until about eleven-thirty, and at ten minutes to midnight the husband was rescued from the closed bar and despatched upstairs with his wife.

'In the old days,' said the elder Rhuna crone beside whom I now found myself, 'it used to be the custom hereabouts for the old folk to stay the night with the bride and bridegroom and then the bride would get up in the mornin' and give the old folks their breakfast.' She sighed regretfully.

'How long ago was all that?' I asked.

'Oh, not more than thirty, maybe forty years ago I can mind it happenin'.'

'And did that happen at your wedding?'

'Me, my dear? Why, bless you I've never been marrit in my life,' she replied innocently.

I laughed unrestrainedly. Several times during the evening I had caught glimpses of her and every time there had been a wine glass in her hand. I put her answer down to too much whisky.

'You're not very sober, are you?' I teased. 'Fancy trying to tell me you've had thirteen children without ever being married.' I laughed again.

'Indeed, Miss Peckwitt, but it's as true as I'm here,' she assured me earnestly. 'I've never been marrit in my life, and surely it's glad I am that I havena' a man to be frettin' me in my old age.'

I stared at her stupidly. 'But the children?' I blurted out unthinkingly.

The crone drew herself up and stared with magnificent virtuousness at the ceiling. 'Indeed,' she said with elaborate piety, ' 'twas the Lord Himself put the breath in them.'

'My God!' I breathed, thunderstruck, and turned to gape at the Madonna-like expression on her old face. She showed no trace of shame or embarrassment at my reaction but merely went on to tell me what a blessing her children had been to her. Providentially a waitress approached us at that moment bearing a tray of drinks for the road, carefully pointing out that there was whisky for the menfolk and sherry for the ladies. Ignoring her

252

reproving glance I helped myself to one of the whiskies. I felt very badly in need of it.

In order to avoid further shattering revelations I went in search of my landlady and, having found her, we said our goodbyes and prepared to depart. On reaching the door of the hotel we found the way blocked by a jostling, rumbustious throng of wedding guests, servants and bar customers.

'It's what we always do when there's a weddin',' Morag informed me. 'Their bedroom is just above the porch here, and when the bride opens the window and throws out her stocking it'll be time for everybody to take themselves off home.'

As soon as she had finished speaking, there was a tumultuous roar from the crowd and the blind was lifted from a window above and the sash raised. A hand appeared and a moment later a white silk stocking came floating down into the midst of the spectators and landed on the policeman, who flourished it victoriously before rolling it up and thrusting it into his pocket. Immediately the swarm of people began to disperse in different directions, some arm-in-arm and singing happily, others barely capable of holding themselves upright.

The next morning Morag had woeful news to impart. Lachy and Johnny were in gaol! According to her they had started to fight soon after the wedding party had broken up and Lachy had crowned Johnny's head with a whisky bottle. It was terrible news, for the relationship normally existing between Lachy and Johnny was of a David and Jonathan-like quality. It sounded impossible for such a thing to have happened to such good friends, but that it was only too true the policeman himself confirmed when I met him later that day.

'Poor Lachy,' I said. 'I'm sure he didn't mean to hurt Johnny. They were always such good friends.'

'No of course he didn't,' agreed the policeman, who was really very decent. 'And that's just what Johnny himself says when he comes around. My, but Johnny was mad when he found out I'd locked up Lachy. He called me all the bad names in the language and more besides. "He's my best pal," he says. "Your best pal," says I, "and he's just split your head open with a bottle!" "He meant me no harm you b——" says Johnny. "Look here," says I, "if you don't stop cursin' at me I'll lock you up along with him." "I'll come right enough too," says Johnny, and by God! Miss Peckwitt, he came so quick I had all I could do to keep in front of him,' finished the policeman.

I clucked sympathetically.

'And when we got to the police station, did you hear what he did then?'

I shook my head.

'Well, the fool grabbed the fire extinguisher off the wall and he turned it full on me and the sergeant. Of course we had to lock him up then. There was nothin' else to do.'

'Ruined our clothes,' he went on in aggrieved tones, 'and I had my best suit on too.'

I gathered from his further remarks that there was but one cell available on the Island for the lodging of offenders. The reunion, he told me, had been absolutely pathetic.

'What will happen to them?' I asked.

The policeman pursed his lips. 'Depends,' he said. 'A fiver maybe.'

'Lachy must have been terribly drunk to have started it,' I said.

'My, if you'd seen him!' rejoined the policeman. 'He was as wild as a bull.'

'How did you manage to get him to the police station?' I asked, knowing just how unhelpful the villagers would have been in such a situation.

'Well, he was a bit of a job, I can tell you,' he confided. 'He needed handcuffs he was that strong, but I didn't have any on me. When you go to a weddin' you don't expect to have to take handcuffs with you.' He glanced at me as though expecting reassurance. 'Well, I was havin' such a struggle and then I remembered somethin' I had in my pocket.' He smiled, a secret, reminiscent smile. 'So I twisted his two hands behind him and I slipped on this thing. "Now Lachy," I says, "I have the handcuffs on you and you're under arrest!" ' Here the policeman laughed outright. 'The trick worked all right and he came quiet as a lamb, his two hands clasped behind him as though he was sayin' his prayers back to front, for he was so blind drunk he couldn't tell the difference between a pair of handcuffs and this.'

With a wry smile he thrust his hand into his tunic pocket and held out the makeshift handcuffs. I recognised it of course. I had discovered a pair of them in a decaying little shop in an insignificant side street; it was speckled with rose-buds, bordered with lace and tufted with swansdown—and the bride had been enchanted with it.

The author offers her apologies to all Gaelic speakers for the way in which she has tortured their beautiful language so as to make it pronounceable for stiff-tongued Sassenachs.

The correct Gaelic spelling and their approximate meanings are as follows:

Tha e breagh (He Breeah)	It is fine
Tha e fliuch (He Fluke)	It is wet
Tha e fuar (He Fooar)	It is cold
Ceilidh (Cayley)	A meeting together for gossip and song
Mo ghaoil	My dear
Ciamar a Tha (Kamera-ha)	How are you?
Tha gu math (Ha-goo-ma)	I am well
Strupach (Strupak)	A cup of tea and a bite to eat